Keep Going With QuickBooks® 2018 for Windows

Technical Learning Resources

This guide is intended for use with QuickBooks Desktop 2018. The practice files will not work properly if QuickBooks Desktop 2018 is not installed on your computer or laptop. Refer to the Before You Get Started lesson in this guide for instructions on downloading and activating the trial software.

technical learning resources

Copyright Notice

Keep Going With QuickBooks® 2018 for Windows
ISBN # 978-1-942020-05-9
Item # KG2018

© TLR, 2018. Published in January 2018.

Disclaimer

Trademark Acknowledgments

Other Acknowledgments

Executive Editors:	Edward F. Thaney and Scott T. Gerken
Project and Production Managers:	Lori Laney and Brandy Halstead
Developer:	Carene Kulis

Technical Learning Resources is affiliated with Thaney & Associates, CPA's

Special Notice

Publisher: Technical Learning Resources
Voice: (877) 223-5740
Web: www.tlr-inc.com

Contents

Before You Get Started

Introduction

This training guide is dedicated to providing you with a flexible, high-performance learning system. This dedication has resulted in a unique and progressive training method. Unlike other training methods that focus on theory or high-tech training products that overwhelm you, this training method provides a simple approach to learning computer software. Each guide is written to assume the user has no prior computer skills. If you are using the software for the first time, you will be introduced to its primary features. If you are familiar with the software, you will quickly learn the new features and functionality of this version. Regardless of your skill level, you will learn with the greatest of ease.

Our Training Philosophy

Three core principles are the foundation of every training guide:

- You learn best by doing.

- The most important evaluation of your progress comes from you.

- Training should be flexible and allow you to focus on only the skills you need to learn.

Training Guide Features

This training guide provides instructions for downloading the accompanying practice files from the www.tlr-inc.com web site. The practice files encourage quick and easy learning and reinforce the development of new skills. This training guide is based on the above principles and uses the following features to ensure that you learn the most skills in the least amount of time.

Step-by-Step Instruction

Lessons are written in a simple and concise language, and use step-by-step instructions to perform software tasks. This hands-on approach is the essence of skills application and ensures successful learning. You can complete each lesson in 45 minutes or less, which will dramatically improve your ability to retain new skills.

Confidence Building

Learning objectives are defined at the beginning of each lesson. The practice section at the end of each lesson allows you to determine whether you have met the objectives. To help you monitor the accuracy and success of your work within each lesson, this guide includes computer responses, narration and screen captures. The combination of continuous feedback and post-lesson practice helps you develop confidence that strengthens ongoing learning.

Self-contained Lessons

Each lesson within a training guide is self-contained. For example, there's no need to complete lessons 1-4 if you prefer to learn lesson 5. Because lesson modules are self-contained, you can pinpoint needed skills, master them, and move on. This flexibility allows for self-paced learning so you can learn what you want, when you want, and apply new skills immediately.

How to Use This Guide

General Conventions

In this lesson, you will learn:

Lesson objectives are stated at the beginning of each lesson. A quick glance at the objectives will give you a brief description of what you will learn in the lesson.

Concept

This paragraph explains why the objectives are important, and how the objectives might be used in an actual situation.

Scenario

The scenario paragraph sets the stage for each lesson. The scenario is explained, and a general overview presents the tasks you will perform in the lesson.

In this lesson, you have learned:

This section provides a summary of the topics covered in the lesson. Check the items listed in this section to see if you have learned them thoroughly.

Practice

The practice section enables you to reinforce new skills with additional tasks similar to those performed in the lesson. If you have trouble completing the practice section, refer back to the lesson for help before proceeding.

Instructional Conventions

Procedural Steps

Step-by-step instructions are in the form of numbered steps.

Example:

1. Click to close the Control Panel

Steps are divided into columns. Following the step number, the first column contains the action. The second column contains the item on which the action is being performed. The third column contains the intent of the step, or additional information that is needed.

Many steps include keystrokes.

Example:

2. Press   Tab   to move to the next field

Multiple keys may appear in a step. If the keys listed are the same, press the keys one after the other; if the keys listed are different, the first key is held while pressing the second key.

Steps may direct you to select a command from a menu.

Example:

3. Select   File : Exit   from the menu bar

Steps directing you to type a specific amount, date, word, or phrase are in boldface.

Example:

4. Type   **30**   in the Amount field

Steps directing you to type variable information, such as the date, are in boldface and are enclosed by square brackets.

Example:

5. Type   **[today's date]**   in the Date field

For example, if today's date is November 1, 2018, you would type 11/01/2018.

Some steps do not fit the three-column structure.

Example:

6. Use the scroll bars to move around the report

A diamond bullet indicates a one-step procedure.

Example:

◆ Use the scroll bars to move around the report

Icons

Lessons frequently contain tips, shortcuts, or warnings for the tasks being performed. Such instances are indicated by the following icons:

The **Quick Tip** icon provides useful shortcuts for common tasks. Quick Tips also explain events or conditions that may occur.

The **Quick Fix** icon provides solutions to small problems and inconsistencies that may arise. Quick Fix icons also mark information that instructs you to change the application's settings or preferences to better fit the lesson.

The **Caution** icon indicates that it may be easy to perform a step incorrectly. Pay close attention to the step-by-step instructions when you see the Caution icon.

Prerequisites

You can successfully complete this training guide without any prior software knowledge or computer experience. A basic understanding of the computer operating system you are using is recommended.

System Requirements

This training guide does not include the Intuit QuickBooks software; however, it does include access codes to the free trial version of the software, so that you may use this guide along with the practice files. Before using this guide, verify that the software is installed on your computer. This training guide works with the following application:

• QuickBooks® Pro or QuickBooks Premier 2018 for Microsoft® Windows

Note: The QuickBooks Simple Start software is not recommended for use with the QuickBooks guides.

Customized Settings for This Guide

Displaying File Extensions

It is recommended that you display file extensions while using this guide. By default, file extensions are hidden, so you must perform the following procedure to display them.

Note: You may want to remember to hide extensions between lessons or upon completion of using this guide.

1. Click (Windows Start button)

The Windows Start menu displays.

Note: Depending on your operating system, these steps and the icons on your computer may be slightly different.

2. Select   **Control Panel**

The Control Panel opens:

Note: Your computer's control panel may look different.

3. Select   Tools : Folder Options   from the Control Panel menu bar

The Folder Options window opens:

Note: Your computer's Folder Options may look different.

4. Select   the View tab

The View page displays:

5. Click   the Hide extensions   to deselect it
            for known file types
            check box

6. Click   [OK]   to close the Folder Options window

You return to the Control Panel.

7. Click   [X]   to close the Control Panel

Dates

The current day, month, and year on your computer are always displayed when using the QuickBooks application. Therefore, the dates that display in this training guide will be different from the dates that display on your screen. We strongly recommend that you temporarily change your computer's date setting to November 1, 2018 while taking this course, so that the dates you see on your screen match the dates in this guide.

Note: The following steps work with a Windows Vista™, Windows 7, and Windows 8 operating system. Depending on your operating system, these steps may be slightly different.

To change your computer's date,

1. Click   the time   displayed in the lower-right corner of your screen

Note: If your computer does not display the time, right-click in the lower-right corner of the screen and select the Adjust date/time option from the menu that displays.

A calendar opens:

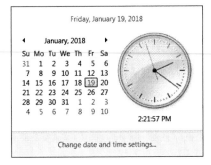

2. Click   the Change date and time settings link

The Date and Time window opens:

3. Click   Change date and time...

Note: If a User Account Control dialog box displays asking for permission to continue, click the Continue button.

The Date and Time Settings window opens:

4. Click ▶ at the top of the calendar to scroll to November, 2018

5. Click   1   in the calendar (if necessary)

6. Click   [OK]   to return to the Date and Time window

7. Click   [OK]   to close the Date and Time window

Your computer's date should now be set to November 1, 2018.

Training Objectives

After completing this training guide, you should be able to:

- Memorize transactions

- Customize forms

- Use other QuickBooks accounts

- Create reports

- Create graphs

- Track and pay sales tax

- Prepare payroll with QuickBooks

- Use online banking

- Manage company files

- Estimate, time track, and job cost

- Write letters

Downloading the Practice Files

The practice files you use to complete the lessons in this guide can be downloaded from the tlr-inc.com web site. This section provides instructions for unzipping the practice files to a folder you create on the C: drive of your computer.

Note: The steps in this section may be different, depending on the web browser and browser version you are using. The following steps work with Internet Explorer.

1. Open   the www.tlr-inc.com   in Internet Explorer
                  web site

The TLR web site opens.

2. Click   the Practice Files tab   at the top of the page

The QuickBooks practice files display.

3. Click   Get Smart with QuickBooks 2018

A dialog box opens asking if you want to open or save the StudentsBooks2018.zip file:

Do you want to open or save **StudentBooks2018.zip** (169 MB) from **tlr-inc.com**?   Open   Save ▼ Cancel   ×

Note: Your dialog box may appear different.

4. Click   [Open]

The StudentBooks2018.zip file downloads. When the file has completed downloading, the WinZip - StudentBooks2018.zip dialog box displays:

5. Click   [Unzip ▼]

A drop-down menu displays:

Note: Your window will be different.

6. Select   Unzip to a selected folder

The Unzip dialog box displays:

Note: *The folder and file locations that display in your window will be different.*

7. Navigate   to the C drive

Note: *If you prefer to install the practice files to another drive, navigate to that drive.*

8. Click   New folder

A blank new folder displays in the Unzip window.

9. Type   **Books2018**   to name the new folder

10. Press   Return

11. Click   Unzip ▾

A Winzip dialog box displays while the practice files are unzipped to the Books2018 folder on the C drive:

The dialog box closes when all files are unzipped.

Quick Tip. *You can use the practice files as many times as you want. To guarantee you perform every lesson with "fresh" files, we recommend that you delete the current Books2018 folder and then follow these steps every time you use this guide.*

Opening Practice Files

Most lessons in this guide have a corresponding practice file, which is indicated at the beginning of each lesson. Before starting a lesson, be sure to open the correct practice file using the method below.

To open a practice file,

1.	Start	QuickBooks 2018	
2.	Select	File : Open or Restore Company	from the menu bar

The Open or Restore Company window opens:

3.	Verify that Open a company file is selected	
4.	Click	Next

The Open a Company window displays:

5.	Navigate	to the Books2018 folder (if necessary)
6.	Select	the file you want to open
7.	Click	Open

This guide demonstrates the process of opening a file in further detail in the first lesson that requires you to open a practice file. The following abbreviated method will be shown after that lesson:

- ◆ Open   the file   using the method described in Before You Get Started

Downloading the Trial Software

This guide is intended for use with QuickBooks Desktop 2018. The practice files will not work properly if QuickBooks Desktop 2018 is not installed on your computer or laptop.

Note: The steps in this section may be different, depending on the web browser and browser version you are using. The following steps work with Internet Explorer.

To download the QuickBooks Desktop Pro trial software:

1. Open   the www.tlr-inc.com web site   in Internet Explorer

The TLR web site opens.

2. Click   the Trial Download tab   at the top of the page

The Intuit QuickBooks web site opens.

Note: If the QuickBooks Desktop Pro 2018 software information does not display, click the Change link next to QuickBooks Desktop Pro. When the Select dialog box opens, click QuickBooks Desktop Pro in the left pane. The right pane of the dialog box is populated with the QuickBooks Desktop Pro versions. Click 2018 to return to the Downloads and Updates page.

3. Click   Download

A dialog box opens asking if you want to open or save the Setup_QuickBooksPro2018.exe file.

4. Click   the down arrow   next to the Save button

A drop-down menu displays.

5. Select   Save as   from the drop-down menu

The Save As dialog box displays.

6. Navigate   to the C drive

Note: If you prefer to download the QuickBooks executable file to another drive, navigate to that drive.

7. Double-click   the Books2018 folder

8. Click   Save   to download the executable file to the Books2018 folder

When the download is complete, a dialog box displays.

  9. Click   Run

Note: If a User Account Control dialog box displays asking if you would like to allow the program to make changes to your computer, click Yes.

The Intuit Download Manager dialog box displays while the file is downloaded. When the download is complete, the QuickBooks Financial Software PRO Series - InstallShield Wizard opens. The InstallShield Wizard will guide you through the QuickBooks installation process.

  10. Click   Next   to extract the installation files

The Intuit QuickBooks Desktop Installer window displays the Welcome to QuickBooks Desktop window.

  11. Click   Next

The License Agreement window displays.

  12. Select   the I accept the terms   check box
                         of the license
                         agreement

  13. Click   Next

The License and Product Numbers window displays. The license and product numbers entered in this window are located on the inside cover of your QuickBooks guide.

  14. Type   **[the License Number]**   in the License Number fields

  15. Type   **[the Product Number]**   in the Product Number fields

  16. Click   Next

The Choose your installation type window displays.

  17. Verify   Express (recommended) is selected

  18. Click   Next

The QuickBooks Desktop Installer window displays while the software is installed. When the software installation is complete, a Congratulations window displays.

  19. Click   Open QuickBooks   to open the QuickBooks application

Note: If you cannot click the Open QuickBooks button, you may need to click the Close button and then restart your computer for QuickBooks to finish the installation.

Evaluation Criteria

The back of this guide contains important materials. Please take a moment to review the materials before using this guide.

Before Training Skill Evaluation

This training guide is designed to meet the course objectives stated at the beginning of each lesson. Prior to using the guide, rate your skill level for each objective.

After Training Skill Evaluation

After completing the guide, rate your skill level again. This evaluation helps to determine whether you met the objectives of each lesson.

Training Guide Evaluation

Rate your satisfaction level with guide objectives. This evaluation allows for comments and suggestions, and is invaluable in helping us to provide you with the best educational materials possible. Please complete the evaluation and return it to the address provided on the evaluation form.

Ordering Training Guides

If you are interested in ordering more copies of this guide, or are interested in other training guides, you may use the order form available at the back of this guide or log on to tlr-inc.com.

1

Memorizing Transactions

In this lesson, you will learn how to:

- ❑ Enter a new memorized transaction
- ❑ Edit a memorized transaction
- ❑ Delete a memorized transaction
- ❑ Group memorized transactions
- ❑ Use a memorized transaction
- ❑ Print the Memorized Transaction List

Concept

A transaction is any business agreement or exchange that you make with another person or business. In QuickBooks, you use various forms, such as invoices, bills, or checks, to perform transactions. In accounting, a transaction can also be a journal entry and some accountants may have you record depreciation expense on a monthly basis. If you have a transaction that you frequently enter, you can save time by memorizing it for future use. For example, you can memorize a monthly rent or utility bill you pay, a monthly invoice or estimate you send, or a monthly depreciation expense you enter.

Scenario

In this lesson, you will memorize a payment transaction for rental property. You will then access the Memorized Transaction List to edit a memorized transaction and delete a memorized transaction. You will also create a new memorized transaction group and add memorized transactions to this group. Finally, you will use a memorized transaction and print the Memorized Transaction List.

Practice Files: B18_Memorizing_Transactions.qbw

Entering a New Memorized Transaction

If you have a transaction that you frequently enter, you can save time by memorizing the transaction for future use. If you continuously enter the same items on a transaction, memorizing the transaction prevents you from having to re-enter the same information each time. If the amounts on the transaction do not change, for example, if you always pay the same monthly rent, you can memorize the transaction and have QuickBooks automatically enter the transaction for you at a scheduled time.

In this exercise, you will memorize a payment transaction to Fairview Properties for monthly rent due on your rental property.

Note: For this lesson, be sure to set your computer's date to 11/1/2018 before opening the QuickBooks file, as recommended in the Before You Get Started lesson. This will ensure that the dates and amounts you see on your screen match the dates and amounts in this lesson.

1. Open   **B18_Memorizing_**   using the method described in
                                 Transactions.qbw   Before You Get Started

The QuickBooks Login dialog box displays:

This dialog box informs you that you must login as a QuickBooks Administrator in order to open the company file.

2. Type   **Canalside2**   in the Password field

Note: Passwords are case-sensitive.

3. Click

QuickBooks opens the file and displays the Home page:

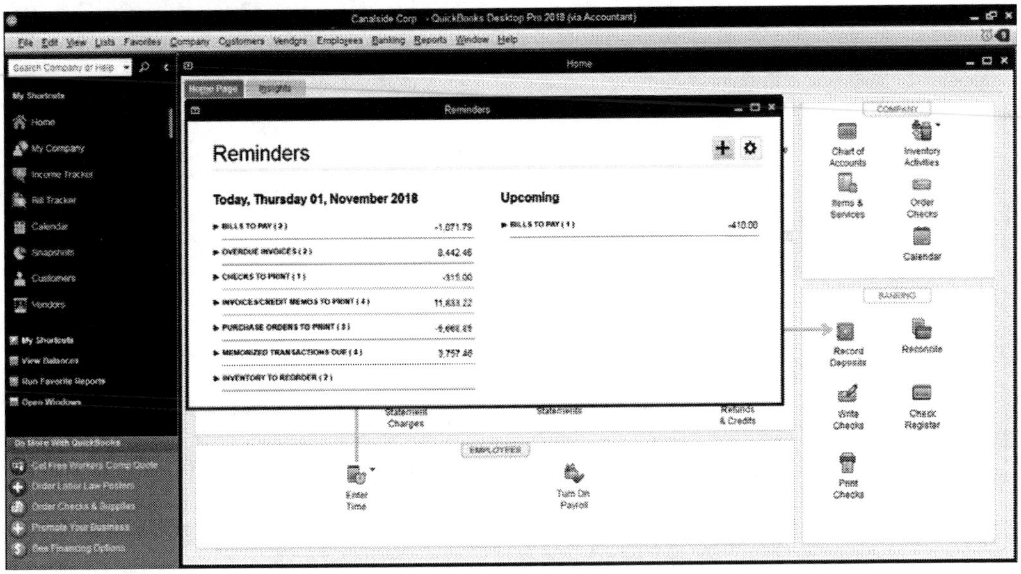

When QuickBooks opens, a Reminders window also opens. This window displays all reminders and notifications in one single location, including overdue items, to-do tasks, system notifications, and even notes from accountants.

Your Reminders window should resemble the figure below:

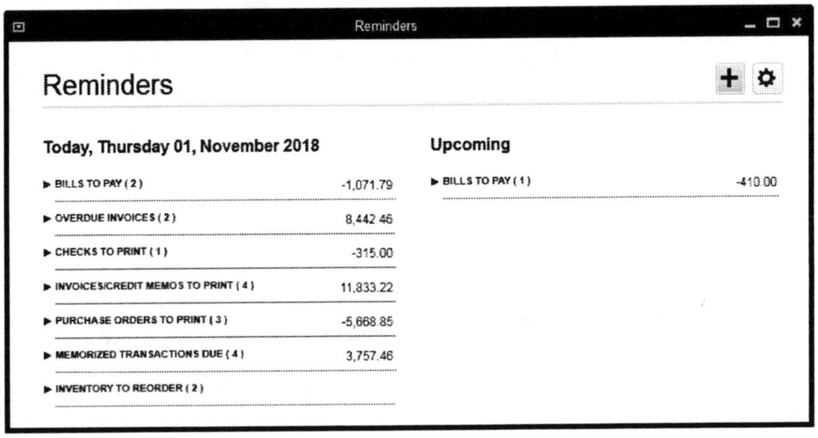

Note: If you did not change your computer's date as recommended in the Before You Get Started lesson, the Reminders that display in your window will be different.

To display the memorized transactions that are currently due,

4. Click   Memorized   in the Reminders window
           Transactions Due

Note: If you did not change your computer's date as recommended in the Before You Get Started lesson, no memorized transactions will display as due. However, you will be able to see all memorized transactions in the Memorized Transaction List later in the lesson.

The Memorized Transactions Due list expands:

Today, Thursday 01, November 2018			**Upcoming**	
▶ BILLS TO PAY (2)		-1,071.79	▶ BILLS TO PAY (1)	-410.00
▶ OVERDUE INVOICES (2)		8,442.46		
▶ CHECKS TO PRINT (1)		-315.00		
▶ INVOICES/CREDIT MEMOS TO PRINT (4)		11,833.22		
▶ PURCHASE ORDERS TO PRINT (3)		-5,668.85		
▼ MEMORIZED TRANSACTIONS DUE (4)		3,757.46		
11/01/2018	75 Sunrise ST.	4,922.46		
11/01/2018	PJ's Plumbing	-850.00		
11/01/2018	Quarterly Payments			
11/01/2018	Smith's Construction Rent...	-315.00		
▶ INVENTORY TO REORDER (2)				

Note: You may need to scroll down to view all of the transactions.

When memorizing a transaction, you can specify when you would like to be reminded about the transaction and QuickBooks will then automatically remind you when the transaction is due. For example, if you memorize a transaction to pay a bill, you can specify that you would like QuickBooks to remind you to pay the bill five days before the bill is actually due.

5. Close the Reminders window

Now, you'll learn how to memorize a transaction and specify when QuickBooks should remind you about the transaction.

6. Click in the Banking area of the Home page

The Write Checks - Checking window opens:

7. Select   Fairview Properties   from the Pay to the Order of drop-down menu

Fairview Properties has already been set up in your Vendors list, so the address information for this vendor is automatically populated. Because you have previously paid rent to Fairview Properties, the Account column on the Expenses tab at the bottom of the window is also automatically populated with the Rent account.

Because you pay the same amount each month for your rental property,

8. Type   **1200.00**   in the $ field

Quick Tip. *If the details of certain fields will change each time you recall a transaction, leave those fields blank. For example, you may want to leave the Amount field blank on your monthly phone bill or electric bill. That way, you can fill in the amount each time you recall the bill.*

9. Press | Tab |

The Amount column to the right of Rent account is updated to display **$1200.00**. Your Write Checks - Checking window should resemble the figure below:

To memorize the transaction,

10. Click   [💬 Memorize]   in the Write Checks - Checking toolbar

The Memorize Transaction window opens:

This window allows you to enter details about the memorized transaction, such as a name for the transaction, whether or not you want to be reminded about this transaction, and if so, how often you want to be reminded.

To help easily identify this transaction in the Memorized Transaction List,

11.	Type	**Rent**	in the Name field to replace Fairview Properties

Now, you can choose to be reminded to enter the transaction, to have QuickBooks automatically enter the transaction for you, or neither. In this exercise, you will have QuickBooks remind you to enter the transaction.

12.	Verify the Add to my Reminders List option is selected

This selection adds the transaction to your Reminders list. You can now enter how often you want the reminder to occur and the next date when the transaction is due.

13.	Select	**Every four weeks**	from the How Often drop-down menu

14.	Type	**12/01/2018**	in the Next Date field

Quick Tip. You can also choose to have QuickBooks automatically enter a transaction for you. When selecting this option, be sure to enter how often you want QuickBooks to enter the transaction and the next date the transaction is due. You can even specify how many times you want QuickBooks to enter the transaction in the Number Remaining field. QuickBooks will then automatically enter the transaction according to your selections.

The Memorize Transaction window should resemble the figure below:

15. Click [OK] to memorize the transaction and return to the Write Checks - Checking window

QuickBooks will now remind you that this transaction is due every four weeks. The next rent payment is due on 12/01/2018, so QuickBooks will display a reminder in your Reminders list prior to that date.

In this exercise, you created a memorized transaction for rent. However, because you don't want to actually pay the monthly rent to Fairview Properties at this time, you need to clear the Write Checks window.

16. Click [Clear] to clear all data in the Write Checks - Checking window

17. Close the Write Checks - Checking window

Editing a Memorized Transaction

You can edit a memorized transaction's name, schedule, or other options using the Memorized Transaction List. In this exercise, you will edit the schedule for a memorized transaction and then change the transaction's line items.

To edit a memorized transaction's schedule,

1. Select Lists : Memorized Transaction List from the menu bar

The Memorized Transaction List opens:

TRANSACTION NA... ▲	TYPE	SOURCE ACCOUNT	AMOUNT	FREQUENCY	AUTO	NEXT DATE
◊ 75 Sunrise ST.	Invoice	Accounts Receivable	4,922.46	Annually		11/01/2018
◊ Dental Office	Invoice	Accounts Receivable	1,392.63	Never		
◊ Fairgrave Gas & Electric	Check	Checking	156.33	Every four w...		12/01/2018
◊ Mason & Son Painting	Bill	Accounts Payable	217.29	Never		
◊ PJ's Plumbing	Bill	Accounts Payable	850.00	Monthly		11/01/2018
◊ **Quarterly Payments**	**Group**			**Quarterly**		**11/01/2018**
◊ D. Raff	Check	Checking	375.00			
◊ Fairgrave Insurance	Check	Checking	225.00			
◊ Remodel Bathroom	Invoice	Accounts Receivable	1,998.13	Never		
◊ Rent	Check	Checking	1,200.00	Every four w...		12/01/2018

Memorized Transaction ▼   Enter Transaction

Note: You can move and resize the Memorized Transaction List as necessary.

This list includes all transactions that have been memorized and the memorized transaction groups that have been created. Individual memorized transactions display in normal font and memorized transaction groups display in bold.

Transactions within a group are indented immediately below the group name. Notice that the memorized transaction you just created for rent displays in the list (you may need to scroll down).

2. Select   Fairgrave   in the Memorized Transaction List
                Gas & Electric

3. Click

Memorized Transaction ▾

A drop-down menu displays:

Edit Memorized Transaction	Ctrl+E
New Group	
Delete Memorized Transaction	Ctrl+D
Customize Columns...	
Print List...	Ctrl+P
Re-sort List	

4. Select   Edit Memorized   from the drop-down menu
                Transaction

The Schedule Memorized Transaction window opens:

When you specify a schedule for a memorized transaction, you can choose for QuickBooks to remind you of the transaction or to automatically record it for you.

QuickBooks is currently scheduled to remind you of this transaction every four weeks beginning on 12/01/2018. You will now edit this transaction's schedule so that QuickBooks will automatically enter it for you.

5. Select   Automate Transaction Entry

The Number Remaining and Days in Advance to Enter fields become active.

6. Type   **12**   in the Number Remaining field

This indicates that you want QuickBooks to enter this payment twelve more times.

7. Type   **3**   in the Days in Advance to Enter field

This indicates that you want QuickBooks to enter this transaction three days in advance of the due date.

The Schedule Memorized Transaction window should resemble the figure below:

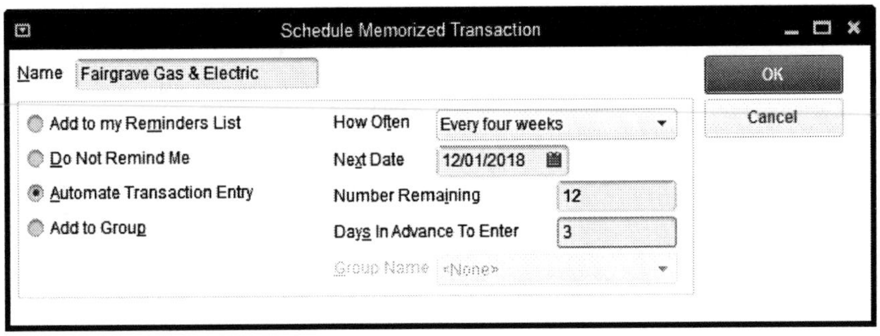

8. Click **OK**

The transaction is memorized with the new schedule and the Schedule Memorized Transaction window closes.

QuickBooks will now automatically enter the payment transaction to Fairgrave Gas & Electric every four weeks beginning on 12/01/2018 for the next twelve months. In addition, QuickBooks will enter the transaction three days in advance of the due date.

You can also edit a memorized transaction if you need to change line items, amounts, or other details of the transaction. In this exercise, you will change the amount of the Fairgrave Gas & Electric memorized transaction.

9. Double-click **Fairgrave Gas & Electric** in the Memorized Transaction List

Note: If you did not change your computer's date as recommended in the Before You Get Started lesson, click the Yes button in the Future Transactions dialog box that displays informing you this transaction is more than 30 days in the future.

The Write Checks - Checking window opens displaying the Fairgrave Gas & Electric transaction:

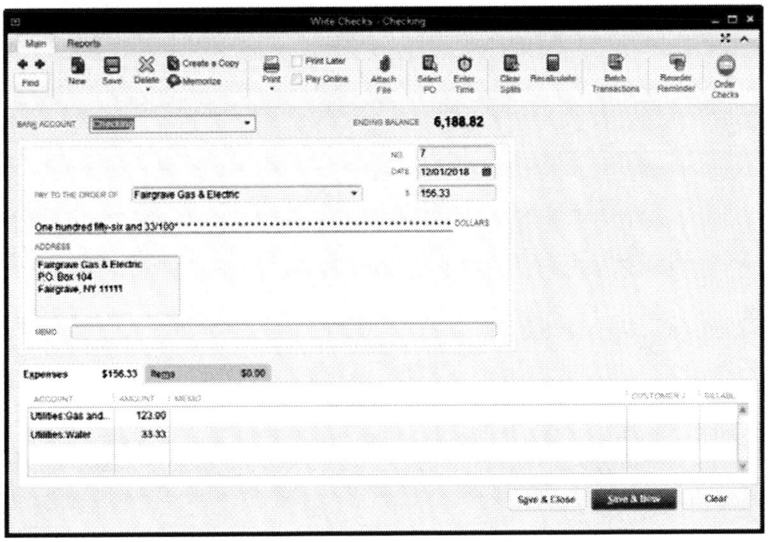

You recently started using Fairgrave Gas & Electric's budgeted billing program and are now paying the same amount for gas and electric each month for the rest of the year.

10. Type **205.00** in the $ field

Because you changed the amount of the transaction, you need to change the amounts on the Expenses tab in the lower portion of the window.

11. Type **205.00** in the Amount column to the right of Utilities:Gas and Electric

Because you no longer pay Fairgrave Gas & Electric for your water bill,

12. Delete the Utilities:Water text in the Account column and 33.33 in the Amount column

13. Press [Tab]

The check will need to be printed and mailed.

14. Select the Print Later check box in the toolbar

Your Write Checks - Checking window should resemble the figure below:

To memorize the transaction with the new amount,

15. Click [🗨 Memorize] in the Write Checks - Checking toolbar

A Replace Memorized Transaction dialog box displays:

This dialog box informs you that Fairgrave Gas & Electric is already in the Memorized Transaction List and asks if you would like to replace the existing transaction or add a new one.

16. Click　　　　　　　| Replace |　　　　　　　to replace the existing transaction

Because you are not actually paying the monthly gas and electric bill at this time, you need to clear the Write Checks window.

17. Click　　　　　　　| Clear |　　　　　　　to clear all data in the Write Checks - Checking window

18. Close the Write Checks - Checking window

You return to the Memorized Transaction List.

Deleting a Memorized Transaction

In addition to editing memorized transactions, you can also delete memorized transactions that you no longer use.

Note: You cannot delete a memorized transaction while using your company file in multi-user mode; the company file must be open in single-user mode.

To delete a memorized transaction,

1. Select　　　　Dental Office　　　　in the Memorized Transaction List

2. Click　　　　| Memorized Transaction ▾ |

A drop-down menu displays.

3. Select　　　　Delete Memorized　　from the drop-down menu
　　　　　　　　　Transaction

The Delete Memorized Transaction dialog box displays:

Delete Memorized Transaction

Are you sure you want to delete this memorized transaction?

| OK |　| Cancel |

4. Click

The Dental Office memorized transaction is deleted.

Grouping Memorized Transactions

If you have several memorized transactions that you always enter on the same day, you can save time if you group them together. For example, suppose you memorize multiple transactions that occur at the end of each month, including your rent check, your gas and electric check, an invoice for a monthly standing order from a customer, and a bill from your cell phone company.

Instead of recalling each memorized transaction separately at the end of each month, you can group them together in a group named "End of Month". Then, you can either have QuickBooks enter the grouped transactions automatically at the end of every month, or have QuickBooks remind you when it's time to recall the grouped transactions.

In this exercise, you will create a new group called "End of Month" and then group specific memorized transactions within this group.

In the Memorized Transaction List,

1. Click **Memorized Transaction** ▼

A drop-down menu displays.

2. Select   New Group   from the drop-down menu

The New Memorized Transaction Group window opens:

To enter a name for this group,

3. Type   **End of Month**   in the Name field

You can now choose how you want to manage the transaction group. You can have QuickBooks remind you about the transaction group on a regular basis, you can have the transaction group available for future use without being reminded about it, or you can have QuickBooks record the transactions in the group on a regular basis.

To have QuickBooks remind you about the transaction group on a regular basis,

4. Verify the Add to my Reminders List option is selected

5. Select | Monthly | from the How Often drop-down menu

6. Type | **12/28/2018** | in the Next Date field

7. Click | OK | to create the new memorized transaction group

The End of Month group is added to the Memorized Transaction List:

TRANSACTION NA. ▲	TYPE	SOURCE ACCOUNT	AMOUNT	FREQUENCY	AUTO	NEXT DATE
◆ 75 Sunrise ST.	Invoice	Accounts Receivable	4,922.46	Annually		11/01/2018
◇ End of Month	Group			Monthly		12/28/2018
◆ Fairgrave Gas & Electric	Check	Checking	205.00	Every four w...	✓	12/01/2018
◆ Mason & Son Painting	Bill	Accounts Payable	217.29	Never		
◆ PJ's Plumbing	Bill	Accounts Payable	850.00	Monthly		11/01/2018
◆ Quarterly Payments	Group			Quarterly		11/01/2018
◇ D. Raff	Check	Checking	375.00			
◇ Fairgrave Insurance	Check	Checking	225.00			
◆ Remodel Bathroom	Invoice	Accounts Receivable	1,998.13	Never		
◆ Rent	Check	Checking	1,200.00	Every four w...		12/01/2018

Memorized Transaction ▼ | Enter Transaction

Notice that End of Month is bolded to indicate it is a group. You can now add memorized transactions to the End of Month group.

8. Select | Fairgrave Gas & Electric | in the Memorized Transaction List

9. Click | Memorized Transaction ▼ |

A drop-down menu displays.

10. Select | Edit Memorized Transaction | from the drop-down menu

The Schedule Memorized Transaction window opens displaying the schedule for the Fairgrave Gas & Electric memorized transaction:

Name [Fairgrave Gas & Electric]   OK   Cancel

○ Add to my Reminders List   How Often [Every four weeks ▼]
○ Do Not Remind Me   Next Date [12/01/2018 📅]
● Automate Transaction Entry   Number Remaining [12]
○ Add to Group   Days In Advance To Enter [3]
　　Group Name [<None> ▼]

To add the Fairgrave Gas & Electric memorized transaction to the End of Month group,

11.   Select   Add to Group

The Group Name field becomes active, while the How Often, Next Date, Number Remaining, and Days in Advance to Enter fields become inactive.

12.   Select   End of Month   from the Group Name drop-down menu

13.   Click   [OK]   to close the Schedule Memorized Transaction window

You return to the Memorized Transaction List:

TRANSACTION NA... ▲	TYPE	SOURCE ACCOUNT	AMOUNT	FREQUENCY	AUTO	NEXT DATE
⬧ 75 Sunrise ST.	Invoice	Accounts Receivable	4,922.46	Annually		11/01/2018
⬧ End of Month	Group			Monthly		12/28/2018
⬧ Fairgrave Gas & Ele...	Check	Checking	205.00			
⬧ Mason & Son Painting	Bill	Accounts Payable	217.29	Never		
⬧ PJ's Plumbing	Bill	Accounts Payable	850.00	Monthly		11/01/2018
⬧ Quarterly Payments	Group			Quarterly		11/01/2018
⬧ D. Raff	Check	Checking	375.00			
⬧ Fairgrave Insurance	Check	Checking	225.00			
⬧ Remodel Bathroom	Invoice	Accounts Receivable	1,998.13	Never		
⬧ Rent	Check	Checking	1,200.00	Every four w...		12/01/2018

[Memorized Transaction ▼]   [Enter Transaction]

Note: You may need to scroll up to view the End of Month group.

The Fairgrave Gas & Electric memorized transaction is now indented below the End of Month group to indicate it is part of this group.

14.   Repeat steps 8-13 to add the Rent memorized transaction to the End of Month group

When you have finished, the Memorized Transaction List should resemble the figure below:

TRANSACTION NA... ▲	TYPE	SOURCE ACCOUNT	AMOUNT	FREQUENCY	AUTO	NEXT DATE
⬧ 75 Sunrise ST.	Invoice	Accounts Receivable	4,922.46	Annually		11/01/2018
⬧ End of Month	Group			Monthly		12/28/2018
⬧ Fairgrave Gas & Ele...	Check	Checking	205.00			
⬧ Rent	Check	Checking	1,200.00			
⬧ Mason & Son Painting	Bill	Accounts Payable	217.29	Never		
⬧ PJ's Plumbing	Bill	Accounts Payable	850.00	Monthly		11/01/2018
⬧ Quarterly Payments	Group			Quarterly		11/01/2018
⬧ D. Raff	Check	Checking	375.00			
⬧ Fairgrave Insurance	Check	Checking	225.00			
⬧ Remodel Bathroom	Invoice	Accounts Receivable	1,998.13	Never		

[Memorized Transaction ▼]   [Enter Transaction]

The Rent memorized transaction is now indented below the End of Month group to indicate it is part of this group. You would repeat these same steps for all transactions you want added to the End of Month group.

Using a Memorized Transaction

After you have created a memorized transaction, it is easy to use the transaction. If you use the transaction on a regular basis (for example, monthly), you can set it up as a recurring transaction when you memorize it. Otherwise, you can use it as needed by entering it from the Memorized Transaction List.

1. Select   Mason & Son Painting   in the Memorized Transaction List

2. Click   Enter Transaction

The Enter Bills window opens:

This windows displays the memorized bill transaction for Mason & Son Painting. You can now make any necessary changes to the transaction before entering it. In this exercise, you will change the amount of the bill, as well as the line items on the Expenses tab.

3. Type   **158.62**   in the Amount Due field

4. Click   in the Memo column
                 on the Expenses tab

The Amount column on the Expenses tab at the bottom of the window is updated to display **$158.62**.

5. Type **Family Room Paint** in the Memo field on the Expenses tab to replace Interior Paint

6. Select Klieier, Patricia Family Room from the Customer:Job drop-down menu to replace Richard Real Estate

7. Deselect the Billable check box

The Enter Bills window should resemble the figure below:

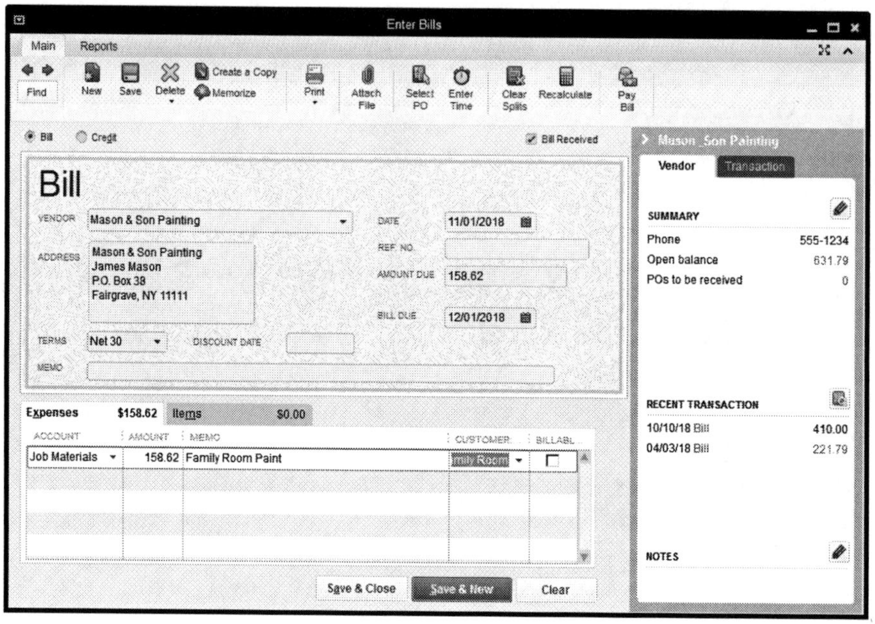

8. Click Save & Close to save the transaction and close the Enter Bills window

You return to the Memorized Transaction List.

Printing the Memorized Transaction List

QuickBooks allows you to easily print the Memorized Transaction List. When printing this list, the name, type, account used, frequency, and amount of each memorized transaction prints.

To print the Memorized Transaction List,

1. Click Memorized Transaction ▼

A drop-down menu displays.

2. Select Print List from the drop-down menu

A List Reports dialog box displays informing you about printing list reports:

```
┌─────────────────────────────────────────────────────┐
│                    List Reports                    ✕ │
├─────────────────────────────────────────────────────┤
│   ⓘ   You may want to try list reports, which allow  │
│       you to customize and format a report before    │
│       printing it. List reports are available from   │
│       the Reports button on the list, as well as the │
│       main Reports menu.                             │
│                                                       │
│       ☐ Do not display this message in the future    │
│                                                       │
│              [    OK    ]    [  Cancel  ]            │
└─────────────────────────────────────────────────────┘
```

3. Click [OK]

The Print Lists window opens:

```
┌──────────────────────────────────────────────────────────────────┐
│                          Print Lists                             ✕ │
├──────────────────────────────────────────────────────────────────┤
│  ┌Settings┐ ┌Fonts┐ ┌Margins┐                                     │
│                                                    [   Print   ]  │
│  Print to:                                                         │
│  ⦿ Printer:  Xerox Phaser 6180N PS on LPT1:  ▼  [ Options... ]    │
│                                                    [  Cancel   ]  │
│  ○ File:     ASCII text file                 ▼                    │
│                                                    [   Help    ]  │
│  Note: To install additional printers or to change port           │
│        assignments, use the Windows Control Panel. [  Preview  ]  │
│                                                                    │
│  ORIENTATION:              PAGE RANGE:                             │
│  ⦿ Portrait                ⦿ All                                   │
│  ○ Landscape               ○ Pages:                               │
│                               From: 1    To: 9999                 │
│                                                                    │
│                            Number of copies:  1                   │
│                            ☑ Collate                              │
│                                                                    │
│                            ☐ Print in color (color printers only) │
│                                                                    │
└──────────────────────────────────────────────────────────────────┘
```

Note: The printer displayed in your Print Lists window will be different.

The Print Lists window allows you to specify the print settings, fonts, and margins.

You will accept the default selections.

Note: If your computer is not set up to print, click Cancel to close the Print Lists window.

4. Click [Print]

All memorized transactions in the list print.

5. Close the Memorized Transaction List

Review

In this lesson, you have learned how to:

- ☑ Enter a new memorized transaction
- ☑ Edit a memorized transaction
- ☑ Delete a memorized transaction
- ☑ Group memorized transactions
- ☑ Use a memorized transaction
- ☑ Print the Memorized Transaction List

Practice:

1. Write a check to Bennet's Insulation for $250.00 and charge the payment to the Building Supplies account.

2. Memorize the check and have QuickBooks remind you about the transaction weekly beginning 11/10/2018.

3. Clear the Write Checks - Checking window and then close the window without recording the transaction.

4. Edit the schedule for the Smith's Construction Rental memorized transaction to have QuickBooks automatically enter the transaction on a quarterly basis beginning 12/01/2018 for three more times. Have QuickBooks enter the transaction five days in advance.

5. Delete the Remodel Bathroom memorized transaction.

6. Create a new memorized transaction group named December 2018 Project Bills. Have QuickBooks remind you about the transaction group on a weekly basis beginning 12/01/2018.

7. Group the PJ's Plumbing memorized transaction in the December 2018 Project Bills group.

8. Use the D. Raff memorized transaction, but change the payment to $200.00.

9. Close the company file.

2

Customizing Forms

In this lesson, you will learn how to:

❑ Create a custom template

❑ Modify a template

❑ Print forms

Concept

The built-in forms provided by QuickBooks can be used to create professional documents. For example, there are three preset forms in QuickBooks that can be used to create invoices: Professional, Service, and Product. However, these preset forms may not always fulfill your needs. As your busine ss grows, you may want to customize a form to suit the needs of your business, such as by adding or deleting fields from the form.

You may also want to customize the appearance of your forms to match the needs of your business. For each form, you can decide which fields and columns to include, what they are called, and where to place them. After you have created these forms, you can save them to use whenever you want. These forms are called templates.

Scenario

As the owner of Canalside Corp., a company that does remodeling and new construction, you are responsible for the company's finances, which includes issuing purchase orders and invoicing your clients. In this lesson, you will create two custom forms, an invoice and a purchase order. First, you will duplicate the Intuit Product Invoice template to create an invoice tailored to your business needs. You will then customize the template by changing the title, deleting fields, renaming a field, adding a custom column, and rearranging columns. You will also use the Layout Designer to move fields, change the width of columns, and change the font attributes for text in a field. You will then modify the purchase order template by adding disclaimer text. Finally, you will print an invoice.

Practice Files: B18_Customizing_Forms.qbw

Creating a Custom Template

Two basic concepts are used to create custom business templates: customizing and designing. You customize templates by specifying information on tabs in the Customize window. You design the layout of templates using the Layout Designer, which allows you to move and resize objects.

Canalside Corp. provides remodeling and construction services, as well as sells product materials for these services. One of the products the company sells most often is interior wood doors. You would like to create a custom invoice for the sale of this product. In this exercise, you'll use both the customize and designer features in QuickBooks to create a custom invoice for interior wood doors.

To create a custom template,

1.	Open	B18_Customizing Forms.qbw	using the method described in Before You Get Started

The QuickBooks Login dialog box displays:

```
┌──────────────────────────────────────────────────────┐
│              QuickBooks Login                       ✕  │
├──────────────────────────────────────────────────────┤
│  You need to log in as QuickBooks Administrator to     │
│  proceed.  Please enter the admin (owner) password     │
│  for the company:                                      │
│                                                        │
│                  Canalside Corp.                       │
│                                                        │
│     Password: [_____]   I forgot my password│
│              Passwords are case sensitive.             │
│                                                        │
│       [   OK   ]    [ Cancel ]    [  Help  ]           │
└──────────────────────────────────────────────────────┘
```

This dialog box informs you that you must login as a QuickBooks Administrator in order to open the company file.

2.	Type	**Canalside2**	in the Password field

Note: Passwords are case-sensitive.

3.	Click	OK

QuickBooks opens the file.

4.	Click	✕	to close the Reminders window

QuickBooks displays the Home page:

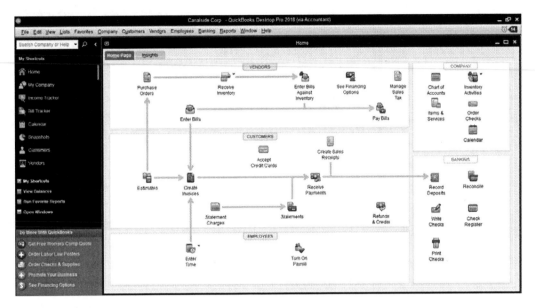

To open the list of templates,

5.   Select   Lists : Templates   from the menu bar

The Templates window opens:

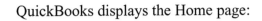

Note: The templates listed in the Templates window depend on the version of QuickBooks you are using.

This window displays a list of the available templates in QuickBooks. To view the Intuit Product Invoice,

6.   Select   Intuit Product   in the Name column
                       Invoice

7.   Click   Open Form

The Intuit Product Invoice displays in the Create Invoices window:

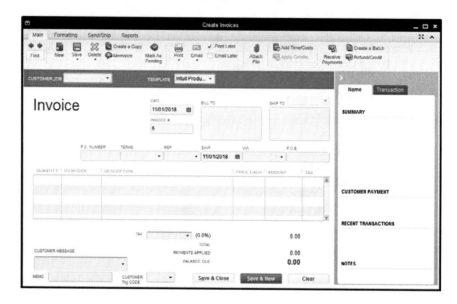

In this exercise, you will change the default title of the form from Invoice to Bill, delete the Terms and Rep fields, and rename the Ship Via field. You will also add a Color column in the lower half of the form and rearrange the columns so that the Color column displays to the right of the Description column. You will then change the color scheme of the form and give the form a new name.

8. Close the Create Invoices window to return to the Templates window with the Intuit Product Invoice selected

Although QuickBooks allows you to customize the predefined Product Invoice, Service Invoice, and Professional Invoice templates, there are several customization options that are not available for these predefined templates, including the Layout Designer. If you want to change the layout of a predefined template, you will need to create a duplicate of the template and customize the duplicate to better suit your needs.

To duplicate the product invoice template,

9. Click | Templates ▾ | at the bottom of the window

A drop-down menu displays:

New	Ctrl+N
Edit Template	Ctrl+E
Delete Template	Ctrl+D
Duplicate	
Make Template Inactive	
Show Inactive Templates	
Customize Columns...	
Import...	
Export...	
Download Templates...	
Create Form Design...	
Use	Ctrl+U
Find in Transactions...	
Print List...	Ctrl+P

10. Select   Duplicate   from the drop-down menu

The Select Template Type window opens:

Select Template Type   ✖
Please select the type of template you are creating:
⦿ Invoice
◯ Credit Memo
◯ Sales Receipt
◯ Purchase Order
◯ Statement
◯ Estimate
OK   Cancel

11. Click   [OK]   to accept Invoice as the type of template to duplicate

A copy of the Intuit Product Invoice is created and displays in the Templates list:

Templates	_ ☐ ✖
NAME	TYPE
Copy of: Intuit Product Invoice	Invoice
Fixed Fee Invoice	Invoice
Intuit Packing Slip	Invoice
Intuit Product Invoice	Invoice
Intuit Professional Invoice	Invoice
Intuit Service Invoice	Invoice
Templates ▼ **Open Form** ☐ Include inactive	

Note: The templates listed in the Templates window depend on the version of QuickBooks you are using.

With the Copy of: Intuit Product Invoice selected,

12. Click   [Templates ▼]   at the bottom of the window

A drop-down menu displays.

13. Select   Edit Template   from the drop-down menu

The Basic Customization window opens:

The Basic Customization window includes different areas displaying various formatting options. For example, the Logo & Fonts area allows you to include a logo on your form, select a color scheme, or change the font attributes on the form.

In this exercise, you will customize the fields on the form first.

14. Click   [Additional Customization...]

The Additional Customization window opens:

The Additional Customization window uses multiple tabs to display several sets of formatting options. Notice that the Header tab is currently selected. The Header tab lets you select the text to use for the titles displayed on the screen or printed on the hard copy of the invoice. You can also select the fields you would like to display on the screen and the printed form, and enter custom titles for each field.

In this exercise, you will change the title on the invoice to Bill, delete the Terms and REP fields since you don't want them to display on the invoice, and change the title of the Ship Via field to Method.

To change the title on the invoice,

| 15. | Select | Invoice | in the Default Title field |
| 16. | Type | **Bill** | to replace the Invoice text |

Because the Screen and Print check boxes are selected, this changes the title of the form from Invoice to Bill on both the screen *and* the printed form.

Quick Tip. *If you want to track information on a form that you would rather not have the customer see, select the Screen check box and deselect the Print check box for the item.*

To delete the Terms and REP fields from the invoice when it is displayed on the screen and when it's printed,

| 17. | Click | the Screen check box | in the Terms row to deselect it |

A Layout Designer dialog box displays informing you how to make changes to the layout of the form:

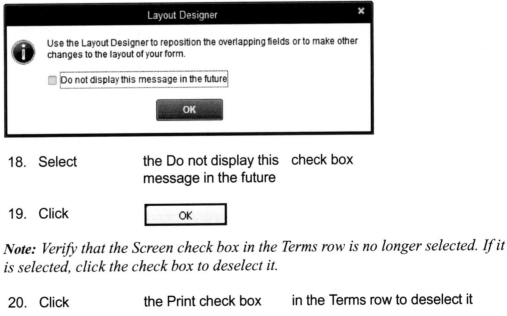

| 18. | Select | the Do not display this message in the future | check box |
| 19. | Click | OK | |

Note: *Verify that the Screen check box in the Terms row is no longer selected. If it is selected, click the check box to deselect it.*

| 20. | Click | the Print check box | in the Terms row to deselect it |
| 21. | Click | the Screen and Print check boxes | in the REP row to deselect them |

Quick Tip. *At any time during the process of creating a new template, you can click the Default button to return a page to its original settings.*

To change the title of the Via field,

22.	Select	Via	in the Title column of the Ship Via row
23.	Type	**Method**	to replace Via

Quick Tip. *You can use the Other row to add a field to the form.*

24.	Press	Tab	to update the preview of the form

Your Additional Customization window should resemble the figure below:

The form has been updated in the Preview area with the new title, the Terms and REP fields have been deleted, and the Via field is now entitled Method.

25.	Click	the Columns tab	

The Columns customization options display:

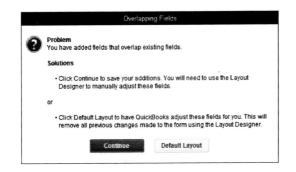

The Columns tab allows you to select the items you would like to display on the screen and the printed form. Notice that a Color option displays at the bottom of the list below the Other options. This option displays here because it is a customized field that was added to the Item List. Custom fields provide a way for you to track information specific to your business.

When you add a customized field for an item, you must add the same field to a template in order for it to display on forms. For example, if you want the Color information for interior wood doors to display, you must customize this template to include the Color field.

To add the Color column on screen and on the printed form,

26.   Click   the Screen and   next to Color to select them
                           Print check boxes

An Overlapping Fields dialog box displays:

This dialog box informs you that you have added fields that overlap existing fields. You can fix the fields at a later time using the Layout Designer or you can allow QuickBooks to automatically adjust the overlapping fields for you.

27. Click   Default Layout   to allow QuickBooks to adjust the overlapping fields

A Warning dialog box displays:

This dialog box warns you that you are about to lose all changes made to the form using the Layout Designer. Because you have not made any changes to the form using the Layout Designer yet,

28. Click   Yes

The fields are automatically adjusted and the Color column displays to the right of the Price Each column in the Preview area. QuickBooks has also placed a number 5 in the Order column next to Color. The number in the Order column indicates the placement of the column on the form.

To rearrange the columns so that the Color column is displayed to the right of the Description column,

29. Select   5   in the Order field of the Color row to highlight it

30. Type   **4**

31. Click   in the Order field   of the Rate row

Note: If the Overlapping Fields dialog box displays, click the Default Layout button and then click the Yes button in the Warning dialog box.

QuickBooks automatically replaces the 4 in the column with a 5. The Color column will now be displayed after the Description column and before the Price Each column.

Your Additional Customization window should resemble the figure below:

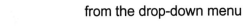

Note: The form in your window may look slightly different.

Quick Tip. *You can use the Other 1 and Other 2 fields to add columns to the form.*

| 32. | Click | OK | to save the form and return to the Basic Customization window |

To apply a new color scheme to the form,

| 33. | Click | ▾ | below Select Color Scheme |

A drop-down menu displays:

✔ Please Select..
Black
Gray
Maroon
Green
Blue
Beige

| 34. | Select | Green | from the drop-down menu |

| 35. | Click | Apply Color Scheme |

The new color scheme is applied and the form now displays in green in the Preview area of the Basic Customization window.

Because you have changed this form to suit your specific business needs, you should now give the form a new name.

| 36. | Click | Manage Templates... |

The Manage Templates window opens:

Note: *The templates listed in the Manage Templates window depend on the version of QuickBooks you are using.*

This window allows you to copy, delete, download, and name templates.

37.	Select	Copy of: Intuit Product Invoice	in the Template Name field in the Preview area of the window
38.	Type	**Invoice for Interior Wood Doors**	
39.	Click	OK	to save the form with the new name

You return to the Basic Customization window and the new name displays in the Selected Template area at the top of the window.

| 40. | Click | OK | to close the Basic Customization window |

The newly named customized template displays in the Templates window:

Note: *The templates listed in the Templates window depend on the version of QuickBooks you are using.*

To view the customized invoice,

41. Click [O**p**en Form]

The custom invoice you just created for interior wood doors opens:

To view how the form will look when it is printed,

42. Click [Print ▾] in the toolbar

A drop-down menu displays.

43. Select   Preview   from the drop-down menu

Note: If a Shipping Labels dialog box displays, select the Do not display this message in the future check box and click the OK button.

The Print Preview window opens:

The title of the form is now Bill, the color scheme is green, the Terms and Rep fields have been deleted, the Ship Via field is now the Method field, and a Color column now displays after the Quantity column.

Quick Tip. Click the Zoom In button if you would like to enlarge the form.

44. Click **Close** to close the Print Preview window

You return to the Create Invoices window.

Using the Layout Designer

With the Layout Designer, you can change the design or layout of a form. You can move and resize fields, change the width of columns, turn borders on or off around fields, and specify fonts.

Next, you will edit the layout of the customized invoice by moving the P.O. Number and Sample fields, changing the width of the Quantity and Color columns, and editing the font properties for text in a field.

With the Invoice for Interior Wood Doors displayed,

1. Click the Formatting tab in the Create Invoices window

The Formatting toolbar displays.

2. Click [Customize Data Layout] in the Formatting toolbar

The Additional Customization window opens:

	Screen	Print	Title
Default Title	✔	✔	Bill
Date	✔	✔	Date
Invoice Number	✔	✔	Invoice #
Bill To	✔	✔	Bill To
Ship To	✔	✔	Ship To
P.O. No.	✔	✔	P.O. Number
S.O. No.	☐	☐	S.O. No.
Terms	☐	☐	Terms
Due Date	☐	☐	Due Date
REP	☐	☐	Rep
Account Number	☐	☐	Account #
Ship Date	✔	✔	Ship
Ship Via	✔	✔	Method
FOB	✔	✔	F.O.B.
Project/Job	☐	✔	Project
Other	☐	☐	
Contract #	☐	☐	

You will use the Layout Designer to change the design of the invoice.

Quick Tip. *The Customize Design toolbar button allows you to open a QuickBooks Forms Customization window where you can create a new design reflecting your business and use it for all your QuickBooks forms, such as invoices and sales receipts.*

3. Click | Layout Designer... | at the bottom of the window

The Layout Designer - Invoice for Interior Wood Doors window opens:

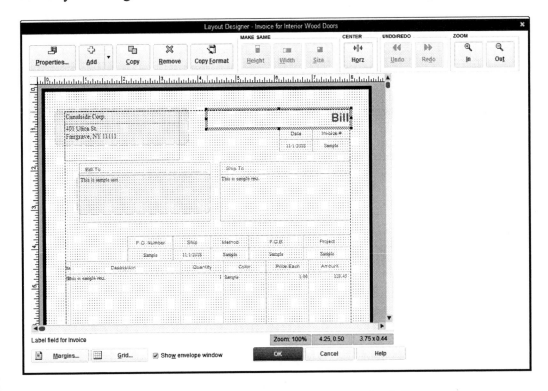

Note: *The size of the invoice (the amount showing) may be different on your screen.*

By clicking the In and Out Zoom buttons in the upper-right corner of the window, you can zoom in for a closer look at a small area of the form or zoom out to see a wider view of the form.

4. Click   one time to zoom out

Your form should resemble the figure below:

Note: The form in your window may look slightly different.

First, you will move the P.O. Number field and corresponding Sample field so they are positioned next to the Date field.

5.   Click   P.O. Number   to select it

Diagonal hashmarks display around the P.O. Number field to indicate that it's selected.

You can select multiple fields at once by holding down the Shift key.

6.   Press and hold   Shift

7.   Click   Sample   (below P.O. Number)

8.   Release   Shift

The P.O. Number and Sample fields should resemble the figure below:

Note: The "Sample" text does not display on the screen or printed version of a form. QuickBooks uses this text to identify empty fields in the Layout Designer.

9. Position   the mouse pointer   over the selected fields

The mouse pointer changes to a four-directional arrow 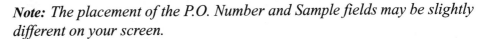 .

10. Click and hold   the left mouse button

11. Drag   the selected fields   up until they are positioned to the
                                                  left of the Date field in the upper-
                                                  right corner of the form

12. Release   the mouse button

Your form should resemble the figure below:

Note: *The placement of the P.O. Number and Sample fields may be slightly*
different on your screen.

Because Canalside Corp. rarely has orders of more than one hundred interior wood
doors, the Quantity field is much wider than it needs to be. Also, you've found that
the Color column is too small. Next, you will decrease the width of the Quantity
column and increase the width of the Color column.

13. Click   anywhere   in the Quantity column heading to
                                                  select it

The Description, Quantity, Color, Price Each, and Amount columns are selected:

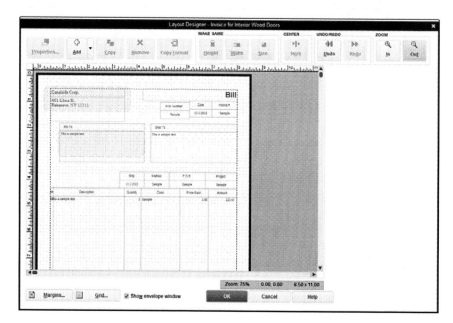

14. Position   the mouse pointer   on the vertical line between the
                                                  Quantity and Color columns

The mouse pointer changes to a bi-directional arrow ✛.

15. Click and hold   the left mouse button

16. Drag   the vertical line   about 1/4 inch to the left
                       between the columns   (so that the word Quantity still
                                                  displays completely in the column)

17. Release   the mouse button

The Quantity column is now smaller while the Color column is wider:

Quick Tip. *If you make a mistake when using the Layout Designer, you can click the Undo button in the toolbar to undo your changes.*

If you want to change the font, border, or background of a field, you can double-click the field to display the Properties window. In this exercise, you will change the Canalside Corp. font properties.

| 18. | Double-click | the Canalside Corp. field | in the upper-left corner of the window |

The Properties window opens:

Quick Tip. *You can also click the Properties button at the top of the Layout Designer to display the Properties window.*

The Properties window allows you to change the font and justification of text in a field, add or remove a border from a field, or change the background of a field.

| 19. | Click | Font... |

The Example window opens:

This window allows you to change the font type, style, size, effects, and color.

| 20. | Select | Bold | from the Font Style list |

21. Select  14 from the Size list

As you change the font attributes, an example of how the text will display on the form appears in the Sample field.

22. Click [OK] to return to the Properties window

23. Click [OK] to return to the Layout Designer

The Canalside Corp. text is now bold and in a 14 point font size:

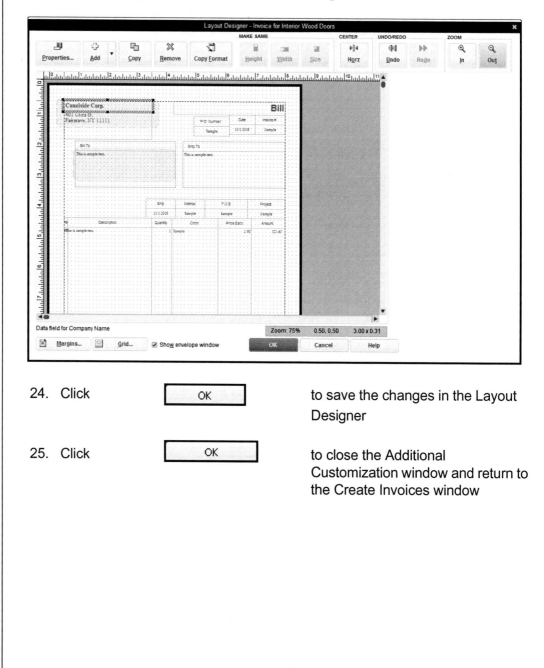

24. Click [OK] to save the changes in the Layout Designer

25. Click [OK] to close the Additional Customization window and return to the Create Invoices window

Your Create Invoices window should resemble the figure below:

The invoice does not show the changes you just made in the Layout Designer. This is because changes made in the Layout Designer sometimes affect only the printed invoice and not the invoice that QuickBooks displays for data entry.

To preview how the printed invoice will look,

26. Click **Preview** in the toolbar

The Print Preview window opens:

The Print Preview window shows you exactly how the printed form will look. The changes you made in the Layout Designer are reflected in this preview.

27. Click [Close] to close the Print Preview window

28. Close the Create Invoices window to return to the Templates window

Modifying a Template

Existing templates can be modified quickly and easily within QuickBooks to create forms that are tailored to your business needs.

Note: You can modify the existing Product Invoice, Service Invoice, and Professional Invoice templates; however, several customization options are not available for these predefined templates, including the Layout Designer.

In this exercise, you will create a custom purchase order by adding a disclaimer to the existing purchase order template.

To modify a template,

1. Select   Custom Purchase   in the Name column of the
                 Order   Templates window (scroll down)

2. Click   [Templates ▼]

A drop-down menu displays.

3. Select   Edit Template   from the drop-down menu

The Basic Customization window opens:

4. Click   [Additional Customization...]

The Additional Customization window opens:

5. Click the | Footer | tab

The Footer tab displays:

The Footer tab enables you to add information to the footer area located at the bottom of a form.

6. Click the Print check box for to select it
Long text (disclaimer)

This indicates that the disclaimer text should be displayed on the printed form. Because you did not select the Screen check box, the disclaimer text will not display on screen.

7.	Click	in the text box	for Long text (disclaimer)
8.	Type	**If the actual amount exceeds the value of this purchase order, call for approval.**	in the text box

9. Click Layout Designer...

The form is displayed in the Layout Designer window.

10. Click In to zoom in

11. Scroll to display the lower-left area of the form

The text entered in the Long text (disclaimer) field is located in the footer of the Custom Purchase Order:

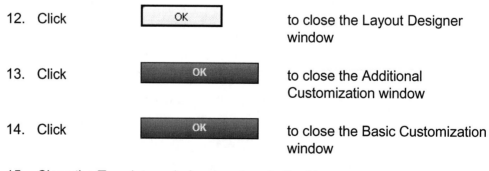

Note: The size of the Layout Designer may be different on your screen.

12.	Click	OK	to close the Layout Designer window
13.	Click	OK	to close the Additional Customization window
14.	Click	OK	to close the Basic Customization window
15.	Close the Templates window to return to the Home page		

Printing Forms

In QuickBooks, you can print several forms at once, such as invoices or purchase orders. In this exercise, you will select and print a group of invoices.

Note: You must have a printer driver and printer installed on your computer or network in order to print forms.

To print several invoices at once,

1. Click 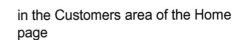 in the Customers area of the Home page

The Create Invoices window opens:

Create Invoices	_ □ ×

Main Formatting Send/Ship Reports

Preview Manage Templates Download Templates Customize Data Layout Spelling Insert Line Delete Line Copy Line Paste Line Customize Design ▾

CUSTOMER:JOB   TEMPLATE Intuit Servic... ▾

Name Transaction

Invoice

DATE 11/01/2018   BILL TO
INVOICE # 5

P.O. NO.   TERMS

SUMMARY

ITEM QUANTITY DESCRIPTION   RATE AMOUNT TAX

CUSTOMER PAYMENT

RECENT TRANSACTIONS

TAX   (0.0%)   0.00
TOTAL
CUSTOMER MESSAGE   PAYMENTS APPLIED   0.00
BALANCE DUE   0.00   NOTES

MEMO   CUSTOMER TAX CODE   Save & Close Save & New Clear

2. Click the Main tab at the top of the Create Invoices window

The Main toolbar displays. There is a check box labeled Print Later in the toolbar. If this check box is selected, the invoice will be displayed in the Select Invoices to Print window.

3. Click ⬅
   (the Previous button) in the toolbar to move to the last invoice you entered

The invoice for the Richard Real Estate : 75 Sunrise St. job displays:

Notice the Print Later check box is selected, indicating this invoice to Richard Real Estate for $3,520.00 will display in the Select Invoices to Print window.

Quick Tip. *The History pane that displays on the right side of the window provides an at-a-glance view of the customer's history. Here, you can quickly see the customer's open balances, active estimates, sales orders to be invoiced, unbilled time and expenses, and recent transactions. You can click any of the links listed to view individual transactions, lists, or reports.*

To view the list of invoices for printing,

4. Select — File : Print Forms : Invoices — from the QuickBooks menu bar

The Select Invoices to Print window opens:

The Select Invoices to Print window allows you to select an individual invoice or several invoices at once for printing. You can also print mailing labels for the invoices by clicking the Print Labels button.

There are four invoices currently waiting to be printed, the last of which is the bill to Richard Real Estate for 3,520.00. If you had deselected the To be printed check box on the Richard Real Estate invoice, it would not display in this list.

To deselect an invoice,

5. Click — the first invoice — (to Kleier, Patricia)

The check mark is removed from the invoice.

6. Click [OK] to print the remaining selected invoices

The Print Invoices window opens:

Note: The printer name will be different on your screen.

This window allows you to select the printer, the type of paper to print on, whether to print lines around each field, and the number of copies to print.

Note: If your computer is not set up to print, click the Cancel button to close the Print Invoices window.

7. Click [Print] to print the invoices (if your computer is set up to print)

QuickBooks sends the invoices to the printer and displays a Print Invoices - Confirmation window:

This window allows you to reprint any invoices that did not print correctly. For the purpose of this exercise, you will assume that all invoices printed correctly.

8. Click [OK] to return to the Create Invoices window

9. Close the Create Invoices window to return to the Home page

Review

In this lesson, you have learned how to:

- ☑ Create a custom template

- ☑ Modify a template

- ☑ Print forms

Practice:

1. Open the Enter Sales Receipt window. (*Hint: Click the Create Sales Receipts icon in the Customers area of the home page.*)

2. Customize the Custom Sales Receipt form by applying a blue color scheme.

3. Change the default title on the header from Sales Receipt to Cash Sale.

4. Rename the Payment Method field to Cash.

5. Delete the Check Number field on both the screen and printed form.

6. Display the Qty column before the Description column.

7. Using the Layout Designer, make the columns for Qty and Rate narrower so the Description column is wider.

8. Edit the Canalside Corp. text so that it is bold and 16 point.

9. Display the Custom Sales Receipt in the Print Preview window and zoom in to view your changes.

10. Close the company file.

3

Using Other QuickBooks Accounts

In this lesson, you will learn how to:

- ❑ Use other QuickBooks account types
- ❑ Work with credit card transactions
- ❑ Work with fixed assets
- ❑ Work with long-term liability accounts
- ❑ Use the Loan Manager

Concept

QuickBooks has many types of accounts. In addition to bank accounts, there are credit card accounts, asset accounts, liability accounts, and equity accounts, to name only a few. These accounts combine to make QuickBooks a complete solution to your financial needs.

Scenario

In this lesson, you will learn how to use other QuickBooks account types. First, you will track credit card transactions by entering a credit card charge, reconciling a credit card statement, and then creating a QuickBooks check to pay for the charges.

Next, you will learn about the different ways to track fixed assets; either by creating fixed asset items or fixed asset accounts. You will first create a fixed asset item as you purchase it. You will then sell the fixed asset item and delete a fixed asset item using the Fixed Asset Item List. After that, you will create a new account for a fixed asset, as well as two subaccounts. You will then make a general journal entry to record a depreciation expense for the fixed asset item you just created. And finally, you will create a long-term liability account for a loan. You will then add the loan to the Loan Manager and record a payment on the loan using the Loan Manager.

Practice Files: B18_Using_Other_QuickBooks_Accounts.qbw

Other QuickBooks Account Types

In this lesson, you will learn about other types of accounts that QuickBooks offers. In addition to bank accounts and income and expense accounts, the account types QuickBooks offers and what they track are as follows:

Account Type	What it Tracks
Credit Card	Transactions that you pay for with a credit card. Create one account for each credit card your business uses.
Fixed Asset	The value of items that have a useful life of more than one year. These items are typically major purchases, such as buildings, land, machinery and equipment, and vehicles. *Note: Consult with your accountant for the minimum value of a fixed asset.*
Other Current Asset	The value of things that can be converted to cash or used up within one year, such as prepaid expenses, employee cash advances, inventory, and loans from your business.
Other Asset	The value of things that are neither Fixed Assets nor Other Current Assets, such as long-term notes receivable and security deposits paid.
Loan	The principal your business owes for a loan or line of credit.
Equity	Money invested in, or money taken out of, the business by owners or shareholders. Payroll and reimbursable expenses should not be included.
Accounts Receivable (A/R)	Money your customers owe you on unpaid invoices. Most businesses require only the A/R account that QuickBooks automatically creates.
Accounts Payable (A/P)	Money you owe to vendors for purchases made on credit. Most businesses require only the A/P account that QuickBooks automatically creates.
Other Current Liability	Money your business owes and expects to pay within one year, such as sales tax, security deposits/retainers from customers, and payroll taxes.
Long Term Liability	Money your business owes and expects to pay back over more than one year, such as mortgages, long-term loans, and notes payable.
Cost of Goods Sold	The direct costs to produce the items that your business sells, such as cost of materials, cost of labor, shipping, freight and delivery, and subcontractors.

Working with Credit Card Transactions

If your business carries a credit card revolving balance — the card is not paid in full every month — the easiest method to track the amount due is by using a Credit Card account. You should set up a Credit Card account for each credit card you use in your business. Like any QuickBooks account, a Credit Card account has its own register, which lists all the charges, credits, and payments for the account.

Caution. *Although QuickBooks has accounts Payable accounts that can also be used for entering charges, it is recommended you use the credit card account feature specifically designed for entering and reconciling credit card charges. This is because the reconciliation process includes balancing the statement from the credit card company and automatically generating a check to pay all or a portion of the amount due.*

Entering Credit Card Charges

Revolving debt is a way of life for many small businesses and keeping track of balances and related charges can be a difficult task. QuickBooks makes this task easier by allowing you to enter your credit card charges either at the time of the transaction or when you receive the bill. Entering charges at the time of the transaction results in more accurate financial information. In this exercise, you will enter a credit card transaction in your World Credit charge account.

Note: *For this lesson, be sure to set your computer's date to 11/1/2018 before opening the QuickBooks file, as recommended in the Before You Get Started lesson. This will ensure that the dates you see on your screen match the dates in this lesson.*

1. Open   B18_Using_Other QuickBooks Accounts.qbw   using the method described in Before You Get Started

The QuickBooks Login dialog box displays:

This dialog box informs you that you must login as a QuickBooks Administrator in order to open the company file.

2. Type   **Canalside2**   in the Password field

Note: *Passwords are case-sensitive.*

3. Click   OK

QuickBooks opens the file.

4. Click to close the Reminders window

QuickBooks displays the Home page:

5. Click

Enter Credit
Card Charges

in the Banking area of the Home page

Quick Tip. *Credit card transactions can also be added directly to the credit card account register.*

The Enter Credit Card Charges - World Credit window opens:

Notice that World Credit is already selected in the Credit Card field.

Quick Tip. *To select a different credit card account, click the drop-down arrow next to the Credit Card field to display the menu of accounts. You can also add a new credit card account from this menu.*

| 6. | Select | Smith's Construction Rental | from the Purchased From drop-down menu |
| 7. | Press | Tab | twice, to move to the Ref No. field |

The Ref No. field allows you to enter a transaction number from the credit card receipt. This field may be left blank, but adding this number to the account gives you extra information about the credit card charge.

8.	Type	**90**	as the reference for the transaction
9.	Press	Tab	to move to the Amount field
10.	Type	**88.50**	to replace 0.00 in the Amount field
11.	Press	Tab	to move to the Memo field
12.	Type	**Generator Rental**	in the Memo field
13.	Press	Tab	

The text in the Account column is selected.

14.	Press	Delete	to delete the text
15.	Type	**E (for Equipment)**	in the Account column
16.	Press	Tab	

QuickBooks completes the entry with **Equipment Rental**:

17. Click [Save & Close] to record the transaction and close the window

QuickBooks adds $88.50 to the Credit Card account register and the Equipment Rental expense account.

Quick Tip. *If you pay your credit card balance in full every month, you can record credit card charges when you enter a bill or write a check. To do this, you would simply record all expenses and finance charges on the Expenses tab of the Enter Bills and Write Checks windows. This method of recording credit card charges does not effect the credit card liability account.*

Reconciling a Credit Card Statement

Just as you reconcile bank accounts, you should compare your credit card receipts to your credit card statement. Reconciling a credit card statement is very similar to reconciling a bank account.

Quick Tip. *You should always reconcile all of your credit card accounts. Reconciliation is an important step in maintaining accurate records.*

In this exercise, you will reconcile the World Credit Card account using the statement below:

World Credit Card
Eastcoast Bank
PO Box 234
Fairgrave, NY 11111

Date	Payee	Charges	Credits
10/08/2018	Bennett's Insulation	275.00	
10/09/2018	Payment		100.00
10/14/2018	David's Lumber	48.00	
10/21/2018	Smith's Construction Rental	179.99	
10/22/2018	Smith's Construction Rental		179.99
10/29/2018	Fields Kitchen	689.27	
11/01/2018	Smiths Construction Rental	88.50	
11/01/2018	Finance Charge	58.30	

Ending Balance: 1059.07

1. Click in the Company area of the Home page

The Chart of Accounts opens:

2. Select   World Credit   in the Chart of Accounts (scroll down)

3. Click   

A drop-down menu of options for the World Credit account displays:

Write Checks
Make Deposits
Enter Credit Card Charges
Transfer Funds
Make General Journal Entries
Reconcile Credit Card
Use Register   Ctrl+R

Note: *If you are using the QuickBooks Premier version, additional options may display in your drop-down menu. In addition, a Reconcile option may display instead of Reconcile Credit Card.*

4. Select   Reconcile Credit Card   from the drop-down menu

The Begin Reconciliation window opens:

Begin Reconciliation ✕
Select an account to reconcile, and then enter the ending balance from your account statement.
Account   World Credit ▼
Statement Date   03/31/2017 📅
Beginning Balance   0.00   What if my beginning balance doesn't match my statement?
Ending Balance   400.00
Enter any finance charge.
Finance Charge   Date   Account
28.30   03/31/2017 📅   Bank Service Charges ▼
Locate Discrepancies   Undo Last Reconciliation   Continue   Cancel   Help

This window is used to enter the information necessary for reconciling your account. World Credit is already entered as the credit card account. The Beginning Balance is entered automatically, and is the cleared balance from the last time you reconciled the account.

Note: *The dates in this window identify the last time the account was reconciled.*

5. Press   Tab   to move to the Statement Date field

6. Type   **11/1/2018**   in the Statement Date field

7. Press   Tab   to move to the Ending Balance field

8. Type   **1059.07**   in the Ending Balance field

Quick Tip. The Ending Balance is the figure that displays as the current balance on your credit card statement.

When you carry a balance from month-to-month on a credit card, you will need to enter finance or interest charges in QuickBooks.

To add finance charges,

9. Press   `Tab`   to move to the Finance Charge field

10. Type   **58.30**   in the Finance Charge field

11. Press   `Tab`   to move to the Date field

12. Type   **11/1/2018**   in the Date field

Bank Service Charges is automatically selected in the Account field.

13. Click   [Continue]

The Reconcile Credit Card - World Credit window opens:

Reconcile Credit Card - World Credit								
For period: 11/01/2018				☐ Hide transactions after the statement's end date				

Charges and Cash Advances

✓	DATE ▲	REF #	PAYEE	AMOUNT
	10/08/2018	2516	Bennet's Insul...	275.00
	10/14/2018	89	Davids Lumber	48.00
	10/21/2018	1393	Smith's Const...	179.99
	10/29/2018	7748	Fields Kitchen...	689.27
	11/01/2018	90	Smith's Const...	88.50

Payments and Credits

✓	DATE ▲	REF #	MEMO	TYPE	AMOUNT
	10/09/2018		Payment	CC CRED	100.00
	10/22/2018	Return	Return of ...	CC CRED	179.99

☑ Highlight Marked   [Mark All]   [Unmark All]   [Go To]   [Columns to Display...]

Beginning Balance	0.00	[Modify] Finance Charge -58.30
Items you have marked cleared		
0 Payments and Credits	0.00	Ending Balance 1,059.07
0 Charges and Cash Advances	0.00	Cleared Balance 58.30
		Difference -1,000.77

[Reconcile Now]   [Leave]

The transaction entered for Smith's Construction Rental for $88.50 displays as the last entry in the Charges and Cash Advances list. The finance charge of 58.30 and the value entered for the ending balance (1059.07) are displayed in the lower-right corner of the window. Because no transactions have been cleared other than the finance charge, the difference between the ending balance and the cleared balance is -1000.77.

To mark a transaction as cleared in the Charges and Cash Advances area,

14. Click   the Bennet's Insulation transaction for $275.00

15. Click   the David's Lumber transaction for $48.00

16. Click   the Smith's Construction transaction for $179.99

17. Click   the Field's Kitchen transaction for $689.27

18. Click   the Smith's Construction transaction for $88.50

A check mark displays next to each transaction.

To mark a transaction as cleared in the Payments and Credits area,

19. Click   the payment of $100.00

20. Click   the return of merchandise for $179.99

Quick Tip. *You can also click the Mark All button to mark all transactions as cleared.*

Your Reconcile Credit Card window should resemble the figure below:

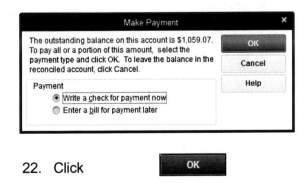

Notice the Difference field in the lower-right corner of the window is now 0.00.

21. Click   [Reconcile Now]

The Make Payment window opens:

The outstanding balance on this account is $1,059.07. To pay all or a portion of this amount, select the payment type and click OK. To leave the balance in the reconciled account, click Cancel.

Payment
- ◉ Write a check for payment now
- ○ Enter a bill for payment later

[OK] [Cancel] [Help]

22. Click   [OK]   to accept Write a check for payment now

Quick Tip. *You can click the Cancel button to leave the amount owed in the credit card account, and not pay or enter the bill. The account will still be considered reconciled and you can make a payment to the account at a later time.*

The Select Reconciliation Report window opens allowing you to select the type of reconciliation report you would like to view:

Select Reconciliation Report ✕

Congratulations! Your account is balanced. All marked items have been cleared in the account register.

Select the type of reconciliation report you'd like to see.

○ Summary
○ Detail
● Both

To view this report at a later time, select the Report menu, display Banking and then Previous Reconciliation.

[Display]   Print...   Close

23. Select ◯ Detail

24. Click [Display]

A Reconciliation Report dialog box displays with a message about the transaction dates in the reconciliation report:

Reconciliation Report ✕

ⓘ This report displays current data. It shows all transactions that were reconciled on the given date. It also shows transactions that were uncleared at the time of the reconciliation, and new transactions.

☐ Do not display this message in the future

[OK]

25. Click the Do not display this message in the future check box

26. Click [OK]

The Reconciliation Detail window opens:

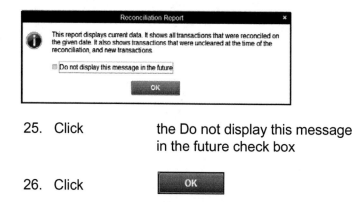

This report may be saved or printed to keep a record of the reconciliation.

27. Close the Reconciliation Detail report

Because you previously selected the option to write a check for payment now, the Write Checks - Checking window opens:

28. Select   Eastcoast Bank   from the Pay to the Order of drop-down menu

The check is now made out to Eastcoast Bank for the full amount of the credit card balance. When you record the transaction, the amount of the check will be deducted from the Checking account and applied to the World Credit account.

Quick Tip. QuickBooks automatically enters the full amount owed as the payment amount. You can make a partial payment by changing the entry in the $ field.

29. Click   Save & Close   to record the transaction, close the Write Checks window, and return to the Chart of Accounts

30. Close the Chart of Accounts

Quick Tip. If you would like to undo your last reconciliation, click the Reconcile icon in the Banking area of the Home page. When the Begin Reconciliation window opens, select the appropriate account from the Account drop-down menu and click the Undo Last Reconciliation button.

Working with Fixed Assets

A fixed asset tracks the value of significant items that have a useful life of more than one year, such as buildings, land, machinery and equipment, and vehicles.

Note: Consult with an accountant for the minimum dollar amount of fixed assets.

Determining How to Track Fixed Assets

Most businesses require some types of fixed assets to run. Vehicles, computers, office equipment, and office space all require a substantial investment. Tracking the book value of such long-term fixed assets over time is important, because the amount by which they depreciate can affect the worth of your business and the size of your tax bill.

When tracking fixed assets, you have the following options:

- You can create fixed asset items to track your assets. Fixed asset items give you one location to store information about an asset, such as the date of purchase, purchase price, where you bought it, and when and for how much you sell the asset. This is especially useful if your accountant uses the QuickBooks Fixed Asset Manager. Your accountant can use the information from the fixed asset item to figure all your depreciation and post a general journal entry back to your company file. In addition, your accountant can create new fixed asset items for you and add them to your company file.

Note: If your accountant does not use the QuickBooks Fixed Asset Manager, you can still use fixed asset items to track information about your assets.

- You can use accounts to track fixed assets. If you have several fixed assets that you're tracking using only accounts, and you don't need additional information tracked in QuickBooks, there is no need to create fixed asset items. You can continue to use only the accounts to track the assets.

Regardless of how you track fixed assets, it's important to develop good record-keeping habits where fixed assets are concerned. You must work with your accountant to make sure you're recording all the necessary information about your assets, so that both financial statements and tax returns are correct.

Tracking Fixed Assets Using Fixed Asset Items

When purchasing fixed assets for your business, it is important that you keep very good records, so you can track the cost of the assets, the cost of any repairs or upgrades, and how much the assets depreciate from year to year. Tracking fixed assets with fixed asset items provides a way to keep important information about your assets in one place.

Creating a Fixed Asset Item

You can create a fixed asset item from the Fixed Asset Item List or from a transaction. The simplest way to create a fixed asset item is while you are entering the transaction used to purchase it.

You can record information about a fixed asset as you purchase it from any of the following:

- Items tab of the Enter Bills window

- Items tab of the Write Checks window

- Items tab of the Enter Credit Card Charges window

- Item column of the Purchase Order window

In this exercise, you are the owner of Canalside Corp. and have recently purchased a pickup truck from Fairgrave Auto Center. You will create the fixed asset item for the truck as you enter the payment transaction.

1. Click in the Banking area of the Home page

The Write Checks - Checking window opens:

2. Select   Fairgrave Auto Center   from the Pay to the Order of drop-down menu

Fairgrave Auto Center has already been set up in your Vendors list, so the address information for this vendor is automatically populated.

3. Press   Tab   to move to the $ field

4. Type   **12,500.00**   in the $ field

5. Click   the Items tab   in the lower portion of the window

6. Select   <Add New>   from the Item drop-down list (scroll to the top of the list)

The New Item window opens:

7. Select   Fixed Asset   from the Type drop-down menu

The New Item window is updated to display fields for a fixed asset:

This window allows you to enter all of the details for the fixed asset. In the Asset Name/Number field, you should enter a name or number that will help you distinguish this item from all others on the list. The name you enter in this field will display on fixed asset item reports.

8. Press   [Tab]

9. Type   **2018 Pickup Truck**   In the Asset Name/Number field

You will now assign the asset item to a fixed asset account that tracks all of your company vehicles.

| 10. | Select | the Vehicles Fixed Asset account | from the Asset Account drop-down menu |

The Purchase Information section allows you to enter purchase information about the fixed asset item, including a brief description of the purchase, whether the item was purchased as new or used, the date of the purchase, the cost of the item, and the vendor from whom you purchased this item.

11.	Type	**Pickup Truck**	in the Purchase Description field
12.	Select	used	in the Item is area, above the Purchase Description field
13.	Type	**11/01/2018**	in the Date field
14.	Press	Tab	to move to the Cost field
15.	Type	**12,500.00**	in the Cost field
16.	Press	Tab	to move to the Vendor/Payee field
17.	Type	**Fairgrave Auto Center**	in the Vendor/Payee field

Note: The Vendor/Payee name will not be saved to the Vendor's list automatically when this transaction is saved. If this vendor was not already in your Vendor's list, you would need to manually enter the vendor using the Vendor Center.

The Sales Information section allows you to enter sales information for the fixed asset item, including whether or not you have sold the item, a description of the sale, the date of the sale, the price of the sale, and any expenses incurred during the sale. You just purchased the pickup truck, so you will leave these fields blank.

The Asset Information section allows you to enter information about your asset, such as a description of the asset (make, model, brand, etc.), the location of the asset (if the asset is land or real estate), the PO number used to purchase the asset, the asset's serial number, when the warranty (if any) expires, and any notes about your asset that you want to track.

18.	Type	**Black, 5 speed, four-wheel drive**	in the Asset Description field
19.	Type	**11/01/2019**	in the Warranty Expires field
20.	Press	Tab	to move to the Notes field
21.	Type	**Full coverage insurance**	in the Notes field

The New Item window should resemble the figure below:

22. Click [OK] to save the fixed asset item

The New Item window closes and you return to the Write Checks - Checking window with the 2018 Pickup Truck displayed on the first row of the Items tab:

23. Click [Save & Close] to record the payment transaction for the pickup truck

Note: You can create a fixed asset item to track a fixed asset at several points during the asset's life cycle, but it is recommended that you create the item as soon as you purchase the asset, just as you did in this exercise.

Using the Fixed Asset Item List

The Fixed Asset Item List displays all fixed asset items you've set up. You can use this list to track changes to the value of your fixed assets, including any repairs or improvements, damage, or anything else that can affect their book value and amount of depreciation.

Quick Tip. The simplest way to create a fixed asset item is while you are entering the transaction used to purchase it. However, sometimes you may want to create a fixed asset item directly from the Fixed Asset Item list. For example, you may want to do this when you intend to purchase or have already purchased several items that you want to track as fixed assets, you pay for a fixed asset with cash, you transfer a personal asset to your business, or you pay for a business asset with personal funds.

To view the Fixed Asset Item List,

1. Select   Lists : Fixed Asset   from the menu bar
                                Item List

The Fixed Asset Item List opens:

NAME	FA...	PURCHASE D...	PURCHASE DESCRIPTION	ACCOUNT	COST	AT...
2018 Pickup Truck		11/01/2018	Pickup Truck	Vehicles	12,500.00	
Cement Mixer		08/04/2015	Cement Mixer	Cement ...	2,500.00	
Desks		06/01/2015	Desks	Desks	5,000.00	
Desktop Computer - 1		05/16/2014	Desktop Computer	Computer	2,800.00	
Laptop - 1		04/15/2014	Laptop	Computer	2,700.00	
Laser Printer		08/25/2013	Laser Printer	Computer	1,575.00	
Stump Grinder		10/04/2013	Stump Grinder	Stump Gr...	16,500.00	

Item ▼   Activities ▼   Reports ▼   Attach   Include inactive

You can use this list to add, edit, or delete fixed asset items. You can also use this list to record transactions that involve the fixed asset item or generate and view reports related to fixed asset items. Notice the fixed asset you just created for the pickup truck displays in this list.

In this exercise, you will sell your Stump Grinder and then mark the fixed asset item as sold. You can perform all of these steps using the Fixed Asset Item List.

Note: The process you use to sell a fixed asset depends on how you track the asset's cost and depreciation. If you track fixed assets using fixed asset items, you must record the sale of the fixed asset item; but if you only use fixed asset accounts to track your fixed assets, you can jump directly to recording the sale with a general journal entry.

2. Select   Stump Grinder   in the Fixed Asset Item List

3. Click   Activities ▼

A drop-down menu displays:

4. Select   Create Invoices   from the drop-down menu

The Create Invoice window opens:

Note: *If your Create Invoices window opens to the Intuit Product Invoice, select Intuit Service Invoice from the Template drop-down menu.*

Because you sold the stump grinder to a private owner,

5. Type   **Tim Johnson**   in the Customer:Job field

6. Press   Tab

A Customer:Job Not Found dialog box displays:

7. Click   Quick Add   to automatically add Tim Johnson to the Customer:Job list

You will leave the current date in the Date field.

8. Select   Stump Grinder Fixed Asset   from the Item drop-down list (scroll down)

Quick Tip. When recording transactions involving your fixed asset, always be sure to choose the appropriate fixed asset item from the Items tab or Item column. This enables you to correctly track depreciation and other costs.

To enter the asset's sales price,

9. Type   **13,000.00**   in the Amount column

10. Click   Save & Close   to record the transaction

The Fixed Asset Item Amount is Different dialog box displays:

Fixed Asset Item Amount is Different   ✕

(i) The fixed asset item amount in this transaction is different than the sales price saved in the Fixed Asset Item List. Do you want to continue? Click Yes to confirm that the transaction amount is correct. Click No to revert the transaction amount to the fixed asset sales price.

☐ Do not display this message in the future

[Yes]   [No]

Because you have not marked the fixed asset item as sold yet, it is okay that the sales values do not match.

11. Click   Yes   to return to the Create Invoices window

12. Click   Save & Close

The Update Fixed Assets dialog box displays:

Update Fixed Assets   ✕

(i) QuickBooks has detected that the item(s) for one or more fixed assets being sold have not been updated with sales information. Do you want QuickBooks to update the item(s) being sold?

☐ Do not display this message in the future

[Yes]   [No]

This dialog box informs you that the item being sold now needs to be updated with sales information and asks if you want QuickBooks to update the item.

13. Click   Yes

QuickBooks automatically updates the Stump Grinder fixed asset item with the sales information.

To view the asset item and the sales information that QuickBooks automatically updated,

14. Select   Stump Grinder   in the Fixed Asset Item List (if necessary)

15. Click   Item ▾

A drop-down menu displays.

16. Select   Edit Item   from the drop-down menu

The Edit Item window opens:

QuickBooks automatically populates the Sales Information section with the information you entered in the Create Invoices window, including a description of the sale, the date of the sale, and the price of the sale.

17. Select   the Item is   check box below the Spelling
                     inactive   button

When you set a fixed asset item to inactive, QuickBooks keeps the information associated with it, but hides it on the Fixed Asset Item List and removes it from any drop-down lists that use items.

18. Click   OK

The Fixed Asset Item List displays:

NAME	FA.	PURCHASE D.	PURCHASE DESCRIPTION	ACCOUNT	COST	AT..
◇ 2018 Pickup Truck		11/01/2018	Pickup Truck	Vehicles	12,500.00	
◇ Cement Mixer		08/04/2015	Cement Mixer	Cement ...	2,500.00	
◇ Desks		06/01/2015	Desks	Desks	5,000.00	
◇ Desktop Computer - 1		05/16/2014	Desktop Computer	Computer	2,800.00	
◇ Laptop - 1		04/15/2014	Laptop	Computer	2,700.00	
◇ Laser Printer		08/25/2013	Laser Printer	Computer	1,575.00	

Item ▼   Activities ▼   Reports ▼   Attach   ☐ Include inactive

The Stump Grinder fixed asset item no longer displays in the list because it is now inactive.

Quick Tip. *If you are working in single-user mode, you can display inactive items at any time by selecting Show Inactive Items from the Item drop-down menu.*

You can also delete items from the Fixed Asset Item List. To delete a fixed asset item,

19. Select   Laptop - 1   from the Fixed Asset Item List

20. Click   Item ▼

A drop-down menu displays

21. Select   Delete Item   from the drop-down menu

A Delete Item dialog box displays:

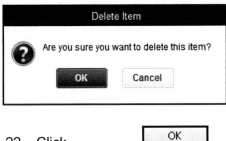

22. Click   OK

The item is deleted from the Fixed Asset Item List.

23. Close the Fixed Asset Item List

Using Accounts to Track Fixed Assets

If you do not use fixed asset items to track fixed assets, you can use accounts. To track fixed assets using accounts, you need to set up the necessary accounts to track depreciation. In this exercise, you have purchased a piece of heavy equipment (a forklift) for Canalside Corp. and will set up a Fixed Asset account for the forklift, as well as create two subaccounts for the Fixed Asset account: one for cost and one for accumulated depreciation.

To set up a fixed asset account,

1. Click  in the Company area of the Home page

The Chart of Accounts opens:

2. Click **Account ▼** at the bottom of the Chart of Accounts

A drop-down menu displays.

3. Select **New** from the drop-down menu

The Add New Account: Choose Account Type window opens:

4. Select **⊙ Fixed Asset (major purchases)**

A description and examples of fixed asset accounts display in the area on the right side of the window. Each fixed asset account can represent a single asset or a group of related assets.

5. Click [Continue]

The Add New Account window opens:

```
┌─────────────────────────────────────────────────────────────────────┐
│ ⊡                    Add New Account                      —  ☐  ✕      │
│                                                                        │
│  ▥   Account Type   [ Fixed Asset            ▼ ]                       │
│                                                                        │
│  ┌──────────────────────────────────────────────────────────────┐    │
│      Account Name  [                                        ]         │
│                    ☐ Subaccount of  [                    ▼ ]          │
│                                                                        │
│    OPTIONAL                                                            │
│         Description  [                                        ]        │
│                      [                                        ]        │
│                                                                        │
│              Note   [                                        ]         │
│     Tax-Line Mapping  [ <Unassigned>         ▼ ]   How do I choose the right tax line? │
│                       [ Enter Opening Balance... ]  Should I enter an opening balance? │
│  └──────────────────────────────────────────────────────────────┘    │
│                                                                        │
│                          [ Save & Close ]  [ Save & New ]  [ Cancel ] │
└─────────────────────────────────────────────────────────────────────┘
```

Notice that Fixed Asset is already displayed in the Account Type field and the cursor is positioned in the Account Name field. You should name the fixed asset account with a name that identifies the asset it is tracking.

6. Type **Forklift** in the Account Name field

You will not enter an opening balance for the forklift account at this time. Later in this lesson, you will set up a separate account to track the loan you took out for the forklift. The amount of the loan will automatically be entered into the Forklift account as the opening balance.

7. Click [Save & Close] to create the account

The Chart of Accounts displays with the new Forklift account selected:

```
┌─────────────────────────────────────────────────────────────────────┐
│ ⊡                    Chart of Accounts                    —  ☐  ✕      │
│                                                                        │
│  Look for account name or number                                      │
│  [                        ]  [ Search ]  [ Reset ]                    │
│                                                                        │
│  ◆  NAME          ⚡  TYPE ▲              BALANCE TOTAL    ATTACH       │
│  ◦ Forklift          Fixed Asset              0.00                     │
│  ◦ Stump Grinder     Fixed Asset         -13,000.00                    │
│  ◦ Vehicles          Fixed Asset          12,500.00                    │
│  ◦ Accounts Payable  Accounts Payable      6,289.00                    │
│  ◦ World Credit      Credit Card              0.00                     │
│  ◦ Office Furniture  Other Current Liability  0.00                     │
│                                                                        │
│  [ Account ▼ ]  [ Activities ▼ ]  [ Reports ▼ ]  [ Attach ]  ☐ Include Inactive │
└─────────────────────────────────────────────────────────────────────┘
```

You have now created a new Fixed Asset account named Forklift, with an opening balance of $0.00. Next, you will create two subaccounts to track the cost of the forklift and its depreciation.

To set up a subaccount for a Fixed Asset account,

8.	Click	Account ▼	at the bottom of the Chart of Accounts
9.	Select	New	from the drop-down menu

The Add New Account: Choose Account Type window opens.

10.	Select	○ **Fixed Asset (major purchases)**
11.	Click	Continue

The Add New Account window opens with Fixed Asset displayed in the Account Type field:

12.	Type	**Cost**	in the Account Name field
13.	Click	the check box next to Subaccount of	to select it
14.	Click	▼	next to the Subaccount of field

A drop-down menu of fixed asset accounts displays:

< Add New >	
Cement Mixer	Fixed Asset
Computer	Fixed Asset
Desks	Fixed Asset
Forklift	Fixed Asset
Stump Grinder	Fixed Asset
Vehicles	Fixed Asset

15. Select   Forklift   from the drop-down menu

16. Click | Save & Close | to create the fixed asset subaccount

The new Cost account is included in the Chart of Accounts as a subaccount of Forklift:

NAME	TYPE ▲	BALANCE TOTAL	ATTACH
◆ Desks	Fixed Asset	0.00	
◆ Forklift	Fixed Asset	0.00	
◆ Cost	Fixed Asset	0.00	
◆ Stump Grinder	Fixed Asset	-13,000.00	
◆ Vehicles	Fixed Asset	12,500.00	
◆ Accounts Payable	Accounts Payable	6,289.00	

17. Follow steps 8-16 in this section to create a second subaccount with the following attributes:

Account Type: Fixed Asset

Account Name: Accumulated Depreciation

Subaccount of: Forklift

The new subaccount displays below Forklift in the Chart of Accounts:

NAME	TYPE ▲	BALANCE TOTAL	ATTACH
◆ Forklift	Fixed Asset	0.00	
◆ Accumulated Depreciation	Fixed Asset	0.00	
◆ Cost	Fixed Asset	0.00	
◆ Stump Grinder	Fixed Asset	-13,000.00	
◆ Vehicles	Fixed Asset	12,500.00	
◆ Accounts Payable	Accounts Payable	6,289.00	

Recording Depreciation Expenses for Fixed Assets using General Journal Entries

Fixed assets tend to last a long time; therefore, you do not charge their full cost to the year in which they were bought, but, instead, spread the cost over several years. Because fixed assets wear out or become obsolete, their value declines over time. The amount of this decline in value is called depreciation.

To determine the estimated value of a fixed asset at any point in time, you need to subtract its accumulated depreciation (the total amount of depreciation since the asset's purchase) from the original cost of the asset. Usually, you will want your balance sheet to show the original cost of an asset (plus any subsequent improvements) on one line, the amount of depreciation on a second line, and the current value (net) on a third line.

If you use accounts to track your fixed assets, most likely, you will need to make certain adjustments when you are closing your books at the end of an accounting period. Adjusting entries are made at the end of an accounting period to account for items that did not get recorded in your daily transactions. In a traditional accounting system, these entries are made in a general journal.

Note: If your accountant uses the QuickBooks Fixed Asset Manager and you track your fixed assets with fixed asset items, you may not need to enter depreciation transactions. Ask your accountant for more information.

A general journal entry includes a record of a transaction in which the total amount in the Debit column equals the total amount in the Credit column and each amount is assigned to the appropriate account in the Chart of Accounts. QuickBooks includes a Make General Journey Entries window that you can use for entering special adjustment transactions, such as recording a depreciation expense.

You can decide whether you want to handle some or all adjusting entries yourself or if you want an accountant to prepare them for you. If your accountant does prepare adjusting entries, they will be able to provide you with a copy of these entries so you can enter them into the General Journal in QuickBooks.

An example of an adjusting entry that typically needs to be made for businesses is one that records a depreciation expense. There are very specific rules regarding the amount of an asset that you can depreciate each year. It is your decision whether or not you compute depreciation for your assets in QuickBooks the same way you compute it for tax purposes. You may also choose to have an accountant compute depreciation and provide you with a schedule showing the amount of depreciation for your assets, which you can then use to make general journal entries.

In this exercise, your accountant has determined that the value of the forklift you purchased for Canalside Corp. has depreciated by $1200.00. You never entered this transaction into QuickBooks, so you now need to make a general journal entry to record this depreciation expense and update the forklift's Accumulated Depreciation subaccount.

To make a general journal entry to record a depreciation expense,

1. Select   Company : Make   from the menu bar
   General Journal
   Entries

The Assigning Numbers to Journal Entries dialog box displays:

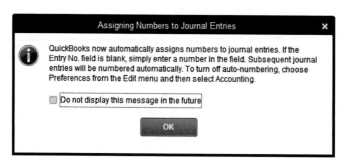

This dialog box informs you that QuickBooks automatically assigns numbers to journal entries.

2. Select   the Do not display this   check box
                  message in the future

3. Click | OK |

The Make General Journal Entries window opens:

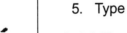

Note: If you are using QuickBooks Premier, the Make General Journal Entries window may be slightly different.

The current date displays in the Date field. You will accept this default.

4. Press | Tab | to move to the Entry No. field

Since this is your first journal entry,

5. Type   **1**   in the Entry No. field

Quick Tip. If you enter a number in the Entry No. field, QuickBooks will automatically number journal entries from this point forward.

To record the depreciation expense,

6. Click   in the Account column

A drop-down arrow displays.

7. Select   Depreciation Expense   from the Account drop-down menu
                                          (scroll down)

Note: If a Depreciation Expense account is not included in your Chart of Accounts when you set up your company file, you will need to create one.

8. Press   to move to the Debit column

9.	Type	**1200.00**	in the Debit column
10.	Press	Tab	twice to move to the Memo column
11.	Type	**To record forklift depreciation for the period ending 12/31/17**	

Quick Tip. *Any information entered in the Memo field will display on reports that include the general journal entry.*

To update the forklift's accumulated depreciation account,

12.	Click	in the second row	of the Account column

A drop-down arrow displays.

13.	Select	Accumulated Depreciation (below the Forklift account)	from the Account drop-down menu
14.	Press	Tab	twice to move to the Credit column
15.	Type	**1200.00**	in the Credit column (if necessary)
16.	Click	in the third row	of the Account column

Your Make General Journal Entries should resemble the figure below:

Note: Depending on the edition of QuickBooks you are using, the text "To record forklift depreciation for the period ending 12/31/17" may be automatically entered in the Memo field of the second line item.

17.	Click	Save & Close	to save the journal entry and display the Chart of Accounts

Note: If a Tracking Fixed Assets on Journal Entries dialog box displays, select the Do not display this message in the future check box and click the OK button.

When you record a depreciation transaction, QuickBooks updates two other accounts:

- The depreciation amount is subtracted from the balance in the Fixed Asset account register. The transaction will be labeled as GENJRNL in the register.

- The depreciation amount is added to the Depreciation Expense account as a depreciation expense.

Working with Long-Term Liability Accounts

Liabilities are your company's debts. Liabilities include the bills you've received, money you owe on credit cards, sales tax you owe the government, employee withholdings you owe the government, and both short-term and long-term debts. Current liabilities are debts your company expects to pay within a year, such as a short-term loan or a bill. Long-term liabilities are debts your company expects to pay off in more than one year.

Creating a Long-Term Liability Account

When you owe money to a lending institution, the amount of the loan is a liability for your company. You can track a loan in QuickBooks by setting up a liability account for it.

You have already created a Fixed Asset account to track the value of a forklift. In this exercise, you will create a Long Term Liability account for a $9,500 loan you took out to purchase the forklift.

Note: If you take out a loan to pay for a new asset (such as a new vehicle for your business) the asset account (for the vehicle) and the liability account (for the loan) are not connected in QuickBooks in any way. On your balance sheet you'll see the value of the vehicle as an asset, which adds to the net worth of your business. The loan will be listed as a liability, which subtracts from the net worth of your business.

To create a Long Term Liability account,

1. Click   Account ▼   at the bottom of the Chart of Accounts

A drop-down menu displays.

2. Select   New   from the drop-down menu

The Add New Account: Choose Account Type window opens:

3. Select   ⊙ **Other Account Types**

A drop-down menu displays:

4. Select   Long Term Liability   from the drop-down menu

A description and examples of long term liability accounts display in the area on the right side of the window.

5. Click   Continue

The Add New Account window opens:

Long Term Liability is already displayed in the Account Type field and the cursor is positioned in the Account Name field.

6. Type   **Forklift Loan**   in the Account Name field

7. Type   **654321**   in the Account No. field

At this time, you will not enter an opening balance.

8. Click | Save & Close | to create the account

The Chart of Accounts displays with the new Forklift Loan account selected:

When you take out a new loan, you either receive money to deposit in your bank account or receive a new asset. In this example, you will record the cost of the forklift and record the opening balance of the forklift loan.

To make a general journal entry to record the cost of the forklift and the opening balance of the forklift loan,

9. Select   Company : Make   from the menu bar
                      General Journal
                      Entries

The Make General Journal Entries window opens:

QuickBooks automatically numbers this as the second journal entry.

To record the forklift cost,

10. Click   in the Account column

A drop-down arrow displays.

11. Select   Forklift : Cost   from the Account drop-down menu

12. Press   [Tab]   to move to the Debit column

13. Type   **9500.00**   in the Debit column

14. Press   [Tab]   twice to move to the Memo column

15. Type   **Cost of forklift**

To credit the forklift's loan account,

16. Click   in the second row   of the Account column

A drop-down arrow displays.

17. Select   Forklift Loan   from the Account drop-down menu (scroll down)

18. Press   [Tab]

QuickBooks automatically populates the Credit column with **9.500.00**:

Note: Depending on the edition of QuickBooks you are using, the text "Cost of forklift" may be automatically entered in the Memo field of the second line item.

19. Click   Save & Close   to save the journal entry

The Chart of Accounts displays the Forklift Long Term Liability Loan for $9,500.00:

20. Scroll up in the Chart of Accounts to view the balance of the Forklift Fixed Asset account

Notice that the $1,200 depreciation expense you recorded as a general journal entry was entered in the Forklift account as an accumulated depreciation. The $9,500 loan (entered into the Cost subaccount) was added to the balance, to provide a starting value for the asset. Finally, the depreciation amount was subtracted from the value of the forklift to produce the estimated value of the forklift today, $8,300.

21. Close the Chart of Accounts to return to the Home page

Using the Loan Manager

The Loan Manager helps you track the loans that you've set up in QuickBooks based on the information in your Long-Term Liability and Other Current Liability accounts. When you use the Loan Manager, you can keep track of all your loans in one location and be reminded of upcoming payments. In the Loan Manager, you can add and remove loans you want to track, view payment schedules, set up loan payments, and analyze different loan scenarios.

Before adding loans to the Loan Manager, you'll need to complete the following:

• Set up a liability account for the loan in QuickBooks. When you add the account and lender details, include any information you want the Loan Manager to use for tracking, such as the account number and lender contact information. This information can be found on your loan documents. Be sure that you enter the correct opening balance for the account. Otherwise, you will not be able to set up payments from the loan manager.

• Set up an expense account for tracking the loan interest.

• Set up an escrow account if you need to make escrow payments to the loan.

• Ensure all transactions for the loan liability and interest accounts are up to date.

1. Select **Banking : Loan Manager** from the menu bar

Note: If a Feature update - reboot required to use this feature dialog box displays informing you QuickBooks has updated this feature to work with Internet Explorer, you must reboot your computer before you can use the Loan Manager.

The Loan Manager opens:

Note: You may resize and move the Loan Manager window as necessary.

The Loan Manager displays any loans you've set up to track, including details about the loans (such as the lender name and origination date), a payment schedule, and contact information. Use this window to enter and track your loans, set up payments, and run "what if" scenarios when considering a new loan or refinancing an existing one.

2. Click   [Add a Loan...]

The first screen in the Add Loan wizard displays:

The Add Loan wizard allows you to enter information about the loans you want to track in the Loan Manager.

The Account Name drop-down list includes both current liability and long-term liability accounts and allows you to select the loan for which you set up the liability account.

3. Select   Forklift Loan   from the Account Name drop-down menu

When you add a loan to the Loan Manager, the liability account information is automatically prefilled, including the current balance of the loan and the account details you entered when you set up the liability account.

4. Select   Eastcoast Bank   from the Lender drop-down menu

5. Type   **11/01/2018**   in the Origination Date field

The Loan Manager uses the loan origination date to calculate the loan maturity date and the number of remaining payments, as shown on the Payment Schedule. The loan origination date must be correct for accurate calculations.

6. Type   **9,500.00**   in the Original Amount field

This is the original amount of the loan. You have not made any payments on the loan yet, so the original amount is the same as the current balance.

7. Type   **48**   in the Term field

This indicates that the term of the loan is 48 months. You can also enter the loan terms in weeks or years.

8. Click   Next

The next screen in the Add Loan wizard displays:

Add Loan

Enter payment information for this loan

DUE DATE OF NEXT PAYMENT [   ]

PAYMENT AMOUNT (PRINCIPAL + INTEREST) [0.00]   NEXT PAYMENT NUMBER [1]

PAYMENT PERIOD [Monthly ▾]

Does this loan have an escrow payment?   ○ Yes   ◉ No

ESCROW PAYMENT AMOUNT [0.00]

ESCROW PAYMENT ACCOUNT [▾]

TOTAL PAYMENT **$0.00**

☑ Alert me 10 days before a payment is due

[Previous] [Next] [Finish] [Cancel] [Help]

This screen of the Add Loan wizard allows you to enter loan payment information. The loan payment information is required to calculate the principal and interest portions of your loan payment and to build your payment schedule.

9. Type **12/01/2018** in the Due Date of Next Payment field

10. Type **275.00** in the Payment Amount field

The payment for the forklift is due on a monthly basis, so you will leave the "Monthly" selection from the "Payment Period" drop-down menu.

You will also leave the "No" option selected in the "Does this loan have an escrow payment?" area, because the Forklift loan does not require an escrow payment.

Quick Tip. *When adding loans to the Loan Manager for your own business, be sure to check your loan information to see if you need to make an escrow payment with your loan payment. Typically, all mortgage loans require escrow payments.*

11. Press Tab

The "Total Payment" field is now automatically updated with $275.00 — the amount of the monthly payment. Also, the "Alert me 10 days before a payment is due" check box is selected. This posts an alert to your Reminders list ten days before your loan is due, so you will be reminded about the upcoming payment.

12. Click Next

The final screen of the Add Loan wizard displays:

Add Loan
Enter interest information for this loan

INTEREST RATE 0.000 %

COMPOUNDING PERIOD Monthly What is an exact days compounding period?

COMPUTE PERIOD 365/365

PAYMENT ACCOUNT

INTEREST EXPENSE ACCOUNT Interest Expense:Loan Interest

FEES/CHARGES EXPENSE Bank Service Charges

Previous Next Finish Cancel Help

13. Type **6.5** in the Interest Rate field

The loan interest information is required to calculate the interest portion of your payment and establish your payment schedule.

14. Verify that Monthly is selected from the Compounding Period field

The compounding period is the frequency that interest is compounded on the loan, such as annually, monthly, weekly, or exact days. The compounding period affects how much interest is owed on the loan. The more frequently the interest is calculated, the higher the total interest.

Quick Tip. *When "Monthly" is selected from the "Compounding Period" drop-down menu, the "Compute Period" field will be inactive. The compute period is the number of days used by your lender to calculate daily interest charges for loans with a compounding period of exact days. The two compute period options are 365/365 or 365/360. When your lender uses a compounding period of exact days, the daily interest charges are calculated on either a 360- or 365-day year. You will find this information in your loan documents.*

15. Select **Checking** from the Payment Account drop-down menu

This selection indicates you will use your Checking account to make payments on the loan.

16. Verify that Interest Expense:Loan Interest is selected from the Interest Expense Account drop-down menu

This selection indicates that interest for this loan will be tracked in the Loan Interest Expense account.

17. Verify that Bank Service Charges is selected from the Fees/Charges Expense Account drop-down menu

This selection indicates that any fees or charges for this loan will be tracked in the Bank Service Charges account.

18. Click **Finish**

The new Forklift Loan displays in the Loan Manager window:

The Summary tab now displays a summary of the loan details, including the lender name and account number, origination date, original amount, and payment and interest information.

Quick Tip. *You can change information about your loan at any time by clicking the Edit Loan Details button in the Loan Manager. However, information that comes from the liability account, such as the balance of the loan, must be edited in the actual loan liability account.*

To view the payment schedule for the loan,

19. Click   the Payment Schedule tab

Note: If you did not set your computer's date to 11/1/2018, as recommended in the beginning of this lesson, the Payment Schedule will not be completed.

The Payment Schedule for the loan displays:

PAYMENT #	DATE	PRINCIPAL (P)	INTEREST (I)	PAYMENT (P+I)	BALANCE
1	12/01/2018	223.54	51.46	275.00	9,276.46
2	01/01/2019	224.75	50.25	275.00	9,051.71
3	02/01/2019	225.97	49.03	275.00	8,825.74
4	03/01/2019	227.19	47.81	275.00	8,598.55
5	04/01/2019	228.42	46.58	275.00	8,370.13
6	05/01/2019	229.66	45.34	275.00	8,140.47

The Payment Schedule tab displays the schedule of your remaining loan payments. The Loan Manager is a payment calculator that computes the principal and interest portion of your loan payment, plus handles any escrow payment or fees and charges. This capability allows you to track loan-related information on a per-payment and per-total-payments basis. When you need to edit or make changes to a loan, the Loan Manager recalculates your payment information and payment schedule.

To view the lender's contact information,

20. Click   the Contact Info tab

The contact information for Eastcoast Bank displays:

The Contact Info tab displays the lender contact name, address, phone and fax numbers, and e-mail address for the selected loan. This information was automatically populated based on the information you entered for EastCoast Bank in the Vendor Center.

Recording a Payment on a Loan

The Loan Manager allows you to track and pay all of your business loans from one convenient location. When you're ready to make a payment, just set up the payment in the Loan Manager. From there, the Loan Manager takes you directly to the Write Checks or Enter Bills windows, where you can edit your payments.

Note: If you have not set up an opening balance for the loan account, you will not be able to set up a payment for it. In addition, if you did not set your computer's date to 11/1/2018 as recommended in the beginning of this lesson, you will not be able to complete this exercise.

To record a loan payment,

1. Select   the Forklift Loan   in the Loan List of the Loan Manager window

2. Click   Set Up Payment...

The Set Up Payment window opens:

Set Up Payment	✖

This payment is [A regular payment ▾]

Why should I pay my loans from the Loan Manager?

What is the difference between a regular and an extra payment?

ACCOUNT INFORMATION

ACCOUNT NAME Forklift Loan

LENDER Eastcoast Bank

BANK ACCOUNT Checking

PAYMENT INFORMATION

PRINCIPAL (P) [223.54]   FEES & CHARGES [0.00]   PAYMENT NUMBER [1]

INTEREST (I) [51.46]   ESCROW [0.00]

TOTAL (P+I) 275.00   TOTAL PAYMENT **275.00**

PAYMENT METHOD

I want to [Write a check ▾]

[OK] [Cancel] [Help]

This window allows you to set up the details for payment of the selected loan. Notice that "A regular payment" is already selected from the "This payment is" drop-down menu. Regular payments are your scheduled payment amounts of principal, interest, and escrow (if any) per your loan terms. An extra payment is any payment made in addition to regular payments. When you set up an extra payment through the Loan Manager, you can specify how much of the extra payment is to be applied to the principal, the interest, and/or to the fees and charges on your loan.

The Account Information section displays the Account Name, Lender, and Bank Account. The Payment Information section displays the amount of the payment that will be applied to the principal ($223.54), the amount of the payment that will be applied to interest ($51.46), and the total amount of the payment ($275.00).

To write a check for your loan payment,

3. Verify   Write a Check   is selected from the I want to drop-down menu

4. Click   [OK]

The Write Checks - Checking window opens:

Eastcoast Bank, the lender, automatically displays in the Pay to the order of field and the amount of the payment, $275.00, displays in the $ field. On the Expenses tab, the loan payment has been broken into the amount applied toward the principal and the amount applied toward the interest. The principal amount of the payment ($223.54) is automatically assigned to the Forklift Loan account and the interest payment (51.46) is assigned to the Interest Expense:Loan Interest account.

5. Select   the Print Later check box

The check will be added to the list of checks waiting to be printed.

6. Click   [Save & Close]   to record the payment

A Recording Transaction dialog box displays:

7. Click   [Yes]

When you record the transaction, QuickBooks automatically updates the accounts affected by this transaction:

*   In the Checking account, the amount of the check is subtracted from your balance.

*   In the expense account that tracks interest, the interest amount is entered as an increase in your company's interest expense.

*   In the Forklift Loan Long Term Liability account, the principal amount is subtracted from the current value of the liability (reducing your debt).

8. Click   [Close]   to close the Loan Manager

Review

In this lesson, you have learned how to:

- ☑ Use other QuickBooks account types
- ☑ Work with credit card transactions
- ☑ Work with fixed assets
- ☑ Work with long-term liability accounts
- ☑ Use the Loan Manager

Practice:

1. Enter a credit card charge of $51.99 for two faucets purchased from Fields Kitchen & Bath. Assign the transaction to the Building Supplies Expense account.

2. Use the Fixed Asset Item List to create a fixed asset with the following information:

Asset Name/Number	Desktop Computer - 2
Asset Account:	Computer
Purchase Description:	Desktop Computer
Item is:	new
Date:	11/01/2018
Cost:	$1800.00
Vendor/Payee:	Linx Computer Store
Asset Description:	Dell, CD ROM/DVD, Intel Processor
Warranty Expires:	11/01/2021
Notes:	Purchased extended warranty for 3 years

3. Use the Chart of Accounts to create a Fixed Asset account with the following information:

Account Type:	Fixed Asset
Account Name:	Accumulated Depreciation
Subaccount of:	Computer

4. Make a general journal entry for $250.00 recording a depreciation expense for the desktop computer. Credit the Computer accumulated depreciation subaccount.

5. Create a Desktop Computer Loan Long Term Liability account to track a loan for the desktop computer.

6. Use the Loan Manager to edit the Forklift Loan and change the payment terms to 60 months.

7. View the new Payment Schedule for the loan to see how changing the terms affected the payment amount.

8. Close the company file.

Notes:

4 | Creating Reports

In this lesson, you will learn how to:

- ❑ Work with QuickReports
- ❑ Work with preset reports
- ❑ Share reports
- ❑ Export reports to Microsoft® Excel®
- ❑ Print reports

Concept

Reports provide you with essential information to help you stay on top of your business's finances. To help analyze your company's performance, QuickBooks provides two kinds of reports: QuickReports and preset reports. QuickReports summarize information about items you are viewing in lists, forms, or registers with one click of a button. The preset reports provide more comprehensive information on all elements of your company and are used for analyzing profit and losses, budget performance, and sales. QuickBooks provides many preset reports, but if you have specific reporting needs, you can customize any QuickBooks report to display only the data you want to see.

Scenario

In this lesson, you will create and customize a QuickReport and then add this customized report to QuickBooks memory so you can retrieve it later. Then, you will run a preset report and use a filter to limit the report to transactions that meet specified criteria. You will then share the report and learn how to access reports shared by other QuickBooks users. As final steps, you will export a report to Microsoft Excel and then print a report.

Practice Files: B18_Creating_Reports.qbw

Working with QuickReports

The fastest method for viewing a report on your QuickBooks data is to create a QuickReport. A QuickReport instantaneously summarizes financial information on a single aspect of your business. For example, selecting a check in the checking account register and running a QuickReport on it displays a report with a list of all the checks in the register made out to that payee.

Creating QuickReports

Whenever you have a list, a register, or a form displayed, you can quickly and easily create a QuickReport.

Note: For this lesson, set your computer's date to 11/1/2018 before opening the QuickBooks file, as recommended in the Before You Get Started lesson. This ensures the dates you see on screen match the dates in this lesson. If you do not change your computer's date, you will need to select All from the Dates drop-down menus or enter dates from 1/1/2018 to 12/31/2018, so the reports on your screen match the reports in the guide.

To display a QuickReport for a vendor,

1. Open   B18_Creating   using the method described in
                   Reports.qbw   Before You Get Started

The QuickBooks Login dialog box displays:

QuickBooks Login   ✖
You need to log in as QuickBooks Administrator to proceed. Please enter the admin (owner) password for the company:
Canalside Corp.
Password: [_____]   I forgot my password
Passwords are case sensitive.
[OK]   [Cancel]   [Help]

This dialog box informs you that you must login as a QuickBooks Administrator in order to open the company file.

2. Type   **Canalside2**   in the Password field

Note: Passwords are case-sensitive.

3. Click   [OK]

QuickBooks opens the file.

4. Click   [✖]   to close the Reminders window

QuickBooks displays the Home page:

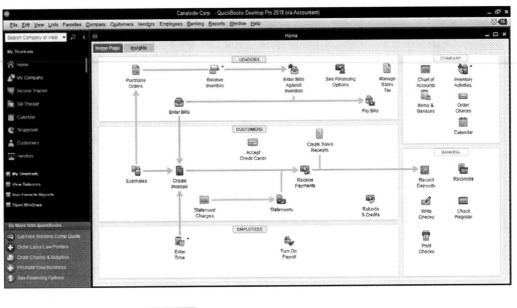

5. Click in the Company area of the Home page

The Chart of Accounts opens:

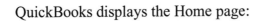

You can easily create QuickReports for any of the accounts listed in the Chart of Accounts.

6. Select   Job Expenses :   in the Name column (scroll down)
                Job Materials

7. Click   **Reports ▼**

A drop-down menu displays:

QuickReport: Job Materials	Ctrl+Q
Income Tax Preparation	
Account Listing	
Reports on All Accounts	▶

8. Select   **QuickReport:**   from the drop-down menu
                          Job Materials

Quick Tip. You can also right-click on any account in the Chart of Accounts and select QuickReport from the drop-down.

The Account QuickReport window opens:

Type	Date	Num	Name	Memo	Split	Amount
Job Expenses						
Job Materials						
Bill	08/10/2018		Fellows Windows...	Large bay w...	Accounts Pa...	250.00
Item Receipt	08/11/2018		Davids Lumber	Decking lum...	Accounts Pa...	1,750.00
Item Receipt	08/11/2018		Davids Lumber	Rough lumber	Accounts Pa...	810.00
Item Receipt	08/11/2018		Davids Lumber	Trim Lumber	Accounts Pa...	375.00
Total Job Materials						3,185.00
Total Job Expenses						3,185.00
TOTAL						3,185.00

Note: If your window does not display the same transactions, select All from the Dates drop-down menu.

This QuickReport chronologically lists all job material expense transactions. The total expenses for job materials is displayed at the bottom of the report.

9. Close the Account QuickReport window and Chart of Accounts

You can also display QuickReports for customers, vendors, and employees.

10. Click   **Vendors**   on the Icon Bar

The Vendor Center opens:

A list of vendors displays on the Vendors tab on the left side of the window.

11. Select — Davids Lumber — in the list of vendors

To display a QuickReport for David's Lumber,

12. Click — | ▪ QuickReport | — in the Reports for this Vendor area (located in the upper-right corner of the window)

The Vendor QuickReport window opens.

13. Select — All — from the Dates drop-down menu

The QuickReport is updated to display all transactions for Davids Lumber:

Vendor QuickReport — ▭ ✕								
Customize Report	Comment on Report	Share Template	Memorize	Print ▼	E-mail ▼	Excel ▼	Hide Header	Refresh
Dates	All	▼	From	🗓 To	🗓	Sort By	Default	▼

Show Filters

11:13 AM
11/01/18

Canalside Corp.
Vendor QuickReport
All Transactions

	Type	Date	Num	Memo	Account	Clr	Split	Amount
Davids Lumber								
▶	Purchase Order	03/10/2010	2		Purchase Orders		-SPLIT-	-2,935.00 ◀
	Item Receipt	08/11/2018		Received ite...	Accounts Payable		-SPLIT-	-2,935.00

Note: The size of your Vendor QuickReport window may be different. You may resize and move the window as necessary. Depending on the size of your window, you may need to scroll to the right to view the entire report.

Note: If you are using the Premier version of QuickBooks, your report will display a Debit column and a Credit column instead of an Amount column.

All QuickReports contain a summary of individual transactions. To help you better understand the information presented in reports, QuickBooks allows you to trace report data to the individual transaction level using QuickZoom.

To display the transactions behind a report item,

14. Position — the mouse pointer — over Item Receipt in the Type column

The mouse pointer changes to a magnifying glass with the letter Z ⊕ for Zoom. The zoom feature allows you to quickly look at the specifics of any transaction in a QuickReport.

15. Double-click — the left mouse button — to zoom in on the Item Receipt

The Create Item Receipts window opens displaying the transaction:

16. Close the Create Item Receipts window to return to the Vendor QuickReport

The QuickReport Toolbar

A QuickReport has a toolbar that enables you to perform tasks such as customizing the report's content and layout, memorizing the report, printing the report, e-mailing the report, or exporting the report.

The commands on this toolbar allow you to:

Customize Report	Modify the report content and layout
Comment on Report	Add comments to any line of a report, which can then be saved, printed, or shared
Share Template	Share a customized report template with other QuickBooks users (this button is inactive until you customize a report)
Memorize	Name and save the report settings
Print ▾	Print a hard copy of the report or save it to a PDF
E-mail ▾	Send the report via e-mail as a PDF or Excel file
Excel ▾	Export the report to a new Excel worksheet or update an existing worksheet
Hide Header	Hide or show the report header

Refresh	Refresh the report to display the latest data

> *Note: You can choose for reports to refresh automatically by opening the My Preferences window, selecting the Reports & Graphs category, and clicking the Refresh automatically option on the My Preferences tab.*

Dates   Filter the report content by date

Sort By   Sort the report content by criteria such as Type, Memo, Account, or Amount

Customizing QuickReports

When you click the Customize Report button on the QuickReport toolbar, a Modify Report window opens allowing you to modify the content and layout of a report. Another useful feature of this window is the ability to use filters and enter criteria that allows you to search for specific data you want displayed in the report.

In this exercise, you will modify the report by adding a transaction number and changing the title.

1. Click   [Customize Report]   on the QuickReport toolbar

The Display tab of the Modify Report: Vendor QuickReport window opens:

The Display tab allows you to edit the report date range, select the columns you want to display on the report, and sort the report data.

To display transaction numbers on the report,

2. Click   Trans #   in the Columns list to select it

A check mark displays next to Trans # indicating it is selected.

3. Click [OK] to accept the change

The transaction numbers (13 and 19) are added to the Vendor QuickReport:

Trans #	Type	Date	Num	Memo	Account	Clr	Split	Amount
Davids Lumber								
13	Purchase Order	03/10/2010	2		Purchase Orders	-SPLIT-		-2,935.00
19	Item Receipt	08/11/2018		Received Ite...	Accounts Payable	-SPLIT-		-2,935.00

11:28 AM 11/01/18 — Canalside Corp. — Vendor QuickReport — All Transactions

Quick Tip. *After a report is customized, the Share Template button becomes enabled. Clicking the Shared Template button allows you to share a customized report with other QuickBooks users.*

To change the title of the report,

4. Click [Customize Report]

The Display tab of the Modify Report: Vendor QuickReport window opens.

5. Click the [Header/Footer] tab

The Header/Footer tab displays:

Modify Report: Vendor QuickReport

SHOW HEADER INFORMATION

- ☑ Company Name — Canalside Corp.
- ☑ Report Title — Vendor QuickReport
- ☑ Subtitle — All Transactions
- ☑ Date Prepared — 12/31/01
- ☑ Time Prepared
- ☑ Print header on pages after first page

SHOW FOOTER INFORMATION

- ☑ Page Number — Page 1
- ☑ Extra Footer Line
- ☑ Print footer on first page

PAGE LAYOUT

Alignment: Standard

The Header/Footer tab allows you to show or hide header information, including the Company Name, Report Title, Subtitle, Date Prepared, and Time Prepared. You can also choose whether to print the header on all pages. In addition, you can show or hide footer information or change the page layout of the report.

6. Select **Vendor QuickReport** in the Report Title field

7. Type   **David's Lumber**   to replace the Vendor QuickReport
                 History   text

Because you do not want a subtitle displayed on the report,

8. Deselect   the Subtitle check box

9. Click   [OK]

The updated Vendor QuickReport displays:

	Vendor QuickReport	_ □ ×
Customize Report	Comment on Report	Share Template	Memorize	Print ▼	E-mail ▼	Excel ▼	Hide Header	Refresh

Dates All ▼ From [ ] To [ ] Sort By Default ▼

Show Filters

| 11:31 AM | | Canalside Corp. | | |
| 11/01/18 | | **David's Lumber History** | | |

	Trans #	Type	Date	Num	Memo	Account	Clr	Split	Amount
Davids Lumber									
	13	Purchase Order	03/10/2010	2		Purchase Orders		-SPLIT-	-2,935.00
▶	19	Item Receipt	08/11/2018		Received ite...	Accounts Payable		-SPLIT-	-2,935.00 ◀

The new title displays on the report and the subtitle has been removed.

Memorizing QuickReports

After you have customized a QuickReport to provide the information you need, in most cases you can have QuickBooks memorize the settings to produce the same report in the future. When QuickBooks memorizes a report, it saves the report settings—not the actual data in the report. For example, if you create a report for David's Lumber that contains month-to-date data and then call up the memorized report next month, the data will be updated to reflect the more recent transactions.

1. Click   [Memorize]   in the Vendor QuickReport toolbar

The Memorize Report window opens:

Memorize Report	×

Name: [David's Lumber History]

☐ Save in Memorized Report Group: Accountant ▼

☐ Share this report template with others

[OK]   [Cancel]

Notice the name of the report is already David's Lumber History.

2. Select   the Save in
                 Memorized Report
                 Group check box

3. Click next to Save in Memorized Report Group

A drop-down menu displays:

> ✓ Accountant
> Banking
> Company
> Customers
> Employees
> Vendors

This menu allows you to categorize your reports by type.

4. Select   Vendors   from the drop-down menu

5. Click   OK   to memorize the report

6. Close the David's Lumber History report window

To display the memorized report,

7. Select   Reports : Memorized   from the menu bar
                 Reports : Vendors :
                 David's Lumber History

The David's Lumber History report you just created opens:

Customize Report	Comment on Report	Share Template	Memorize	Print ▼	E-mail ▼	Excel ▼	Hide Header	Refresh

Dates [All] From [ ] To [ ] Sort By Default

Show Filters

11:44 AM
11/01/18

Canalside Corp.
David's Lumber History

Trans #	Type	Date	Num	Memo	Account	Clr	Split	Amount
Davids Lumber								
13	Purchase Order	03/10/2010	2		Purchase Orders		-SPLIT-	-2,935.00 ◄
19	Item Receipt	08/11/2018		Received ite...	Accounts Payable		-SPLIT-	-2,935.00

Quick Tip. After you have memorized reports, you can take advantage of QuickBooks multiple reports option, a time-saving feature allowing you to quickly generate multiple memorized reports. This feature is useful if you frequently run the same reports and want to generate them all at once, rather than one at a time. For example, you can group together all end-of-month financial reports and run them at the same time. To generate multiple reports, select Reports : Process Multiple Reports from the menu bar. When the Process Multiple Reports window opens, select either All Reports, Ungrouped Reports, or a specific memorized report group (such as Vendors or Customers) from the Select Memorized Reports From drop-down menu. Then, simply select the reports you want to generate and click the Display or Print button.

8. Close the David's Lumber History report window to return to the Vendor Center

Quick Tip. For customers and vendors, QuickBooks also has open balance reports that work much like QuickReports, but show only the open, unpaid transactions. For example, if you want to view a report of only unpaid bills and unapplied credits for this vendor, you can click the Open Balance link to display a Vendor Open Balance QuickReport.

9. Close the Vendor Center to return to the Home page

Working with Preset Reports

QuickBooks includes numerous preset reports that provide a more comprehensive view of your company, allowing you to see the big picture quickly. These reports help answer business questions, such as:

- How much money is owed to me?

- How much money do I owe for purchases?

- Overall, how is my business doing?

All preset reports are accessible through the Reports menu or the Report Center. The following are the major report groups:

- **Company & Financial:** Includes profit and loss reports to provide a global view of your company's income, expenses, and net profit or loss over a specific period of time; balance sheet reports to show the financial position of your business by listing assets, liabilities, and equity; and cash flow reports to help forecast how much cash you will have by projecting your cash inflows, cash disbursements, and bank account balances on a week-by-week basis.

Note: QuickBooks Premier and Enterprise Solutions include a Balance Sheet by Class report. This report shows a financial snapshot of your company as of a specific date and calculates how much your business is worth (equity) by subtracting all the money your company owes (liabilities) from everything it owns (assets). QuickBooks segments this report by class. It is important to note that the Balance Sheet by Class report is an advanced report that differs from other QuickBooks reports and users may experience unexpected results. Understanding and fixing these results requires a strong background in accounting and a good working knowledge of QuickBooks. Therefore, you should only use this report if you need a balance sheet broken down by class and you should work with your QuickBooks accountant to create this report.

- **Customers & Receivables:** Includes Accounts Receivable (A/R) reports that provide information about the "receivables" side of your business: which invoices are due (or overdue), how much each customer owes your company, and so on; customer reports that provide balance summaries and details, open invoices, and unbilled jobs by cost; and reports listing customer phone numbers, customer contacts, and item prices.

- **Sales:** Includes reports that provide information about what you have sold and to whom, such as a Sales by Item Summary report and a Sales by Customer Summary report.

- **Jobs, Time & Mileage:** Includes reports that provide information about the time, cost, and profitability of a job, as well as any vehicle mileage.

- **Vendors & Payables:** Includes reports that provide information about Accounts Payable (A/P), vendor balances, 1099s, sales tax information, and vendor phone and contact lists.

- **Purchases:** Includes reports that provide information about the goods and services you buy.

- **Inventory:** Includes reports that provide information about the status of your inventory, such as the quantities you have on hand or on order, and the value of your inventory.

- **Employees & Payroll:** Includes reports that summarize the information you need to pay your current employees and payroll liabilities.

- **Banking:** Includes reports that display details for deposits, checks, and reconciliation.

- **Accountant & Taxes:** Includes reports that provide information about the general ledger and journal, a report that displays an audit trail, reports that list transactions that match specific criteria you enter, and reports that track income tax data.

- **Budgets:** Includes reports that show how your income and expenses compare with the budgets you have set up.

- **List:** Includes reports that allow you to report on any information stored in a QuickBooks list.

Running a Preset Company & Financial Report

The preset Company & Financial reports include profit and loss reports, income and expense reports, balance sheet and net worth reports, and cash flow reports.

To run a preset Company & Financial report using the Report Center,

1. Click on the Icon Bar (scroll down if necessary)

Note: If a dialog box displays informing you that some views in the Report Center may be slow based on the graphics capabilities of your computer, click the OK button. In this lesson, you will switch to List View, as QuickBooks recommends.

The Report Center opens with the Company & Financial reports displayed:

To switch to List View,

2. Click [the List View icon] in the upper-right corner, below the Search field

The Report Center lists all reports in the Report Center:

From the Report Center, you can easily view all of QuickBooks preset reports.

The following icons display below each report name:

 (Run)   Runs and displays the report.

 (Info)   Displays more information about the report, including an example and description.

 (Fave)   Marks the report as a favorite. A red heart indicates the report is not marked as a favorite. A light gray heart indicates the report is marked as a favorite and will be included in your favorites list.

 (Help)   Displays the QuickBooks help allowing you to learn more about the selected report.

In addition to the icons that display, there is a Dates section for each report. This allows you to select a date range for the report from a drop-down menu.

To run a profit & loss report,

3. Click   below Profit & Loss Detail

A Collapsing and Expanding Transactions dialog box displays:

4. Select the Do not display this message in the future check box

5. Click   OK

The Profit & Loss Detail report opens:

Note: You will need to scroll down to view the entire report.

This report displays year-to-date transactions for all income and expense accounts. The Report Basis area allows you to toggle between accrual or cash basis reporting.

6. Select   the Cash option   in the Report Basis are below the toolbar

The report is updated to display profit and loss on a cash basis:

7. Close the Profit & Loss Detail report to return to the Report Center

A Memorize Report dialog box opens asking if you want to memorize the report:

8. Select the Do not display this message in the future check box

9. Click to return to the Report Center

Now, you will run a balance sheet report.

10. Click ⊙ below Balance Sheet Prev Year Comparison in the Balance Sheet & Net Worth section (scroll down)

The Balance Sheet Prev Year Comparison report opens:

Customize Report	Comment on Report	Share Template	Memorize	Print ▼	E-mail ▼	Excel ▼	Hide Header	Collapse	Refresh

Dates This Fiscal Year-to-date ▼   As of 11/01/2018 🗓   Show Columns Total only ▼   Sort By Default ▼

Report Basis: ⦿ Accrual ◯ Cash   Show Filters

12:14 PM
11/01/18
Accrual Basis

Canalside Corp.
Balance Sheet Prev Year Comparison
As of November 1, 2018

	Nov 1, 18	Nov 1, 17	$ Change	% Change
▽ ASSETS				
▽ Current Assets				
▽ Checking/Savings				
Checking	▶ 14,788.82 ◀	10,450.50	4,338.32	41.5%
Savings - Money Market	27,500.00	0.00	27,500.00	100.0%
Total Checking/Savings	42,288.82	10,450.50	31,838.32	304.7%
▽ Accounts Receivable				
Accounts Receivable	6,007.27	-2,952.37	8,959.64	303.5%
Total Accounts Receivable	6,007.27	-2,952.37	8,959.64	303.5%
▽ Other Current Assets				
Inventory Asset	7,563.45	3,469.00	4,094.45	118.0%
Total Other Current Assets	7,563.45	3,469.00	4,094.45	118.0%
Total Current Assets	55,859.54	10,967.13	44,892.41	409.3%
TOTAL ASSETS	55,859.54	10,967.13	44,892.41	409.3%
▽ LIABILITIES & EQUITY				
▽ Liabilities				
▽ Current Liabilities				
▽ Accounts Payable				
Accounts Payable	6,289.00	0.00	6,289.00	100.0%

Note: You will need to scroll down to view the entire report.

This report compares the worth of your business as of a specific date to the same date last year. The report calculates how much your business is worth (your business's equity) by subtracting all the money your company owes (liabilities) from everything it owns (assets). The total for equity includes your company's net income for the fiscal year to date. Notice the toolbar at the top of the report is similar to the one used for QuickReports.

11. Close the Balance Sheet Prev Comparison report to return to the Report Center

To mark this report as a favorite,

12. Click below the report name

The red heart changes to light gray to indicate the report is marked as a favorite.

To view the report in your favorites list,

13. Select   Reports :   from the menu bar
               Favorite Reports

Notice the Balance Sheet Prev Year Comparison report is now listed as a Favorite in the Favorite Reports menu.

Note: The Favorite Reports item will not display in the Reports menu until you have marked at least one report as a Favorite.

Quick Tip. You can also click the Favorites tab in the Report Center to display all reports marked as a Favorite.

Running a Preset Vendors & Payables Report

The Vendors & Payables reports include Accounts Payable (A/P) aging reports, vendor balances reports, 1099 reports, sales tax reports, and vendor phone and contact lists.

The A/P Aging Summary report summarizes the status of unpaid bills in accounts payable, showing what you owe, who you owe it to, and how much is overdue.

To run a preset A/P Aging Summary report,

1. Click   Vendors & Payables   in the list of report categories
                                      displayed on the left side of the
                                      Report Center

All preset vendor and payables reports are displayed in the Report Center:

2. Click below A/P Aging Summary

The A/P Aging Summary report opens:

A/P Aging Summary									_ □ ✗
Customize Report	Comment on Report	Share Template	Memorize	Print ▾	E-mail ▾	Excel ▾	Hide Header	Collapse	Refresh

Dates Today ▾ 11/01/2018 🗓 Interval (days) 30 Through (days past due) 90 Sort By Default ▾

Show Filters

12:22 PM
11/01/18

Canalside Corp.
A/P Aging Summary
As of November 1, 2018

	Current	1 - 30	31 - 60	61 - 90	> 90	TOTAL
Davids Lumber ▶	0.00 ◀	0.00	0.00	2,935.00	0.00	2,935.00
Joshua Hardware Supp...	0.00	2,094.00	0.00	0.00	0.00	2,094.00
Mason & Son Painting	410.00	0.00	0.00	0.00	0.00	410.00
PJ's Plumbing	0.00	850.00	0.00	0.00	0.00	850.00
TOTAL	410.00	2,944.00	0.00	2,935.00	0.00	6,289.00

For each vendor to whom your company owes money, the report shows how much your company owes for the current and previous billing periods, as well as the total amount owed. The report also displays the total amount owed to all vendors.

3. Close the A/P Aging Summary report to return to the Report Center

Customizing Preset Reports

Just as with QuickReports, when you click the Customize Report button on the report window toolbar, a Modify Report window opens, allowing you to modify the content and layout of the report, including using filters to limit a report to transactions that meet criteria you specify.

Canalside Corp. does new construction, remodeling, and repairs and also has a small mail-order business for custom wood doors and hardware, which it keeps in stock. In this exercise, you will create a sales report in order to view sales figures for your customers and jobs. You will then add a filter to the report so that you can find out how much of your customer sales went towards inventory purchases.

To create a Sales report,

1. Click Sales in the list of report categories displayed on the left side of the Report Center

All preset sales reports are displayed in the Report Center:

2. Click   [This Month-to-date ▾]   below Sales by Customer Summary

A drop-down menu displays.

3. Select   All   from the drop-down menu

4. Click   [○]   below Sales by Customer Summary

The Sales by Customer Summary report opens:

This report displays your total sales figures for each customer and job. If you want to find out the amount of customer sales that went towards inventory purchases from Canalside Corp. this fiscal year-to-date, you can add a filter to the report.

To use filters to search for and display specific sales information,

5. Click   Customize Report   on the report toolbar

The Modify Report: Sales by Customer Summary window opens:

6. Click   the Filters tab

The Filters tab displays:

This tab allows you to set custom criteria for the transactions to be included in the report. You can filter reports by accounts, amounts, names, transaction types, due dates, and a variety of other options.

7. Select   Item   in the Choose Filter list (scroll down)

The tab changes to reflect the Item filter selections:

8. Select   All inventory items   from the Item drop-down menu

Your selection, All inventory items, is added to the list of Current Filter Choices in the table on the right side of the tab.

Quick Tip. *To remove a filter from a report, select the filter in the Current Filter Choices list and click the Remove Selected Filter button.*

9. Click   the Header/Footer tab

The Header/Footer tab displays:

10. Select   Sales by Customer   in the Report Title field
                    Summary

11. Type   **Inventory Sales**   to replace the Sales by Customer
                                                Summary text

12. Click   OK

The filtered Inventory Sales report displays:

Sales by Customer Summary									
Customize Report	Comment on Report	Share Template	Memorize	Print ▼	E-mail ▼	Excel ▼	Hide Header	Collapse	

Dates All ▼   From 📅 To 📅   Show Columns Total only ▼   Sort By Defa

Report Basis: ⦿ Accrual ○ Cash   Show Filters

12:33 PM
11/01/18
Accrual Basis

Canalside Corp.
Inventory Sales
All Transactions

	Oct 11, 18
▽ James Wilson DDS	
Dental office ▶	535.00 ◀
Total James Wilson DDS	535.00
TOTAL	**535.00**

The report is now limited to only the customer whose sales included inventory item purchases.

Quick Tip. *Clicking the Show Filters button displays all filters applied to the report. These will also display on the PDF and printed report.*

As with all QuickBooks reports, you can QuickZoom on any item in the report.

To use QuickZoom,

13. Position   the mouse pointer   over any 535.00 dollar figure

The mouse pointer changes to a magnifying glass with a Z 🔍Z .

14. Double-click   the left mouse button

The Sales by Customer Detail report opens:

Sales by Customer Detail								
Customize Report	Comment on Report	Share Template	Memorize	Print ▼	E-mail ▼	Excel ▼	Hide Header	Refresh

Dates Custom ▼   From 📅 To 📅   Sort By Default ▼

Report Basis: ⦿ Accrual ○ Cash   Show Filters

12:38 PM
11/01/18
Accrual Basis

Canalside Corp.
Sales by Customer Detail
All Transactions

Type	Date	Num	Memo	Name	Item	Qty	Sales Price	Amount	Balance
James Wilson DDS									
Dental office									
▶ Invoice	10/09/2018	2	Exterior woo...	James Wilson DDS...	Wood D...	1	145.00	145.00	145.00 ◀
Invoice	10/09/2018	2	Interior woo...	James Wilson DDS...	Wood D...	3	85.00	255.00	400.00
Invoice	10/09/2018	2	Locking inte...	James Wilson DDS...	Hardwa...	3	45.00	135.00	535.00
Total Dental office						7		535.00	535.00
Total James Wilson DDS						7		535.00	535.00
TOTAL						7		**535.00**	**535.00**

This report allows you to take a closer look at the sales made to James Wilson DDS. Notice that all of the sales items listed in the report are inventory items. From this report, you can zoom in even further to look at an individual invoice.

15. Position   the mouse pointer   over the first invoice on the report for Exterior wood doors

The mouse pointer turns to the QuickZoom pointer ⊛ .

16. Double-click   the left mouse button

The Invoice for James Wilson's Dental office job opens:

By using QuickZoom, you have easily returned to the origin of the report data.

17. Close the Create Invoices window to return to the Sales by Customer Detail report

18. Close the Sales by Customer Detail report to return to the Inventory Sales report

Sharing Reports

QuickBooks allows you to access and use reports that other QuickBooks users have contributed. You can also share customized report templates with QuickBooks users who may need a report just like yours.

With the Inventory Sales report displayed,

1. Click | Share Template | on the report toolbar

Note: The Share Template button on the report toolbar will not be active until you have customized a report.

The Share Template window opens:

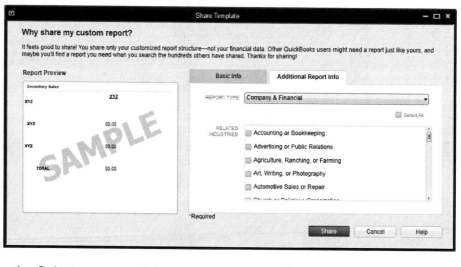

This window allows you to enter the necessary information for sharing a report. Notice the title of the report is already displayed in the Report title field.

2. Type   Summary of inventory   in the Description field
                  sales by customer

Note: All required fields have an asterisk next to them.

For this exercise, you will leave the Your name and Your email fields blank. You will also accept the default selection of Share anonymously.

3. Click   the Additional Report Info tab

The Additional Report Info tab displays:

4. Select   Sales   from the Report Type drop-down
                                                     menu

5. Click   the Select All check box

A check mark displays next to all industries in the Related industries list.

6. Click [Share]

A Share Template dialog box opens indicating the report was shared:

Share Template

Thanks!

We shared your report!

[View my shared reports] [Close]

Note: *If you set your computer's date to 11/1/2018 as recommended at the beginning of this lesson, this dialog box will not display.*

7. Click [Close]

The Share Template dialog box closes and the customized report is saved to the QuickBooks library of contributed reports for others to use. Only the report structure will be shared, not your actual data.

To access reports contributed by other QuickBooks users,

8. Select   Reports : Contributed   from the menu bar
             Reports : Sales

All Sales reports contributed by other users display on the Contributed tab:

Each report displays a description of the report, who the report was created by, the popularity of the report, the average rating of the report, and the number of reviews completed for the report.

Quick Tip. If you are using the QuickBooks Premier edition, you can access industry-specific report templates created by other QuickBooks Premier users.

9. Close the Report Center and the Inventory Sales report

Exporting Reports to Microsoft Excel

Note: To use this feature, you must have Microsoft Excel 2010 or later installed on your computer.

You may find it is helpful to work with the contents of a report in Microsoft Excel, because Excel allows you to perform certain modifications and calculations that aren't available in QuickBooks. For example, in Excel you can create What-if scenarios, which are helpful in predicting future earnings based on current data.

In this exercise, you will use the Reports menu to display a report and then export this report to Excel.

1. Select   Reports : Company   from the menu bar
                           & Financial : Income
                           by Customer Detail

The Income by Customer Detail report opens:

		Income by Customer Detail						
Customize Report	Comment on Report	Share Template	Memorize	Print ▼	E-mail ▼	Excel ▼	Hide Header	Refresh

Dates This Fiscal Year-to-date ▼   From 01/01/2018   To 11/01/2018   Sort By Default ▼

Report Basis: ● Accrual ○ Cash   Show Filters

12:56 PM
11/01/18
Accrual Basis

Canalside Corp.
Income by Customer Detail
January 1 through November 1, 2018

Type	Date	Num	Memo	Account	Clr	Split	Amount	Balance
James Wilson DDS								
Dental office								
Bill	10/08/2018		Painting	Subcontractors		Accounts Pa...	-410.00	-410.00
Invoice	10/09/2018	2	Painting	Subcontractors		Accounts Re...	520.00	110.00
Invoice	10/09/2018	2	Exterior woo...	Materials		Accounts Re...	145.00	255.00
Invoice	10/09/2018	2	Exterior woo...	Cost of Goods Sold		Accounts Re...	-105.00	150.00
Invoice	10/09/2018	2	Interior woo...	Materials		Accounts Re...	255.00	405.00
Invoice	10/09/2018	2	Interior woo...	Cost of Goods Sold		Accounts Re...	-180.00	225.00
Invoice	10/09/2018	2	Locking inte...	Materials		Accounts Re...	135.00	360.00
Invoice	10/09/2018	2	Locking inte...	Cost of Goods Sold		Accounts Re...	-104.85	255.15
Invoice	10/09/2018	2	Installation la...	Labor		Accounts Re...	297.50	552.65
Total Dental office							552.65	552.65
Total James Wilson DDS							552.65	552.65
Kleier, Patricia								
Remodel Bathroom								
Bill	10/07/2018		Plumbing	Subcontractors		Accounts Pa...	-850.00	-850.00
Total Remodel Bathroom							-850.00	-850.00
Total Kleier, Patricia							-850.00	-850.00
Richard Davis								
Stmt Charge	10/10/2018		Painting	Subcontractors		Accounts Re...	0.00	0.00
Total Richard Davis							0.00	0.00

Note: If data does not display in your report window, select All from the Dates drop-down menu.

Note: If you are using the Premier version of QuickBooks, your report will display a Debit column and a Credit column instead of an Amount column.

2. Click   Excel ▼   on the report toolbar

A drop-down menu displays:

Create New Worksheet
Update Existing Worksheet

3. Select   Create New Worksheet from the drop-down menu

The Send Report to Excel window opens:

Send Report to Excel ✕

WHAT WOULD YOU LIKE TO DO WITH THIS REPORT?

◉ Create new worksheet
    ◉ in new workbook
    ○ in existing workbook
○ Update an existing worksheet   How it works
○ Replace an existing worksheet
○ Create a comma separated values (.csv) file

Advanced...

Export   Cancel   Help

This window allows you to do any of the following:

*   Send the report to a new worksheet. You can choose to create a new worksheet in a new workbook or an existing workbook.

*   Update an existing Excel worksheet. If you have already exported a Quick-Books report into an Excel file and modified and saved the Excel file, this option allows you to run the QuickBooks report again for a new time period and export it into the existing Excel file. Any formatting updates made to the existing Excel file will be applied to the new report. For example, Excel will apply modifications, such as formatted fonts, new formulas, renamed rows, columns, and headers, and resized columns to the new report.

*   Replace an existing Excel worksheet.

*   Send the report to a comma separated values (.csv) Excel file.

Quick Tip. *You can also update an existing Excel worksheet by selecting the Update Existing worksheet option from the Excel drop-down menu.*

For this exercise, you will accept the default selection of Create new worksheet in new workbook.

4. Click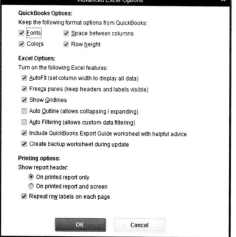

The Advanced Excel Options window opens:

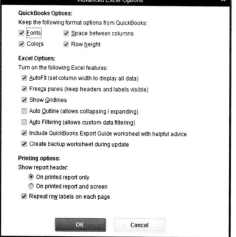

This window allows you to specify settings for the Excel file prior to exporting the report. From this window, you can set options to keep the same font, color, and row height used in the QuickBooks report, turn on various Excel features, such as freezing panes and showing gridlines, and setting print options, such as where to show report headers and whether or not to repeat row labels on each page.

For this exercise, you will leave the default selections.

5. Click   OK   to return to the Send Report to Excel window

6. Click   Export   to export the report to a new Excel workbook

QuickBooks launches Excel and exports the data:

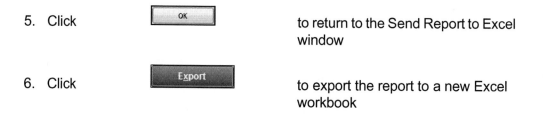

Note: If you are using the Premier version of QuickBooks, your Excel file will display a Debit column and a Credit column instead of an Amount column.

QuickBooks exports the following information into the Excel worksheet:

- Data in the report, in the format it was displayed in QuickBooks
- Formulas for subtotals, totals, and other calculations
- Column and row labels
- Headers and footers from the QuickBooks report

Quick Tip. *The QuickBooks Export Tips tab includes tips for updating QuickBooks reports in Excel.*

To exit Excel,

7. Select   File : Exit   from the Excel menu bar

Note: If the Exit option does not display, select File : Close and then click the x in the upper-right corner to close Excel.

A Microsoft Excel dialog box displays:

Microsoft Excel	✕
⚠ Do you want to save the changes you made to 'Book2'?	
[Save] [Don't Save] [Cancel]	

Note: Depending on the version of Microsoft Office you are using, your dialog box may be slightly different and you may have to click the No button, rather than the Don't Save button in the next step.

8. Click   [Don't Save]   to exit Excel without saving the report

Excel closes and QuickBooks displays the Income by Customer Detail report.

Printing Reports

When you have a report displayed in a report window, you can print it by clicking the Print button in the report toolbar.

Note: You must have a printer driver and printer installed on your computer or network in order to print reports.

To print the Income by Customer Detail report,

1. Click   [Print ▼]   in the report toolbar

A drop-down menu displays:

> Report
> Save As PDF

2. Select   Report   from the drop-down menu

The Print Reports window opens:

> **Print Reports**   ✕
>
> **Settings** | Margins
>
> Print to: **Print**
> ◉ Printer: Brother HL-2170W series on USB001 ▾   Options...   Cancel
> ○ File: ASCII text file ▾   Help
> Note: To install additional printers or to change port   Preview
>   assignments, use the Windows Control Panel.
>
> **ORIENTATION:**   **PAGE RANGE:**
> ○ Portrait   ◉ All
> ◉ Landscape   ○ Pages:
>   From: 1   To: 9999
>
> **PAGE BREAKS:**
> ☐ Smart page breaks (widow/orphan control)   Number of copies: 1
> ☐ Page break after each major grouping   ☑ Collate
>
> ☑ Fit report to 1 page(s) wide   ☐ Print in color (color printers only)
> ☐ Fit report to   page(s) high

Note: The printer displayed in your window will be different.

Because this report has many columns and is rather wide, it should be printed in Landscape orientation to fit on one page.

3. Verify   Landscape   in the Orientation area
                     is selected

4. Select   the Smart page breaks   in the Page Breaks area
                     (widow/orphan control)
                     check box

When this check box is selected, QuickBooks will automatically improve the presentation of the printed report by preventing awkward page breaks. Within small groupings of data, QuickBooks avoids splitting related data across two pages. Within larger groupings, QuickBooks chooses the most logical place to insert a page break.

Quick Tip. Some reports group information into major categories such as customer, vendor, employee, or even type of account. When printing a report that contains major groupings, select the Page break after each major grouping check box to start each major grouping on a new page.

To preview the report,

5. Click   Preview

A Print Preview window opens:

Print Preview – Page 1 of 1

| Print | Prev page | Next page | Zoom In | Help | Close |

Canalside Corp.
Income by Customer Detail
January 1 through November 1, 2018

1:51 PM
11/6/18
Accrual Basis

Type	Date	Num	Memo	Account	Clr	Split	Amount	Balance
James Wilson DDS								
Dental office								
Bill	10/06/2018		Painting	Sub-contractors		Accounts Paya...	-410.00	-410.00
Invoice	10/09/2018	2	Painting	Sub-contractors		Accounts Rece...	520.00	110.00
Invoice	10/09/2018	2	Exterior wood ...	Materials		Accounts Rece...	145.00	255.00
Invoice	10/09/2018	2	Exterior wood ...	Cost of Goods Sold		Accounts Rece...	-105.00	150.00
Invoice	10/09/2018	2	Interior wood ...	Materials		Accounts Rece...	255.00	405.00
Invoice	10/09/2018	2	Interior wood ...	Cost of Goods Sold		Accounts Rece...	-180.00	225.00
Invoice	10/09/2018	2	Locking interi...	Materials		Accounts Rece...	135.00	360.00
Invoice	10/09/2018	2	Locking interi...	Cost of Goods Sold		Accounts Rece...	-104.85	255.15
Invoice	10/09/2018	2	Installation la ...	Labor		Accounts Rece...	297.50	552.65
Total Dental office							552.65	552.65
Total James Wilson DDS							552.65	552.65
Kleier, Patricia								
Remodel Bathroom								
Bill	10/07/2018		Plumbing	Sub-contractors		Accounts Paya...	-850.00	-850.00
Total Remodel Bathroom							-850.00	-850.00
Total Kleier, Patricia							-850.00	-850.00
Richard Davis								
Strct Charge	10/10/2018		Painting	Sub-contractors		Accounts Rece...	0.00	0.00
Total Richard Davis							0.00	0.00
Richard Real Estate								
75 Sunrise St.								
Invoice	07/10/2018	3	Decking lumber	Materials		Accounts Rece...	1,750.00	1,750.00
Invoice	07/10/2018	3	Rough lumber	Materials		Accounts Rece...	810.00	2,560.00
Invoice	07/10/2018	3	Trim Lumber	Materials		Accounts Rece...	375.00	2,935.00
Invoice	07/10/2018	3	Framing labor	Labor		Accounts Rece...	1,760.00	4,695.00
Invoice	09/10/2018	4	Framing labor	Labor		Accounts Rece...	3,520.00	8,215.00
Total 75 Sunrise St.							8,215.00	8,215.00
Total Richard Real Estate							8,215.00	8,215.00
TOTAL							7,917.65	7,917.65

Page 1

Quick Tip. *You can click the Zoom In button to take a closer look at the report.*

You can print the report directly from the Print Preview window.

Note: *If your computer is not set up to print, click the Close button to close the Print Preview window, and the Cancel button to close the Print Reports window.*

6. Click [Print] to print the report (if your computer is set up to print)

QuickBooks sends the report to the printer and closes the Print Preview window.

7. Close the Income by Customer Detail report to return to the Home page

Review

In this lesson, you have learned how to:

- ☑ Work with QuickReports
- ☑ Work with preset reports
- ☑ Share reports
- ☑ Export reports to Microsoft® Excel®
- ☑ Print reports

Practice:

1. Display the Customer Center and create a Customer QuickReport for Patricia Kleier for this fiscal year-to-date.

2. Customize the report by excluding the Memo column, sorting the data by invoice number, and changing the report title to Bathroom Remodeling.

3. Have QuickBooks memorize the new report and save it with the Customers memorized report group.

4. Using the Report Center, run the Vendors & Payables Vendor Balance Detail report.

5. Filter the report to display only balances greater than or equal to $1000.00.

6. Use QuickZoom to display the item receipt for Joshua Hardware Supplies.

7. Share the report using the following data:

Description:	Vendor balances greater than $1000.00
Report type:	Vendors & Payables
Related industries:	Select all

8. Export the report to a new Excel workbook and then close Excel without saving changes.

9. Close the company file without memorizing any reports.

5 | Creating Graphs

In this lesson, you will learn how to:

- ❑ Create QuickInsight graphs
- ❑ Use QuickZoom with graphs
- ❑ Work with the Sales graph
- ❑ Customize graphs
- ❑ Print graphs

Concept

A graph is a valuable tool that provides you with a visual picture of your financial data—a picture that can help you plan current or future business decisions. Because graphs are often easier to understand than numerical reports, you can use QuickBooks's graphing capabilities to display bar graphs and pie charts of your company's data and to identify trends quickly.

Scenario

To help you recognize the trends in income, expenses, and sales for Canalside Corp., you will create a series of graphs using historical data. You will then trace the data back to the individual transactions to get a closer look at some of the figures. You will also customize and print a graph.

Practice Files: B18_Creating_Graphs.qbw

Creating QuickInsight Graphs

A QuickInsight graph allows you to easily create a pictorial view of your company's financial data. QuickBooks has six types of graphs, providing up to 15 different views of your data. The graphs are as follows:

- **Income & Expense graph:** Income compared to expenses over a specified period.

- **Net worth graph:** Changes in your company's net worth (assets, liabilities, and equity).

- **Accounts Receivable graph:** How much your customers owe you and what, if any, portion is overdue.

- **Sales graph:** Sales revenue over a specified period.

- **Accounts Payable graph:** How much you currently owe your vendors and what, if any, portion is overdue.

- **Budget vs. Actual graph:** The variance between your budgeted amounts and the actual amount you earned or spent.

If you want your business to be profitable, you need to keep an eye on your expenses. The Income and Expense graph shows you exactly what you are spending and where. In this exercise, you will create an Income and Expense QuickInsight graph for the last three months of the current year.

Note: For this lesson, set your computer's date to 11/1/2018 before opening the QuickBooks file, as recommended in the Before You Get Started lesson. This ensures the dates you see on screen match the dates in this lesson. If you do not change your computer's date, you will need to select All from the Dates drop-down menus, so the graphs on your screen match the graphs in the guide.

To create an Income and Expense graph,

1. Open   B18_Creating Graphs.qbw   using the method described in Before You Get Started

The QuickBooks Login dialog box displays:

```
                QuickBooks Login                    ✕

You need to log in as QuickBooks Administrator to proceed.  Please enter the
admin (owner) password for the company:

                      Canalside Corp.

    Password: [                    ]    I forgot my password
              Passwords are case sensitive.


        OK            Cancel            Help
```

This dialog box informs you that you must login as a QuickBooks Administrator in order to open the company file.

2. Type   **Canalside2**   in the Password field

Note: Passwords are case-sensitive.

3. Click | OK |

QuickBooks opens the file.

4. Click | ✖ | to close the Reminders window

QuickBooks displays the Home page:

You can create graphs using the QuickBooks Report Center or Reports menu. To create an income and expense graph using the Report Center,

5. Click | 📊 Reports | on the Icon Bar (scroll down)

Note: If a dialog box displays informing you that some views in the Report Center may be slow based on the graphics capabilities of your computer, click OK.

The Report Center opens with the Company & Financial reports and graphs displayed:

Note: The size of your Report Center may be different. If your Report Center does not display in Grid View, click *(Grid View) in the upper-right corner.*

The Report Center allows you to easily view all of QuickBooks reports and graphs.

6. Scroll down to view the Income & Expense Graph in the Income & Expenses section of the Report Center

The Income & Expense graph information displays in the Report Center:

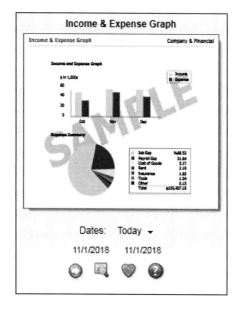

The following icons display below each graph name:

 (Run)   Runs and displays the graph.

 (Info)   Displays more information about the graph, including an example and description.

 (Fave)   Marks the graph as a favorite. A red heart indicates the graph is not marked as a favorite. A light gray heart indicates the graph is marked as a favorite and will be included in your favorites list.

(Help)   Displays the QuickBooks help allowing you to learn more about the graph.

In addition to the icons, there is a Dates section that displays below the graph. This allows you to select a date range for the graph from a drop-down menu.

7. Select   This Fiscal Year   from the Dates drop-down menu below the Income & Expense graph

Note: If you did not change your computer's date as recommended in the Before You Get Started lesson, type 1/1/2018 and 12/31/2018 in the Dates fields.

8. Click below the graph

The QuickInsight: Income and Expense Graph opens displaying income and expenses for the specified period of time:

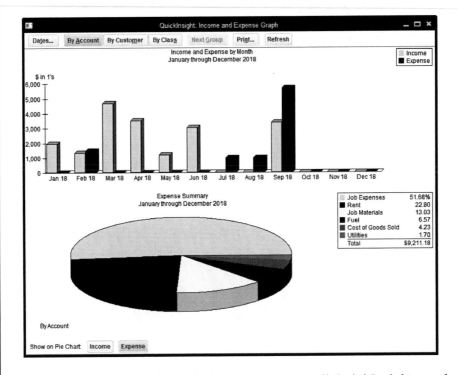

The following are features that are common to all QuickInsight graphs:

*   Every graph window, except for the Net Worth and Budget vs. Actual Graphs windows, shows a bar graph in the top half of the window with a legend, and a pie chart in the bottom half of the window with a legend. The bar graph usually shows totals. For example, this Income and Expense bar graph shows the total for income and the total for expenses for each month of the period. The pie chart shows a breakdown of the information shown in the bar graph; each pie slice in the Income and Expense Graph window represents a type of income or expense. To the right of the pie chart is a legend that shows you which income or expense account corresponds to the colors in the pie chart; it also shows you what percentage of the pie each slice represents.

*   Just as you can use QuickZoom in a report to get more detail on the numbers, it can also be used in a graph to see the numbers behind the picture. For example, when you zoom in on a pie slice, you can find out exactly how much you received or spent (in dollars) for each account.

*   Every graph window has a toolbar with buttons used to customize the graph. For example, you can change the time period shown in the graph by clicking the Dates button. If you want the pie chart to show a breakdown by customer or class rather than by account, click the By Customer or By Class buttons.

Dates...	By Account	By Customer	By Class	Next Group	Print...	Refresh

The following commands on the toolbar allow you to customize the graph data:

 Select the date range for the graph

 Display the graph by account types

 Display the graph by customers

 Display the graph by classes (classes may be used to assign transactions to a department, site, product, and so on)

 Display the next group of accounts (QuickBooks displays only ten accounts at a time)

Print... Print a hard copy of the graph

Refresh Update the graph to display the most recent data

To change the pie chart to display income by customer,

9. Click **Income** at the bottom of the window

10. Click **By Customer** at the top of the window

The Income and Expense Graph is updated to display Canalside Corp.'s income by customer for last fiscal quarter:

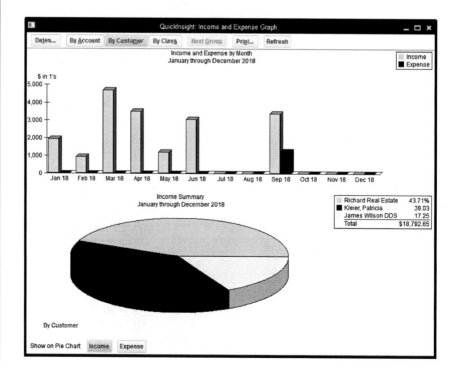

Using this graph, you can see what percentage of your income came from the three customers you serviced this year.

Using QuickZoom with Graphs

The QuickZoom Graphs feature can be used to help you trace the information shown in graphs. In this exercise, you will display the sales data for James Wilson DDS and then use QuickZoom Graphs to look more closely at the sales figures associated with this account.

To display the sales data for a specific customer,

1. Position   the mouse pointer   over the James Wilson DDS wedge
                                             of the pie chart (yellow)

The mouse pointer changes to a magnifying glass with the letter Z 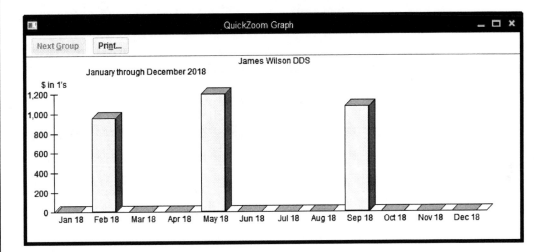 .

2. Double-click   the left mouse button

Quick Tip. *If a wedge is too small to click, click the legend for the wedge instead.*

The QuickZoom graph for James Wilson DDS opens:

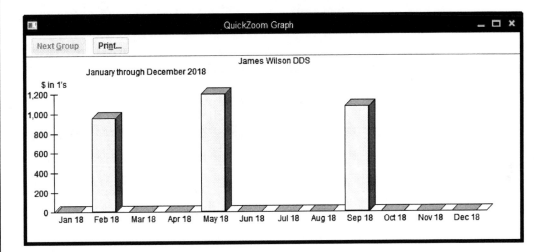

Note: The size of your QuickZoom Graph window may be different. You may resize and move the window as necessary.

To look more closely at these transactions,

3. Position   the mouse pointer   over the bar representing Feb 18

The mouse pointer changes to a magnifying glass with the letter Z 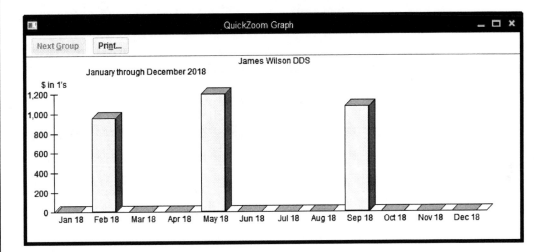 .

4. Double-click   the left mouse button

The Custom Transaction Detail Report opens:

Note: *If you are using QuickBooks Premier, your report will display Debit and Credit columns instead of the Amount column.*

This report shows you the individual transaction that make up the total figure on the QuickZoom Graph.

To display a transaction,

5. Position   the mouse pointer   over the first transaction on the report

6. Double-click   the left mouse button

The invoice for the transaction displays in the Create Invoices window:

The QuickZoom Graph feature has allowed you to quickly access the data behind the Income and Expense Graph.

7. Select   Window : Close All   from the QuickBooks menu bar

All open windows are closed.

Working with the Sales Graph

The Sales graph can be used to view your sales figures by item.

To display the Sales graph from the menu bar,

1. Select   Reports : Sales :   from the menu bar
                       Sales Graph

The QuickInsight: Sales Graph window opens:

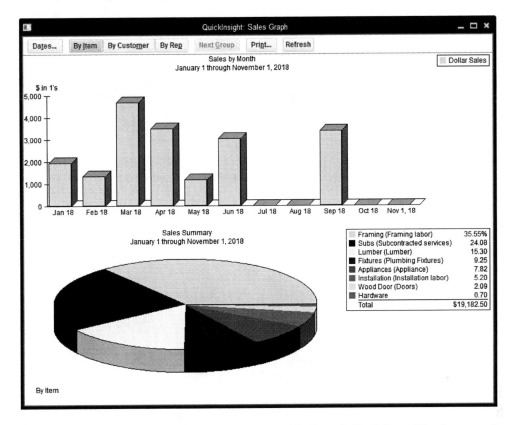

This graph shows sales income for the specified period of time. The bar graph shows the net sales income from invoices, credit memos, and cash sales receipts. The pie chart provides a breakdown of sales income by item.

Note: If data does not display in your graph, click the Dates button in the toolbar of the QuickInsight window. When the Change Graph Dates window opens, enter 1/1/2018 in the From field and 11/1/2018 in the To field and click the OK button.

Quick Tip. Right-click on any piece of the pie on the graph to display its dollar amount.

As with the Income and Expense graph, you can position the mouse pointer on any part of the graph and QuickZoom down to the transaction level.

To look at the sales breakdown for February,

2. Position   the mouse pointer   over the bar for Feb 18 in the bar graph

The mouse pointer changes to a magnifying glass with the letter Z 🔍 .

3. Double-click   the left mouse button

The QuickZoom Graph for February opens:

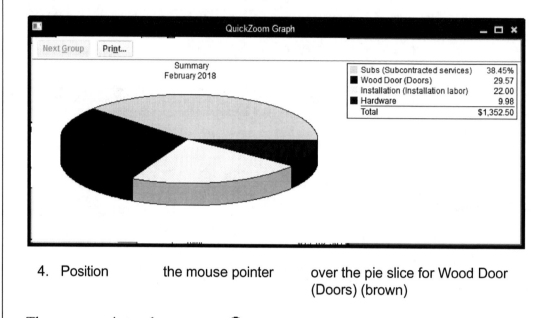

4. Position   the mouse pointer   over the pie slice for Wood Door
                                                 (Doors) (brown)

The mouse pointer changes to a 🔍 .

5. Double-click   the left mouse button

The Custom Transaction Detail Report opens:

From this report, you can QuickZoom to view actual invoices.

6. Position   the mouse pointer   over the first transaction for James
                                                 Wilson DDS

The mouse pointer changes to a 🔍 .

7. Double-click   the left mouse button

The invoice for the selected transaction opens:

8. Close the Create Invoices window

9. Close the Custom Transaction Detail Report

10. Close the QuickZoom Graph

Quick Tip. *Another method for closing a window is to press the Esc key.*

You return to the QuickInsight: Sales Graph.

Customizing Graphs

By customizing graphs you can display your data in a way that is visually appealing and easy to understand. The default for displaying graphs in QuickBooks is three-dimensional (3D). You may find that you would like to change the format to two-dimensional (2D) to display and print graphs more quickly. Also, on a graph that contains a great deal of data, a 2D look may be easier to read.

In this exercise, you will change the format for a graph from 3D to 2D and then customize the Sales graph to display sales by customer.

To create a 2D graph,

1. Select   Edit : Preferences   from the menu bar

The Preferences window opens:

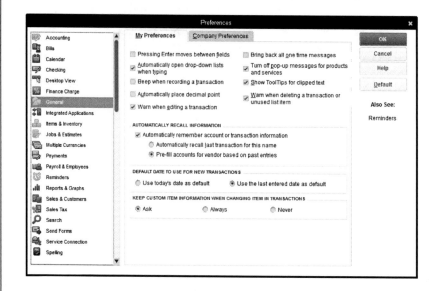

Note: *Your window may display a different selected preference.*

2. Select   the Reports &   from the list of preferences
           Graphs preference

The My Preferences tab of the Reports and Graphs preferences displays:

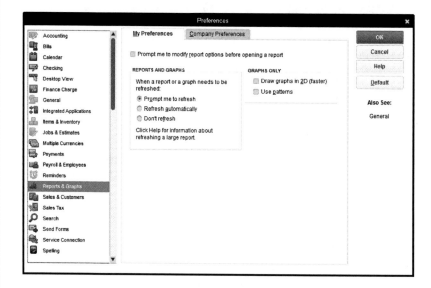

This tab allows you to set preferences for reports and graphs, including when to refresh reports and graphs and how to draw graphs.

3. Select   the Draw graphs in   in the Graphs Only area
           2D (faster) check box

By changing the format of the graph from 3D to 2D in the Preferences window, the new formatting will be applied to all the graphs you create in this company file.

4. Click   to close the Preferences window

The QuickInsight: Sales Graph window now displays a two-dimensional bar graph and pie chart:

To display the sales by customer,

5. Click [By Customer] in the toolbar

The sales data is changed to display the data by customer:

To examine the Richard Real Estate data more closely,

6. Double-click   Richard Real Estate   in the pie chart legend

The QuickZoom Graph for Richard Real Estate opens:

This graph shows the sales to Richard Real Estate totaled over $4,000 in March and over $3,000 in April.

To look at the invoices for these transactions,

7. Position   the mouse pointer   over the bar for Mar 18

The mouse pointer changes to a (Z).

8. Double-click   the left mouse button

The Custom Transaction Detail Report opens for Richard Real Estate:

9. Close the Custom Transaction Detail Report

10. Close the QuickZoom Graph to return to the QuickInsight: Sales Graph

Printing Graphs

After you have created a graph that displays your data in an acceptable format, it's easy to print a hard copy.

Note: You must have a printer driver and printer installed on your computer or network in order to print graphs.

To print the sales graph that is currently displayed,

1. Click **Print...** in the toolbar of the QuickInsight: Sales Graph window

The Print Graphs window opens:

Note: The name of your printer will be different.

This window allows you to select a printer, indicate whether to print in portrait or landscape orientation, and indicate how many copies to print.

2. Click **Print** to print the graph (if your computer is set up to print)

Note: If your computer is not set up to print, click the Cancel button to close the Print Graphs window.

QuickBooks sends the graph to the printer and closes the Print Graphs window.

Review

In this lesson, you have learned how to:

☑ Create QuickInsight graphs

☑ Use QuickZoom with graphs

☑ Work with the Sales graph

☑ Customize graphs

☑ Print graphs

Practice:

1. Using the Report Center, display the Accounts Receivable graph in the Accounts Receivable section for last fiscal quarter.

2. QuickZoom on Patricia Kleier's portion of the pie chart.

3. Use QuickZoom again to see the amount of money owed by Patricia Kleier that is 90 days past due.

4. Using the Preferences window, change the format for graphs back to three-dimensional.

5. Using the Reports menu, display the Accounts Payable graph.

6. Close the company file.

6

Tracking and Paying Sales Tax

In this lesson, you will learn how to:

❑ Use sales tax in QuickBooks

❑ Set up tax rates and agencies

❑ Indicate who and what gets taxed

❑ Apply tax to each sale

❑ Determine what you owe

❑ Pay your tax agencies

Concept

Determining the amount of sales tax your business needs to pay can be a complicated and time-consuming process. QuickBooks reduces the work involved in this task by letting you apply sales tax automatically to specific sales transactions and by tracking the taxes you collect from each customer.

Scenario

In this lesson, you will set up a new tax item for both a county and state, grouping these tax items so both are charged to invoices and cash sales. You will assign your most common tax as the default and create an invoice on a taxable item. Then, you will check what you owe the tax agencies and use QuickBooks to write checks for the amounts you owe.

Practice Files: B18_Tracking_And_Paying_Sales_Tax.qbw

Using Sales Tax in QuickBooks

Your business may deal with some of the following issues when collecting sales tax:

- You may have to collect and pay more than one tax (for example, one rate for local taxes and another rate for state taxes).

- You may have some items that are taxable and some that are not.

- You may need to tax some customers and not others.

If you want QuickBooks to track and pay your sales tax, you need to do the following:

1. Set up your tax rates and agencies.

   In the QuickBooks Item List, set up the separate tax rates you need to charge. In the Vendors List, set up the agencies responsible for collecting your taxes.

2. Indicate who and what gets taxed.

   Not all the items you sell are taxable, and not all your customers pay tax. In your Item and Customers & Jobs Lists, you must indicate which items are taxable and which customers pay tax.

3. Apply tax to each sale.

   When you complete an invoice or sales receipt form and choose a taxable item from your Item List, QuickBooks applies the appropriate sales tax automatically.

4. Determine what you owe.

   As you record taxable sales, QuickBooks automatically keeps track of the tax you have collected in your Sales Tax Payable account. When you are ready to pay your sales tax agency, you can open the Sales Tax Payable register to see how much you owe, or you can create a Sales Tax Liability report.

5. Pay your tax agencies.

   When you access the Pay Sales Tax window, QuickBooks displays the amount you owe and writes a check to the tax agency for that amount.

Setting Up Tax Rates and Agencies

The first step in setting up tax information in QuickBooks is to enter your sales tax rates and provide information about the tax agencies to which you pay the taxes.

Creating a Tax Item for Each Single Tax You Apply

Some businesses need to apply more than one sales tax to their sales. For example, they may collect a state sales tax as well as several county, municipal, or other sales taxes. You need to create a separate sales tax item for each tax that needs to be reported (not necessarily for each tax you collect; some states want you to report state sales tax and county sales tax as separate items, while others let you report them as one item).

Even if you are paying more than one type of tax, you usually want your customers to see one overall tax amount, not separate taxes for the state and county. You will learn how to do that in this lesson.

On the Item List, you already have sales tax for Jefferson and Oswego counties. Because Canalside Corp. now does most of its business in Oneida County, you need to add tax items for Oneida County and set up the New York State sales tax item.

Note: For this lesson, set your computer's date to 11/1/2018 before opening the QuickBooks file, as recommended in the Before You Get Started lesson. This will ensure that the dates you see on your screen match the dates in this lesson.

To add a sales tax item,

1.	Open	B15_Tracking_And Paying_Sales Tax.qbw	using the method described in Before You Get Started

The QuickBooks Login dialog box displays:

```
                QuickBooks Login                    ✕

You need to log in as QuickBooks Administrator to proceed.  Please enter the
admin (owner) password for the company:

                    Canalside Corp.

   Password: [_____]    I forgot my password

              Passwords are case sensitive.


         OK            Cancel            Help
```

This dialog box informs you that you must login as a QuickBooks Administrator in order to open the company file.

2.	Type	**Canalside2**	in the Password field

Note: Passwords are case-sensitive.

3.	Click	OK

QuickBooks opens the file.

4.	Click	✕	to close the Reminders window

QuickBooks displays the Home page:

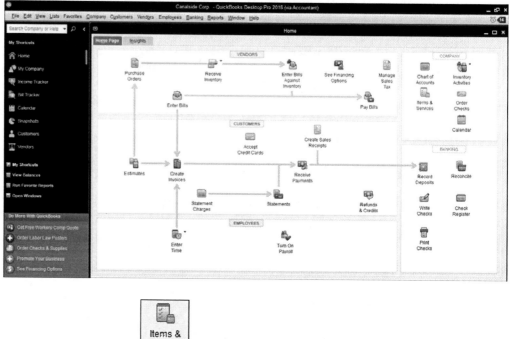

5. Click Items & Services in the Company area of the Home page

The Item List opens:

NAME	DESCRIPTION	TYPE	ACC..	TOTAL ..	PRICE	ATTACH
Framing	Framing labor	Service	Const..		55.00	
Installation	Installation labor	Service	Const..		35.00	
Subs	Subcontracted services	Service	Const..		0.00	
Drywall	Install drywall	Service	Const..		0.00	
Painting	Painting	Service	Const..		0.00	
Plumbing	Plumbing	Service	Const..		0.00	
Hardware		Inventor..	Const..	0	0.00	

Note: The size of your Item List may be different. You may resize and move the window as necessary.

6. Click Item ▼ at the bottom of the window

A drop-down menu displays:

New	Ctrl+N
Edit Item	Ctrl+E
Duplicate Item	
Delete Item	Ctrl+D
Add/Edit Multiple Items	
Edit Markup...	
Make Item Inactive	
Show Inactive Items	
✓ Hierarchical View	
Flat View	
Customize Columns...	
Use	Ctrl+U
Find in Transactions...	
Print List...	Ctrl+P
Re-sort List	

7. Select   New   from the drop-down menu

The New Item window opens:

8. Select   Sales Tax Item   from the Type drop-down menu

The New Item window is updated to display sales tax item fields.

9. Press   [Tab]   to move to the Sales Tax Name field

10. Type   **Oneida**   in the Sales Tax Name field

11. Press   [Tab]   to move to the Description field

QuickBooks automatically populates the Description field with **Sales Tax**.

12. Type   **Oneida County**   in the Description field to replace Sales Tax

13. Press   [Tab]   to move to the Tax Rate field

14.	Type	**3**	in the Tax Rate field
15.	Press	Tab	to move to the Tax Agency field
16.	Type	**Oneida County**	in the Tax Agency field
17.	Press	Tab	

Because Oneida County is not yet in your Vendor List, the Vendor Not Found dialog box displays:

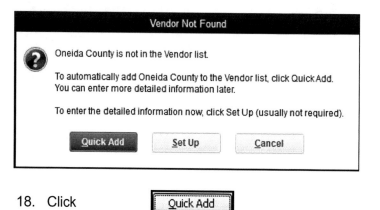

18. Click   Quick Add

Oneida County is added to the Vendor List.

The New Item window should resemble the figure below:

19. Click   OK

Note: *If a Check Spelling on Form dialog box displays, click the Add button. This adds the word "Oneida" to the QuickBooks internal dictionary.*

The Oneida sales tax item is added to the Item List:

NAME	DESCRIPTION	TYPE	ACC...	TOTAL ...	PRICE	ATTACH
◆ Reimb Group	Time and materials	Group				
◆ Discount	10% Discount	Discount	Const...		-10.0%	
◆ Payment	Down payment received	Payment	Unde...			
◆ Jefferson County	NY sales tax, Jefferson County	Sales T...	Sales...		7.75%	
◆ Oneida	Oneida County	Sales T...	Sales...		3.0%	
◆ Oswego	NY sales tax, Oswego County	Sales T...	Sales...		7.5%	
◆ Out of State	Out-of-state, exempt from sales ...	Sales T...	Sales...		0.0%	

20. Follow steps 6 -18 in this section to set up another sales tax item with the following attributes:

Type:	Sales Tax Item
Sales Tax Name:	NY State
Description:	NY Sales Tax
Tax Rate (%):	5.0
Tax Agency:	New York State

The NY State sales tax item displays in the Item List:

NAME	DESCRIPTION	TYPE	ACC...	TOTAL ...	PRICE	ATTACH
◆ Reimb Group	Time and materials	Group				
◆ Discount	10% Discount	Discount	Const...		-10.0%	
◆ Payment	Down payment received	Payment	Unde...			
◆ Jefferson County	NY sales tax, Jefferson County	Sales T...	Sales...		7.75%	
◆ Oneida	Oneida County	Sales T...	Sales...		3.0%	
◆ Oswego	NY sales tax, Oswego County	Sales T...	Sales...		7.5%	
◆ Out of State	Out-of-state, exempt from sales ...	Sales T...	Sales...		0.0%	

Grouping Single Taxes Together

QuickBooks lets you combine some or all of your tax items into groups, so items such as invoices and sales receipts contain only one tax amount. Grouping single taxes together allows you to create reports for your customers with a single, total tax figure.

In this exercise, you will create a sales tax group for county and state sales tax.

To create a tax group,

1. Click   [Item ▼]

2. Select   New   from the drop-down menu

The New Item window opens:

3. Select   Sales Tax Group   from the Type drop-down menu

The New Item window is updated to display fields for a sales tax group:

4. Press   [Tab]   to move to the Group Name/ Number field

5. Type   **Oneida Group**   in the Group Name/Number field

6. Press   [Tab]   to move to the Description field

7.	Type	**Sales Tax, Oneida County**	in the Description field
8.	Press	Tab	to move to the Tax Item column
9.	Click	▼	in the Tax Item column

A drop-down menu displays:

< Add New >		
Jefferson County	Sales Tax Item	NY sales tax, Jefferson County
NY State	Sales Tax Item	NY Sales Tax
Oneida	Sales Tax Item	Oneida County
Oswego	Sales Tax Item	NY sales tax, Oswego County
Out of State	Sales Tax Item	Out-of-state, exempt from sales tax

| 10. | Select | Oneida | from the drop-down menu |

QuickBooks automatically completes the Rate, Tax Agency, and Description information.

| 11. | Press | Tab | to move to the second line of the Tax Item column |
| 12. | Select | NY State | from the Tax Item drop-down menu |

QuickBooks automatically completes the Rate, Tax Agency, and Description information.

The New Item window should resemble the figure below:

TYPE				OK
Sales Tax Group ▼	Use to calculate and individually track two or more sales tax items that apply to the same sale. The customer sees only the total sales tax.			Cancel

Group Name/Number

Oneida Group

Description

Sales Tax, Oneida County

Enter each individual sales tax you need to charge in this district. QuickBooks will collect tax for these items as a group, but will report on each one individually.

TAX ITEM	RATE	TAX AGENCY	DESCRIPTION
Oneida	3.0%	Oneida County	Oneida County
NY State ▼	5.0%	New York State	NY Sales Tax
Group Rate	8.0%		

Notice that the group rate for this tax is 8.0%.

13. Click [OK] to create the tax group

Oneida Group is added to the Item List:

NAME	DESCRIPTION	TYPE	ACC.	TOTAL	PRICE	ATTACH
◆ Payment	Down payment received	Payment	Unde...			
◆ Jefferson County	NY sales tax, Jefferson County	Sales T...	Sales...		7.75%	
◆ NY State	NY Sales Tax	Sales T...	Sales...		5.0%	
◆ Oneida	Oneida County	Sales T...	Sales...		3.0%	
◆ Oswego	NY sales tax, Oswego County	Sales T...	Sales...		7.5%	
◆ Out of State	Out-of-state, exempt from sales ...	Sales T...	Sales...		0.0%	
◆ Oneida Group	Sales Tax, Oneida County	Sales T...			8.0%	

14. Close the Item List to return to the Home page

Identifying Your Most Common Tax

If you want QuickBooks to apply sales tax automatically to invoices and cash sales receipts, you have to tell it which of your sales tax items or groups you use most often. After you do that, QuickBooks applies the sales tax automatically when you fill out an invoice or cash sales receipt.

Note: You can always choose a different sales tax from the sales form if you do not want to use the default tax.

To set the most common tax,

1. Select **Edit : Preferences** from the menu bar

The Preferences window opens:

Note: Your window may display a different selected preference.

2. Select   Sales Tax   from the list of preferences on the left

3. Click   the [Company Preferences] tab

The Company Preferences tab displays Sales Tax information:

> **Quick Tip.** *If you select a frequency (Monthly, Quarterly, Annually) below When do you pay sales tax? on the Company Preferences tab, QuickBooks will automatically display Sales Tax reports and the Pay Sales Tax window to match that same frequency so that it is easy to determine how much you owe.*

4. Select   Oneida Group   from the Your most common sales tax item drop-down menu

5. Click   OK   to close the Preferences window

The Oneida group sales tax will now automatically be used as the default tax rate on invoices and other forms.

Indicating Who and What Gets Taxed

The next step in setting up sales tax is to indicate who and what gets taxed. You must tell QuickBooks whether or not a customer should be taxed and assign a default tax item or tax group to that customer.

You must also distinguish between taxable and nontaxable items in the Item List. When you add an item to the Item List, there is a field that allows you to indicate whether tax is charged for that item. QuickBooks remembers this information and automatically shows whether an item is taxable when you enter the item on a sales form.

In this exercise, you will view an item on the Item List to see how you identify a taxable item.

1. Click in the Company area of the Home page

The Item List opens:

NAME	DESCRIPTION	TYPE	ACCO...	TOTAL ...	PRICE	ATTACH
◇ Framing	Framing labor	Service	Constr...		55.00	
◇ Installation	Installation labor	Service	Constr...		35.00	
◇ Subs	Subcontracted services	Service	Constr...		0.00	
◇ Drywall	Install drywall	Service	Constr...		0.00	
◇ Painting	Painting	Service	Constr...		0.00	
◇ Plumbing	Plumbing	Service	Constr...		0.00	
◇ Hardware		Inventor...	Constr...	0	0.00	

Item List — Look for [ ] in All fields — Search — Reset — Search w

Item ▼   Activities ▼   Reports ▼   Excel ▼   Attach   ☐ Include inactive

2. Select   Standard Doorknobs   in the Description column (scroll down, if necessary)

3. Click   [Item ▼]

A drop-down menu displays.

4. Select   Edit Item   from the drop-down menu

The Edit Item window opens:

Edit Item

TYPE
Inventory Part — Use for goods you purchase, track as inventory, and resell.

OK
Cancel
Notes
Custom Fields
Spelling

Item Name/Number   ☑ Subitem of   Manufacturer's Part Number
Doorknobs Std   Hardware

PURCHASE INFORMATION   SALES INFORMATION
Description on Purchase Transactions   Description on Sales Transactions
Doorknobs Par # JH 2314   Standard Doorknobs

Cost   27.00   Sales Price   30.00   ☐ Item is inactive
COGS Account   Cost of Goods Sold   Tax Code   Tax
Preferred Vendor Joshua Hardware Sup...   Income Account Construction:Materials

INVENTORY INFORMATION

Asset Account	Reorder Point	On Hand	Average Cost	On P.O.
Inventory Asset	50	20	27.00	0

Because Tax is displayed in the Tax Code field, QuickBooks will apply tax to this item. When you choose this item to be included on a sales form, QuickBooks knows that the item is taxable and automatically applies the Oneida Group default sales tax (Oneida County sales tax with a rate of 3% plus New York State sales tax with a rate of 5.0%).

5. Click

The Edit Item window closes and the Item List displays.

6. Close the Item List

You can also apply sales tax to a particular customer when you initially create the customer or when you edit the customer's information.

To view a customer record,

7. Click [Customers] on the Icon Bar

The Customer Center opens:

A list of all customers and jobs displays on the Customers & Jobs tab on the left side of the window.

8. Select Richard Davis in the Name column

9. Click (Edit) in the Customer information area

The Address Info tab of the Edit Customer window displays:

10. Click [Sales Tax Settings]

The Sales Tax Settings tab displays:

On this tab, you can see that the customer is marked as taxable and the Oswego tax item is assigned. Because Richard Davis just moved to Oneida County, you will change the tax item to Oneida Group.

11. Select   Oneida Group   from the Tax Item drop-down menu

12. Click   OK

The Edit Customer window closes and the Customer Center displays.

13. Click   🏠 Home   on the Icon Bar to return to the Home page

Applying Tax to Each Sale

If you have set up a default sales tax, assigned taxes to your customers, and marked taxable items, QuickBooks will automatically calculate and apply the tax when you make a sale.

To apply tax to a sale,

1. Click   Create Invoices   in the Customers area of the Home page

The Create Invoices window opens:

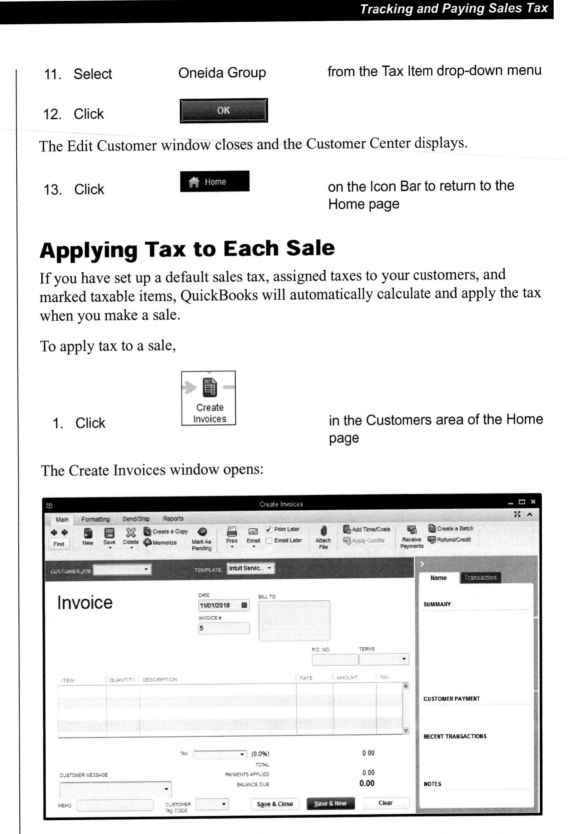

Note: If your window displays the Intuit Product Invoice, select the Intuit Service Invoice from the Template drop-down menu.

2. Select   Richard Davis   from the Customer:Job drop-down menu

The Available Estimates window opens:

You will be creating a new invoice for Richard Davis, so you do not need to select an existing estimate.

3. Click | Cancel | to close the Available Estimates window

4. Click   in the Item column   on the Create Invoices window

A drop-down arrow displays.

5. Select   Doorknobs Std. (below Hardware)   from the Item drop-down menu

The Description, Rate, Amount, and Tax data for the item are added to the invoice:

When you enter a taxable item, the word "Tax" is displayed in the Tax column. If the customer is taxable, QuickBooks will automatically apply the appropriate rate when calculating the amount of tax to apply to the invoice.

Quick Tip. *You can override a customer's default taxable status by selecting Tax (for taxable sales) or Non (for non-taxable sales) from the Tax drop-down menu.*

6.	Press	Tab	to move to the Quantity column
7.	Type	**10**	in the Quantity column
8.	Press	Tab	to calculate the invoice total

Your Create Invoices window should resemble the figure below:

QuickBooks automatically calculates the tax on the doorknobs and adds a total tax of $24.00 to the invoice.

9.	Click	Save & Close	to save the invoice, close the Create Invoices window, and return to the Home page

Determining What You Owe

If you collect sales tax from customers, you have to make periodic payments of the sales tax you have collected. You can quickly determine the amount of your sales tax liability using the Sales Tax Liability report or the Sales Tax Payable register.

Creating a Sales Tax Liability Report

The Sales Tax Liability report provides complete information about the sales tax your company owes for a particular period of time.

To display the Sales Tax Liability report,

1.	Select	Reports : Vendors & Payables : Sales Tax Liability	from the menu bar

The Sales Tax Liability report displays.

2. Select   **All**   from the Dates drop-down menu (scroll to the top of the list)

The Sales Tax Liability report is updated to display all transactions:

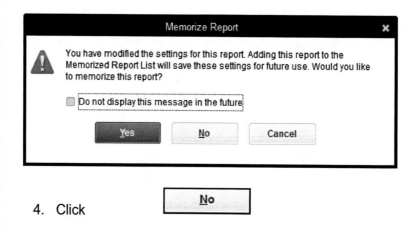

The Sales Tax Liability report shows the total non-taxable sales, total taxable sales, and the amount of sales tax you owe each tax agency.

Note: QuickBooks displays your Sales Tax Liability report on an accrual basis (unless you change the default settings in the Sales Tax Company Preferences window).

Quick Tip. QuickZoom can be used to see the details behind the Sales Tax Liability report.

3. Close the Sales Tax Liability window

A Memorize Report dialog box displays asking you if you want to memorize the report:

Memorize Report ✕

⚠ You have modified the settings for this report. Adding this report to the Memorized Report List will save these settings for future use. Would you like to memorize this report?

☐ Do not display this message in the future

[Yes]   [No]   [Cancel]

4. Click   **No**

Using the Sales Tax Payable Register

Each time you write an invoice or sales receipt that includes sales tax, QuickBooks enters the information in your Sales Tax Payable register. QuickBooks keeps track of transactions for all tax vendors in the same Sales Tax Payable account.

To view the Sales Tax Payable register,

1. Click [Chart of Accounts] in the Company area of the Home page

The Chart of Accounts opens:

NAME	⚡ TYPE	BALANCE TOTAL	ATTA...
◇ Checking	Bank	6,788.82	
◇ Savings - Money Market	Bank	15,000.00	
◇ Accounts Receivable	Accounts Receivable	12,157.22	
◇ Inventory Asset	Other Current Asset	3,918.00	
◇ Undeposited Funds	Other Current Asset	0.00	
◇ Accounts Payable	Accounts Payable	6,289.00	

Look for account name or number [Search] [Reset]

[Account ▼] [Activities ▼] [Reports ▼] [Attach] ☐ Include inactive

Note: The size of your Chart of Accounts may be different. You may resize and move the window as necessary.

2. Select Sales Tax Payable in the Name column (scroll down, if necessary)

3. Click [Activities ▼] at the bottom of the window

A drop-down menu of activities displays:

Write Checks
Make Deposits
Enter Credit Card Charges
Transfer Funds
Make General Journal Entries
Reconcile
Use Register   Ctrl+R

Note: If you are using the QuickBooks Premier version, your drop-down menu will display an additional option for a Working Trial Balance.

4. Select Use Register from the drop-down menu

Quick Tip. You can also double-click the Sales Tax Payable account in the Chart of Accounts to display the Sales Tax Payable register.

The Sales Tax Payable register opens:

Each entry in the register is a single tax transaction. Taxes you record on invoices and sales receipts display as increases, and payments you make to tax agencies display as decreases. The ending balance of the register is your current tax liability.

It is possible for separate tax transactions to have the same invoice number. When you record two tax rates on the same invoice or cash sale, the register shows a separate transaction for each tax agency. This is because you have to make separate payments to individual tax agencies.

5. Close the Sales Tax Payable register and the Chart of Accounts

Paying Your Tax Agencies

When it is time to pay sales tax, the Pay Sales Tax window can be used to write a check to your tax agency or agencies.

To pay sales tax,

1. Select   Vendors : Sales Tax :   from the menu bar
                              Pay Sales Tax

The Pay Sales Tax window opens:

2.	**Press**	Tab	twice to move to the Show sales tax due through field
3.	Type	**11/1/2018**	in the Show sales tax due through field
4.	Press	Tab	

QuickBooks adds all tax agencies to the Pay Sales Tax window.

Some states offer an allowance for collecting sales tax. If your state offers an allowance, you will need to adjust the amount of sales tax paid by the amount of the collection credit.

To adjust the amount of sales tax paid to New York State,

| 5. | Select | NY State | in the Item column |
| 6. | Click | Adjust | |

The Sales Tax Adjustment window opens:

Sales Tax Adjustment	✕
Adjustment Date	11/01/2018 📅
Entry No.	
Sales Tax Vendor	New York State ▼
Adjustment Account	▼
ADJUSTMENT	
⦿ Increase Sales Tax By	
○ Reduce Sales Tax By	Amount
Memo	Sales Tax Adjustment
	OK Cancel Help

| 7. | Type | **11/20/2018** | in the Adjustment Date field |
| 8. | Press | Tab | to move to the Entry No. field |

Because this is the first time you are entering an adjustment in this company file, the Entry No. field is blank.

| 9. | Type | **1** | in the Entry No. field |

After you enter a number in the Entry No. field, QuickBooks will automatically number entries from this point forward.

To apply the adjustment to New York State,

10. Verify that New York State displays in the Sales Tax Vendor field

11. Select   the Sales   from the Adjustment Account
                   Income account   drop-down menu (scroll up)

Note: If you are making an adjustment for a credit or discount you received, you should select an income account from the Adjustment Account drop-down menu. You may want to set up a specific income account, such as Sales Tax Commission, to track a collection credit. If you are making an adjustment for a penalty or for interest due, you should select an expense account.

Because you are adjusting for a credit, you want to decrease the sales tax.

12. Select   the Reduce Sales   in the Adjustment area
                   Tax By option

13. Type   **30.00**   in the Amount field to decrease the
                                    sales tax payment by $30.00

Notice the Memo field is automatically populated with Sales Tax Adjustment. You will accept this default.

14. Click   [OK]

A Warning dialog box displays informing you that the amount paid to each vendor has been reset, because you have made a sales tax adjustment.

> **Warning**
>
> ⚠ Because you made a Sales Tax Adjustment, the Amount Paid to each vendor has now been reset.
>
> [OK]

15. Click   [OK]   to return to the Pay Sales Tax
                                    window

To mark agencies for payment,

16. Click   in the Pay column   to the left of the NY State item for
                                    15.00

17. Click   in the Pay column   to the left of the New York State
                                    30.00 collection credit

18. Click   in the Pay column   to the left of the Oneida County item
                                    for 9.00

19. Select   the To be printed   check box

The Pay Sales Tax window should resemble the figure below:

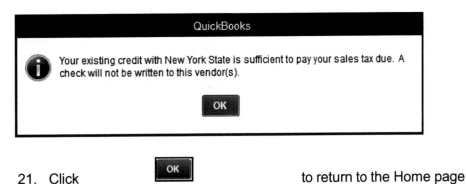

Note: *Many states require you to file your sales tax return and payment electronically. If you file and pay your sales tax electronically, you will need to deselect the To be printed check box and change the entry in the Starting Check No. field to EFT/DBT.*

Quick Tip. *If you want to make a partial payment, you can edit any amount in the Amt. Paid column.*

20. Click

A QuickBooks dialog box displays informing you that because your existing credit with New York State is sufficient to pay your sales tax due, a check will not be written to this vendor.

QuickBooks

ⓘ Your existing credit with New York State is sufficient to pay your sales tax due. A check will not be written to this vendor(s).

OK

21. Click **OK** to return to the Home page

QuickBooks automatically writes a check to the other tax agency you selected, Oneida County, and records the transaction in your Checking account. Because you selected the To be printed check box, you can print the check at any time and send it to the agency. QuickBooks also updates the Sales Tax Liability report and Sales Tax Payable register to show that you have paid the tax agencies.

Review

In this lesson, you have learned how to:

- ☑ Use sales tax in QuickBooks
- ☑ Set up tax rates and agencies
- ☑ Indicate who and what gets taxed
- ☑ Apply tax to each sale
- ☑ Determine what you owe
- ☑ Pay your tax agencies

Practice:

1. Create a new sales tax item with the following criteria:

Type:	Sales Tax Item
Sales Tax Name:	Monroe
Description:	Monroe County
Tax Rate (%):	3.5%
Tax Agency:	Monroe County

2. Create a new sales tax group with the following criteria:

Type:	Sales Tax Group
Group Name/Number:	Monroe Group
Description:	Monroe County Sales Tax
Tax Items:	Monroe
	NY State

3. Create an invoice for 75 Sunrise St. for Richard Real Estate that is an order for 10 interior wood doors and 2 exterior wood doors. Assign the Tax to the Monroe Group. Notice that QuickBooks automatically calculates the total tax for the invoice. Save and close the Invoice.

4. Create a Sales Tax Liability report for the current calendar quarter. Notice the new tax due to Monroe County.

5. Close the company file without memorizing any reports.

7

Preparing Payroll with QuickBooks

In this lesson, you will learn how to:

- ❑ Use payroll tracking
- ❑ Set up for payroll
- ❑ Set up employee payroll information
- ❑ Set up a payroll schedule
- ❑ Write a payroll check
- ❑ Print paycheck stubs
- ❑ Track your tax liabilities
- ❑ Pay payroll taxes
- ❑ Prepare payroll tax forms

Concept

If you have employees, you need to generate a payroll. Payroll tasks include making calculations, writing checks with deductions, tracking data for payroll taxes, and filling out payroll tax forms. QuickBooks has a built-in payroll function that lets you process your payroll with just a few keystrokes.

Scenario

In this lesson, you will learn how QuickBooks tracks payroll and will set up your company file to manually calculate payroll taxes. You will add a new employee to the payroll and set up their hourly rate and filing status. You will then learn how to set up a payroll schedule to pay your employees. Next, you will use QuickBooks to write a payroll check for an hourly employee and print a paycheck stub. You will also see how to track your payroll expenses and liabilities. You will then determine how much you owe various tax agencies and write a check to pay for the taxes. And last, you will learn how to prepare payroll tax forms by importing information from your company file into Excel.

Practice Files: B18_Preparing_Payroll_With_QuickBooks.qbw

Using Payroll Tracking

QuickBooks payroll function calculates each employee's gross pay and then subtracts taxes and deductions to arrive at the employee's net pay. QuickBooks then writes a paycheck, records the transaction in your QuickBooks checking account, and keeps track of your tax liabilities. To calculate payroll, QuickBooks uses built-in tax tables. To be sure you have the most recent tax tables, you can subscribe to one of the QuickBooks payroll services and receive automatic updates to these tables whenever your tax rates change.

You, as the employer, must subtract taxes and other deductions before issuing an employee's paycheck. Some typical paycheck deductions are federal and state withholding (income) taxes, Social Security taxes (FICA), Medicare taxes, and state disability insurance. You may also deduct for such benefits as a 401(k) plan or contributions to your company's medical/dental plan.

When you withhold taxes from employees' paychecks, you must submit regular deposits of the withheld tax money (weekly, monthly, or quarterly, depending on the size of your payroll) to the tax agency and file yearly forms that list the total amounts you withheld from each employee's paycheck. You must also pay quarterly employer payroll taxes, such as your share of Social Security and Medicare taxes, and federal and state unemployment taxes.

To calculate payroll, QuickBooks needs four kinds of information:

1. Information about your company

   This includes the company name and address, and its federal and state tax ID numbers. Enter this information when you set up your QuickBooks company. You can view the company information at any time by selecting Company : My Company from the menu bar.

2. Information about your employees

   The QuickBooks Employees list stores general information about each of your employees and specific information related to payroll (such as the employee's salary or hourly rate, filing status, number of exemptions, and miscellaneous additions, deductions, and company contributions). You can store payroll information that most employees have in common on an employee template. Whenever you have a new employee to add, you can simply enter information that is specific to that employee (name, address, and so on).

3. Information about your payroll items

   QuickBooks maintains a list, called the Payroll Item List, of everything that affects the amount on a payroll check, including any company expenses related to payroll. When you specify you want to use payroll, QuickBooks creates a number of payroll items for you automatically. You add other items as you need them.

4. Tax tables for federal, state, and local withholdings

    The tax tables are built into QuickBooks. It is strongly recommended that you sign up for a QuickBooks payroll service to ensure you have the most current tax tables available. A payroll service allows you to automatically download tax table updates and federal forms directly from the QuickBooks application. In addition to providing current tax tables, QuickBooks payroll services provide additional features, such as calculating earnings, deductions, and payroll taxes for you and managing business finances and payroll in one place.

Quick Tip. To have QuickBooks automatically calculate taxes and provide payroll tax forms, you must sign up for a QuickBooks payroll service. This service will keep tax tables current. To find out how to subscribe, refer to the QuickBooks Desktop Help or select Employees : Payroll Service Options : Learn About Payroll Options from the menu bar. There is an additional fee to obtain a payroll subscription.

After you have set up your company, employee data, and payroll items, all you need to do to run a payroll is enter the number of hours worked during the pay period for each employee. QuickBooks calculates the gross wages for the employee and then refers to its tax tables and the company/employee information you have entered to calculate all withholdings and deductions and arrive at the net pay figure. QuickBooks also calculates your company payroll expenses (for example, your contributions to Social Security and Medicare).

Setting Up for Payroll

If you do not sign up for a QuickBooks payroll service, you will need to manually calculate your payroll tax figures and enter them for each paycheck. Businesses that don't use a QuickBooks payroll service typically use one of the following methods to calculate payroll figures:

*   A spreadsheet or pen and paper. You must then manually enter payroll amounts and deductions for each paycheck in QuickBooks.

*   An outsourced service, such as USA Payroll or Paychex. You or your accountant will need to manually enter or upload payroll figures in QuickBooks to balance your books.

To manually calculate payroll taxes in QuickBooks, you must set your company file to use the manual payroll calculations setting. You will not be able to access the various payroll menu options until you have properly set up your company file.

In this exercise, you are the owner of Canalside Corp. and have decided that you will manually calculate payroll taxes.

Note: For this lesson, be sure to set your computer's date to 11/1/2018 before opening the QuickBooks file, as recommended in the Before You Get Started lesson. This will ensure that the dates you see on your screen match the dates in this lesson.

To set your company file to use the manual payroll calculations setting,

1. Open   B18_Preparing_Payroll   using the method described in
                      With_QuickBooks.qbw   Before You Get Started

The QuickBooks Login dialog box displays:

QuickBooks Login   ✖

You need to log in as QuickBooks Administrator to proceed. Please enter the admin (owner) password for the company:

Canalside Corp.

Password: [   ]   I forgot my password

Passwords are case sensitive.

OK   Cancel   Help

This dialog box informs you that you must login as a QuickBooks Administrator in order to open the company file.

2. Type   **Canalside2**   in the Password field

Note: Passwords are case-sensitive.

3. Click   OK

QuickBooks opens the file.

4. Click   ✖   to close the Reminders window

QuickBooks displays the Home page:

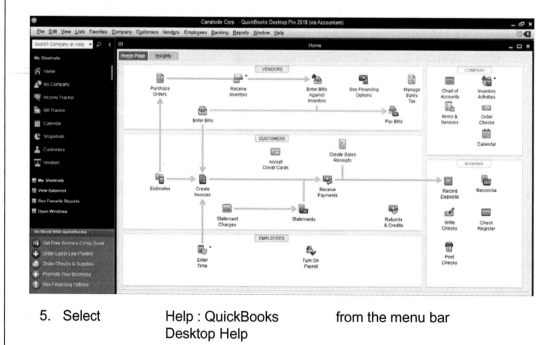

5. Select   Help : QuickBooks   from the menu bar
                     Desktop Help

The Have a Question? window opens:

Note: Your window may display different help topics.

6. Type **set your company file to use manual calculations** in the blank search field at the top of the window

7. Click to the right of the search field

The Have a Question? window is updated to display the relevant help topics:

Note: Your window may be different.

8. Click the "Set your company file to use manual calculations" link below the Answers in Help heading

Additional information about calculating payroll manually displays:

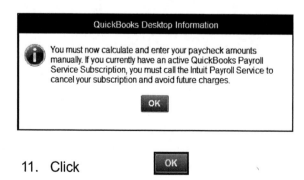

9. Read the help article and then click the "Set my company file to use manual calculations" link at the bottom of the help article

This link automatically applies the manual calculations setting.

Caution. *If you decide that you are going to manually calculate your taxes for your business, you should read through all information pertaining to this topic in the QuickBooks Desktop Help. After you click this link, the manual calculations setting is applied immediately. If you click this link inadvertently, and want to reinstate payroll calculations in your company file, you will need to sign up for a QuickBooks payroll service.*

10. Close the Have a Question? window

A QuickBooks Desktop Information dialog box displays informing you that you must now calculate and enter your paycheck amounts manually:

11. Click   OK

Note: *QuickBooks will only set up the company file that is currently open for manual payroll calculations. If you have more than one company file, you will need to set up each file for manual calculations separately. In addition, you must be in single-user mode to set up a file for manual calculations.*

You return to the QuickBooks Home page:

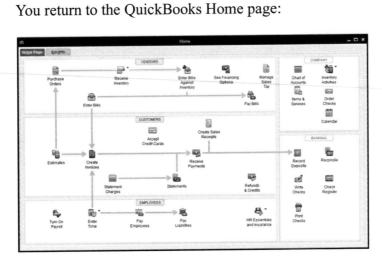

QuickBooks adds Pay Employees and Pay Liabilities icons to the Employees section of the Home page allowing you to quickly pay your employees and your liabilities. An HR Essentials and Insurance icon is also added to the Employees section. You can click this icon to learn about labor law posters, workers compensation, Intuit health benefits, and to view online pay stubs (if you subscribe to Intuit payroll services).

Quick Tip. You can click the Turn on Payroll icon at any time to subscribe to Intuit QuickBooks payroll services.

Setting Payroll Preferences

When you install QuickBooks, the payroll feature is automatically turned on by default. However, you may want to turn this feature off if you do not have any employees or if you use another program to track your payroll. You can use the Preferences window to verify that payroll is turned on or to turn this feature off.

To verify the payroll feature is turned on,

1. Select   Edit : Preferences   from the menu bar

The Preferences window opens with the General preference selected:

Note: Your window may display a different selected preference.

2. Select   Payroll & Employees   from the list of preferences on the left side of the window

3. Click   the Company Preferences tab

The Company Preferences tab for Payroll & Employees displays:

From this tab, you can turn payroll features on or off and set preferences for pay stub and voucher printing, workers compensation, and sick and vacation time. You can also select whether or not you want to copy earning details from previous paychecks, recall quantity and hour fields on paychecks, or use job costing and item tracking for paycheck expenses.

Quick Tip. You can also set employee preferences on this tab.

4. Verify Full payroll is selected in the QuickBooks Desktop Payroll Features section

Note: If the Full payroll option is not selected, select it to turn on payroll.

5. Click   to close the Preferences window

Gathering Information about Tax Obligations

Before you begin working in QuickBooks, you need to gather information about your tax obligations. QuickBooks provides the tools you need to process payroll; however, you must know your own obligations as an employer. Verify you know:

*   Your company's federal and state tax ID numbers

*   All payroll taxes that apply to your company, both employee withholdings and employer contributions

*   Personal information about each employee, such as Social Security Number, filing status, and number of exemptions

- Each employee's payroll totals for the current calendar year for gross compensation, taxes, other deductions, and other additions (unless you are beginning your QuickBooks payroll at the start of a new year)

- Your company's payroll expenses for the current year, such as contributions to Social Security, Medicare, and other company-paid expenses or liabilities (unless you are beginning your QuickBooks payroll at the start of a new year)

QuickBooks uses payroll services, so you do not need to know federal and state withholding rates, state disability rates, the rates for Social Security, Medicare, and federal unemployment, or the amount for each personal exemption or allowance.

Viewing Payroll Items

QuickBooks maintains a list for everything that affects the amount on a payroll check and for every company expense related to payroll. This list is called the Payroll Item List. QuickBooks adds some of the items for you automatically, and you add others as you need them.

To view the Payroll Item List,

1. Select   Employees : Manage   from the menu bar
                    Payroll Items : View / Edit
                    Payroll Item List

Note: The View / Edit Payroll Item List option will not display in the Employees menu unless you have signed up for a QuickBooks payroll service or set your company file to use manual calculations.

The Payroll Item List opens:

ITEM NAME	TYPE	A...	A...	TAX T...	PA...	ACCO...
Salary	Yearly Salary			Comp...		
Sick Salary	Yearly Salary			Comp...		
Vacation Salary	Yearly Salary			Comp...		
Hourly Rate 1	Hourly Wage			Comp...		
Hourly Rate 2	Hourly Wage			Comp...		
Sick Hourly Rate	Hourly Wage			Comp...		

Payroll Item ▼   Activities ▼   Reports ▼   Include inactive

A payroll item can be a Yearly Salary, Hourly Wage, Company Contribution, Federal Tax, and so on. In this exercise, you will view the Medicare Company payroll item.

2. Select   Medicare Company   in the Item Name column (scroll down)

3. Click   Payroll Item ▼

A drop-down menu displays:

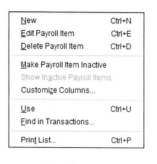

New	Ctrl+N
Edit Payroll Item	Ctrl+E
Delete Payroll Item	Ctrl+D
Make Payroll Item Inactive	
Show Inactive Payroll Items	
Customize Columns...	
Use	Ctrl+U
Find in Transactions...	
Print List...	Ctrl+P

4. Select　　　Edit Payroll Item　　　from the drop-down menu

The first Edit payroll item (Medicare Taxes) window displays:

Edit payroll item (Medicare Taxes)

Name used in paychecks and payroll reports

Enter name for company-paid portion of Medicare tax:

Medicare Company

Enter name for employee-paid portion of Medicare tax:

Medicare Employee

☐ Payroll item is inactive
To hide this item on the Payroll Item list, select the checkbox.

Back　　Next　　Finish　　　Help　　Cancel

This window identifies the name that should be used on paychecks and payroll reports for this payroll item. QuickBooks has automatically completed the information in this window.

5. Click　　　Next

The next Edit payroll item (Medicare Taxes) window displays:

Edit payroll item (Medicare Taxes)

Liability agency

Enter name of agency to which liability is paid:

Liability account (company-paid):　Payroll Liabilities

Liability account (employee-paid):　Payroll Liabilities
This liability account tracks Medicare tax to be paid. You can change this account at any time.

Back　　Next　　Finish　　　Help　　Cancel

This window allows you to select the agency liable for this payroll item.

6. Type **E (for Eastcoast)** in the Enter name of agency to which liability is paid field

7. Press Tab

QuickBooks automatically completes the field with **Eastcoast Bank**

Note: Most payroll tax liabilities are now paid to the IRS through Electronic Funds Transfer (EFT) rather than a bank. However, in this lesson, you will record the payment to Eastcoast Bank.

You work directly with payroll items as you do payroll tasks. Behind the scenes, QuickBooks tracks your payroll liabilities in an Other Current Liability account and your payroll expenses in an Expense account. When you create a new payroll item, QuickBooks helps you assign the item to the correct account or accounts by filling in the account name.

The Edit payroll item (Medicare Taxes) window displays the information stored about the Medicare Company payroll item. Both employers and employees have to pay for Medicare, so this item is both a company-paid payroll expense and an employee-paid payroll expense (a deduction from an employee's paycheck).

8. Click [Next]

The next Edit payroll item (Medicare Taxes) window displays:

Edit payroll item (Medicare Taxes) ✕

Expense account

Enter the account for tracking this expense.

Payroll Expenses ▼

Company-paid Medicare is an expense to your company. You can change this account at any time.

Back | Next | Finish | Help | Cancel

QuickBooks allows you to choose the account to which you will charge this expense. You will accept the default Payroll Expenses account.

9. Click [Next]

The next Edit payroll item (Medicare Taxes) window displays:

Edit payroll item (Medicare Taxes)   ✕

Company and employee tax rates

Company rate

1.45%

Rate provided by tax table

Employee rate

1.45%

Rate provided by tax table

| Back | Next | Finish | Cancel |

The company and employee tax rates are automatically populated. Because these rates are provided in the QuickBooks tax tables, you can not change these entries.

10. Click   Next

The next Edit payroll item (Medicare Taxes) window displays:

Edit payroll item (Medicare Taxes)   ✕

Taxable compensation

Select the items subject to Medicare tax.

✓	PAYROLL ITEM ▲
✓	Salary
✓	Sick Salary
✓	Vacation Salary
✓	Hourly Rate 1
✓	Hourly Rate 2
✓	Sick Hourly Rate

Click Default to revert to QuickBooks automatic settings.

Default

| Back | Next | Finish | Help | Cancel |

All of the selected items are subject to Medicare taxes, so you will accept the defaults.

11. Click   Finish   to return to the Payroll Item List

12. Close the Payroll Item List window

Setting Up Employee Payroll Information

QuickBooks calculates payroll for each employee on the basis of that employee's pay rate, marital status, exemptions, and so on. The Employee Center includes an Employees list and stores general information about each employee, as well as payroll information.

What Information Does QuickBooks Store?

QuickBooks stores a wealth of information about each employee, but you do not need to enter the same information over and over. When you have information that applies to most of your employees, you can enter it on an employee template. Then, when you add a new employee, QuickBooks automatically fills in the information stored on the template. You just need to add or change any information that is different for a particular employee.

Before you add a new employee to Canalside Corp., it would be helpful to look at the default information QuickBooks stores for employees. To view the default settings for employees in this company,

1. Click | Employees | on the Icon Bar

The Employee Center opens:

Notice the Employees tab that displays on the left side of the page.

2. Select   Joseph Rogers   on the Employees tab

On the Employee Center toolbar,

3. Click | Manage Employee Information ▾ |

A drop-down menu displays:

Add / Edit Sales Rep
Change New Employee Default Settings

4. Select   Change New Employee   from the drop-down menu
                 Default Settings

The Employee Defaults window opens:

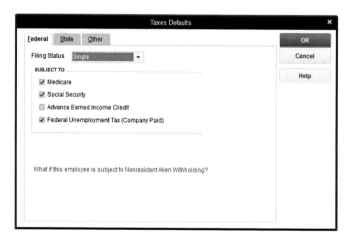

This window is used to specify the payroll information that most of your employees have in common. QuickBooks saves the information so you do not need to re-enter it when you set up the payroll record for an individual employee.

 Quick Tip. *You do not need to create a separate Hourly Wage item for each hourly rate you pay. You enter an employee's specific hourly rate when you set up the employee's payroll record.*

5. Click | Taxes... |

The Taxes Defaults window opens with the Federal tab selected:

The withholding taxes that should be deducted from each employee's paycheck are specified in this window. Employees at Canalside Corp. are subject to Medicare, Social Security, and company-paid Federal Unemployment Tax.

6. Click | Cancel | to close the Taxes Defaults window

7. Click | Sick/Vacation... | in the Employee Defaults window

The Sick and Vacation Defaults window opens:

Default information about accruing sick days and vacation days is specified in this window. QuickBooks will keep track of the hours accrued each pay period.

8. Click [Cancel] to close the Sick and Vacation Defaults window

9. Click [Cancel] to close the Employee Defaults window and return to the Employee Center

Adding a New Employee

By using the information already stored in QuickBooks, you can quickly add a new employee to payroll.

To add a new employee to payroll,

1. Click [New Employee...] on the Employee Center toolbar

The New Employee window opens with the Personal tab selected:

The Personal tab includes information such as an employee's legal name, Social Security number, gender, and date of birth, as well as disability, I-9, and military information.

2. Enter the following information into the fields on the Personal tab for the new employee, Robert Rhodes:

Mr./Ms./ ...	**Mr.**
First Name	**Robert**
M.I.	**T**
Last Name	**Rhodes**
Social Security No.	**111-22-3333**
Gender	**Male**
Date of Birth	**07/25/1973**
Marital Status	**Married**
U.S. Citizen	**Yes**
Disability / Disabled	**No**
I-9 Form / On File	**Yes**
Military / U.S. Veteran	**No**

3. Click [Address & Contact]

The Address and Contact tab displays:

The Address and Contact tab allows you to enter an employee's address and contact information.

4. Enter the following information into the fields on the Address & Contact tab for the new employee, Robert Rhodes:

Home Address

Address	**123 Dublin Avenue**
City	**Fairgrave**
State	**NY**
Zip	**11111**
Work Phone	**555-555-4321**
Mobile	**555-555-4322**

Emergency Contact Info

Contact Name	Janet Rhodes
Contact Phone	555-555-4444
Relation	Spouse

Quick Tip. *Some employers assign employee numbers to their employees. Employee numbers can be entered in the Account No. (Employee ID) field on the Additional Info tab.*

To add payroll information for Robert Rhodes,

5. Click | Payroll Info |

The Payroll Info tab displays:

The Payroll Info tab stores an employee's earnings and any additions, deductions, or company contributions to their paycheck. There are also buttons to access tax information for this employee (the type of information you get from a W-4), sick and vacation time information for this employee, or information about the Direct Deposit feature.

6. Click   in the Hourly/Annual   for Hourly Rate 1
                            Rate column

7. Type   **20**   as the hourly rate

8. Click   [Taxes...]

The Taxes for Robert T Rhodes window opens with the Federal tab selected:

The checked items in the Subject To area indicate the taxes the employees at Canalside Corp. have deducted from each paycheck. A check mark in the Federal Unemployment Tax (Company Paid) box indicates that this employee's pay is subject to the employer-paid federal unemployment tax.

9. Select   Married   from the Filing Status drop-down
                                                 menu

To modify state tax withholdings for this employee,

10. Click   the State tab

The State tab displays:

This tab stores information about state withholding taxes, state unemployment insurance (SUI), and state disability insurance (SDI).

11.	Select	NY	from the State Worked drop-down menu

12.	Select	NY	from the State Subject to Withholding drop-down menu

Additional fields display based on this selection.

13.	Select	Married	from the Filing Status drop-down menu

14.	Click	the Other tab

The Taxes for Robert T Rhodes window displays the Other tab:

This tab displays any other taxes that were added for the employee based on the selections already made. The NY - Yonkers City Resident tax is automatically selected in the Item Name column. Because Robert is not subject to New York City taxes, you will delete these taxes.

15.	Click	Delete	to delete the NY - Yonkers City Resident tax

The NY - Yonkers City Resident tax is deleted and the NY - Yonkers City Nonresident tax becomes selected.

16.	Click	Delete	to delete the NY - Yonkers City Nonresident tax

17.	Select	NY - MCTMT (Transit Tax)	in the Item Name column

18. Click   Delete   to delete the NY - MCTMT (Transit Tax)

19. Click   Delete   to delete the NY - City Resident tax

20. Click   OK   to close the Taxes for Robert T Rhodes window

The New Employee window displays the Payroll Info tab. The Additions, Deductions and Company Contributions table can be used to enter deductions from an employee's paycheck.

21. Click   in the Item Name column   in the Additions, Deductions and Company Contributions table

A drop-down arrow displays.

22. Select   Health Insurance   from the Item Name drop-down menu

23. Press   Tab   to move to the Amount column

24. Type   **65.00**   in the Amount column

This is the company's contribution for health insurance.

To track sick and vacation time for this employee,

25. Click   Sick/Vacation...   in the New Employee window

The Sick and Vacation for Robert T Rhodes window opens:

Note: If you did not change your computer's date as recommended in the Before You Get Started lesson, the dates that display in your window will be different.

To enter the number of paid sick hours that are currently available to this employee,

26. Type   **40**   in the Hours available as of 11/01/2018 field

27. Press | Tab |

You will accept the default of 0.00 in the Hours used in 2018 field. This indicates the employee has not used any paid sick hours yet.

28. Select   Every paycheck   from the Accrual period drop-down menu

This selection grants a specific amount of sick hours per paycheck. QuickBooks will accrue the amount you specify for every paycheck you write for the employee.

Quick Tip. Selecting Beginning of year from the Accrual period drop-down menu grants a specific amount of sick time an employee can accrue over the course of a year. Selecting Every hour on paycheck grants a specific amount of sick hours for every hour the employee works.

29. Type   **4**   to replace 40:00 in the Hours accrued per paycheck field

30. Type   **40**   in the Maximum number of hours field

The employee will now receive four hours of sick time for every paycheck they receive up to a maximum of 40 hours per accrual year. An employee's accrual year is the twelve-month period over which they accrue sick or vacation time. You can set an accrual day to begin on any day of the year, such as an employee's hire date. This employee started on October 25, 2018, so you will tie his accrual period to his hire date.

31. Verify the Reset hours each new year? check box is selected

32. Select   October   from the Year begins on drop-down menu

33. Type   **26**   in the Day field

34. Type   **10/26/2018**   in the Begin accruing sick time on field

You can enter vacation accrual time using the same method you did for sick time.

35. Enter vacation accrual information using the following:

Hours Available as of 11/01/2018:	80
Hours used in 2018	0
Accrual period	Every paycheck
Hours accrued per paycheck	8
Maximum number of hours	80
Reset hours each new year?	Select
Year begins on	October
Day	27
Begin accruing vacation time	10/27/2018

Your window should resemble the figure below:

Sick and Vacation for Robert T Rhodes ✕

SICK

Hours available as of 11/01/2018	40:00
Hours used in 2018	0:00

Accrual period

Every paycheck ▾

Hours accrued per paycheck	4:00
Maximum number of hours	40:00

☑ Reset hours each new year?

Year begins on   October ▾   Day 26

Begin accruing sick time on   10/26/2018 📅

VACATION

Hours available as of 11/01/2018	80:00
Hours used in 2018	0:00

Accrual period

Every paycheck ▾

Hours accrued per paycheck	8:00
Maximum number of hours	80:00

☑ Reset hours each new year?

Year begins on   October ▾   Day 27

Begin accruing vacation time on   10/27/2018 📅

OK
Cancel
Help

Note: If you did not change your computer's date as recommended in the Before You Get Started lesson, the dates that display in your window will be different.

36. Click to close the Sick and Vacation for Robert T Rhodes window and return to the New Employee window

You can now start entering sick and vacation time on this employee's paycheck.

Quick Tip. *If most of your employees accrue sick and vacation time at the same rate, you should add sick and vacation accrual information in the Employee Default window. QuickBooks will then automatically use this information when you set up payroll information for individual employees.*

Setting Up a Payroll Schedule

A payroll schedule allows you to specify how often you pay your employees, the day their paycheck is due, and the day you run payroll. You only need to set up a payroll schedule one time and assign the payroll schedule to the appropriate employees. QuickBooks will then use this information to calculate the due dates for each upcoming pay period, so that you pay your employees on time.

Caution. *Before setting up a payroll schedule and creating your first paychecks in your own company file, you need to run QuickBooks Payroll Setup. The Payroll Setup interview guides you through setting up payroll in QuickBooks and helps you receive your first payroll update, in which QuickBooks downloads information such as current tax forms and federal and state calculations. After payroll information is current, the interview process guides you through setting up payroll taxes for your company, setting up common compensation and benefits correctly, and leads you through setting up individual employees and year-to-date payroll amounts so you can start doing payroll through QuickBooks. For further information about Payroll Setup, refer to the QuickBooks Desktop Help.*

Before you can start paying your employees using payroll schedules, you need to set up at least one payroll schedule. In this exercise, you will set up a payroll schedule directly from the New Employee window for Robert T Rhodes.

1. Select   <Add New>   from the Payroll Schedule drop-down menu in the New Employee window

The New Payroll Schedule window opens:

New Payroll Schedule   ✕

The information you provide will be used to create a payroll schedule.   What is a payroll schedule?
You can set up multiple payroll schedules if you need to.   Why do I need multiple schedules?

Tell us how you'll be processing payroll using QuickBooks: How do I set up a payroll schedule?

What do you want to name this payroll schedule? (e.g., "Weekly", "Biweekly", "Monthly", etc)   [   ]

How often will you pay your employees on this schedule?   [Biweekly (Every other week)   ▾]

What is the pay period end date?   [🔲]

What date should appear on paychecks for this pay period?   [🔲]

The following is based on the information supplied above:
You pay your employees DD days after the pay period end date in this payroll schedule.

☐ Schedule is inactive   [OK   ]   Cancel

When you set up a payroll schedule, you must determine the employee's pay period. A pay period is the duration of time for which the employee is being paid, such as weekly or biweekly.

In this exercise, you will set up a biweekly payroll schedule. The first step in this process is to determine a name for the payroll schedule. For convenience, QuickBooks suggests you name the payroll schedule the same as the pay period.

2. Type   **Biweekly**   in the What do you want to name this payroll schedule? field

To specify the pay period for this payroll schedule,

3. Verify Biweekly (Every other week) is selected from the How often will you pay your employees on this schedule? drop-down menu

You must now specify the next pay period end date for the pay schedule. The pay period end date is the last date of the pay period that a paycheck should cover. QuickBooks will use this date to calculate the number of weeks an employee has worked in a year and the time information to include in the paycheck.

4. Type   **11/09/2018**   in the What is the pay period end date? field

5. Type   **11/16/2018**   in the What date should appear on paychecks for this pay period? field

This date is the date that employees are actually paid and is the date the paycheck affects your bank account. In this example, the pay period end date is Friday, November 9, and the paycheck date is 5 business days later on the following Friday, November 16.

 Quick Tip. *The IRS bases your tax liability and your employees' tax liabilities on the check date.*

6. Click   OK

An Assign Payroll Schedule dialog box displays:

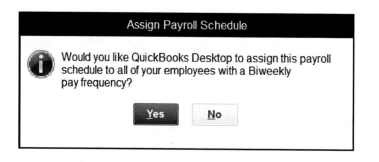

This dialog box asks if you would like to assign this payroll schedule to all of your employees with a Biweekly pay frequency.

7. Click

Note: All employees grouped in the same payroll schedule must have the same pay frequency, such as weekly or biweekly.

A QuickBooks Information dialog box displays:

This dialog box informs you how many employees have been assigned to this payroll schedule.

8. Click   OK   to return to the New Employee window

QuickBooks has created the payroll schedule for each pay period based on the information you entered and Biweekly now displays in the Payroll Schedule field.

9. Click   OK   to close the New Employee window

The Employee Center displays with the new employee Robert T Rhodes listed below Joseph Rogers in the Employees list:

![Employee Center screenshot showing Employee Information for Robert T Rhodes, with employees list including Amy S Parker, Carene Sheridan, Fred J Centofanti, Jerry M Mathew, Joseph Rogers, Robert T Rhodes, Tracy Harper]

Writing a Payroll Check

In addition to using payroll schedules, QuickBooks allows you to write an individual paycheck or several at one time. You may want to process the paychecks of salaried employees in a batch or on a payroll schedule, but complete payroll for the hourly employees one at a time.

For this exercise, you will create a paycheck for Jerry M Mathew, an hourly employee who gets paid weekly. In order to run his paycheck, you will need to run QuickBooks Payroll Setup first.

To run QuickBooks Payroll Setup,

1. Select   Employees :   from the QuickBooks menu bar
                           Payroll Setup

Note: The Payroll Setup option will not display in the Employees menu unless you have signed up for a QuickBooks payroll service or set your company file to use manual payroll calculations.

A QuickBooks Payroll Setup dialog box displays as the payroll information is configured:

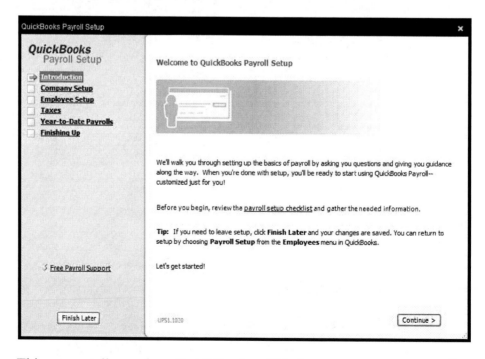

When the Payroll Setup has loaded, the Introduction screen of the QuickBooks Payroll Setup wizard opens:

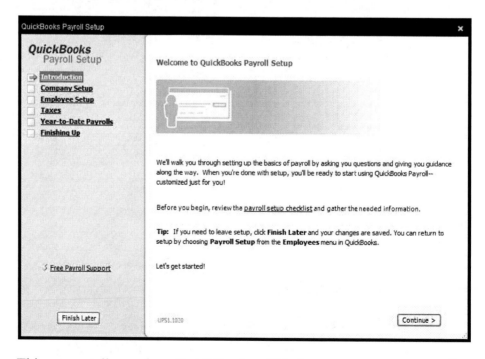

This screen tells you how QuickBooks will help you set up your payroll.

2. Click

The Company Setup screen of the QuickBooks Payroll Setup wizard displays:

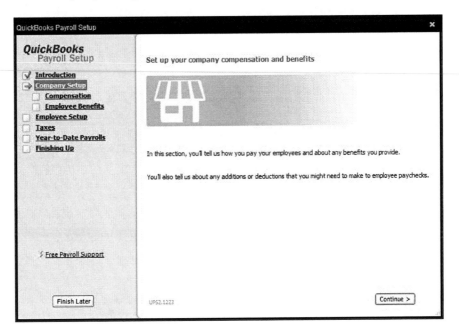

This screen makes you aware of the information you need to have on hand to set up company compensation and employee benefits.

3. Click   Continue >

The Compensation screen of the QuickBooks Payroll Setup wizard displays:

This screen allows you to review your current compensation list, and add, edit, or delete compensation items.

4. Click   Continue >

The Employee Benefits screen of the QuickBooks Payroll Setup wizard displays:

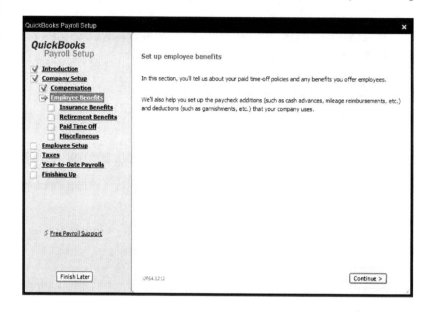

This screen displays information about employee benefits.

5. Click   Continue >

The Add New window opens:

This window allows you to add the types of insurance benefits you provide for your employees.

Quick Tip. *You can click any underlined text in the wizard to display the QuickBooks Payroll Setup Help. The help displays further information about completing the payroll setup process.*

To accept the default selection,

6. Click   Finish

The Add New window closes and the Insurance Benefits page of the QuickBooks Payroll Setup wizard displays:

This screen allows you to review your insurance benefits. You can also set up employee retirement benefits, paid time off, and any miscellaneous benefits in this section.

7. Click   **Employee Setup**   in the left pane of the wizard

The Employee Setup screen of the QuickBooks Payroll Setup wizard displays:

This screen tells you about the information you will need to complete the Employee Setup section.

8. Click   [Continue >]

The Employee List screen of the QuickBooks Payroll Setup wizard displays:

This screen allows you to review your employees' information, add information where it is missing, and fix any errors. An exclamation point will display to the left of any employee with missing information. To add missing information, click the employee name and then click the Edit button.

9. Click [Continue >]

The Taxes screen of the QuickBooks Payroll Setup wizard displays:

This screen tells you the information you will need to set up payment methods for your payroll taxes.

10. Click [Continue >]

The Federal Taxes screen of the QuickBooks Payroll Setup wizard displays:

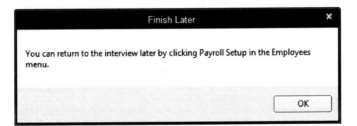

This screen allows you to review and edit any of the Federal taxes QuickBooks has set up for your company. You can also review and edit state taxes and scheduled tax payments in this section.

When you are setting up payroll services for your own company, you should complete the entire QuickBooks Payroll Setup interview. For this exercise, you will not complete the setup.

11. Click   Finish Later

A Finish Later dialog box displays:

This dialog box informs you how to return to the QuickBooks Payroll Setup at a later time.

12. Click   OK   to return to the Employee Center

13. Select   Employees :   from the QuickBooks menu bar
               Pay Employees

Note: The Pay Employees option will not display in the Employees menu unless you have signed up for a QuickBooks payroll service or set your company file to use manual calculations.

The Enter Payroll Information window opens:

This window allows you to enter hours for each employee directly in the table. You can also click an employee's name to enter information directly in their paycheck. Notice that the checking account is selected as the bank account to use for paying employees. If you wanted to change this account, you would simply select the new account from the drop-down menu.

14.	Type	**10/19/2018**	in the Pay Period Ends field
15.	Type	**10/26/2018**	in the Check Date field
16.	Click	in the ✓ column	to the left of Jerry M Mathew

QuickBooks places a check mark next to the name to indicate it is selected.

To enter the number of hours worked by Jerry,

| 17. | Click | in the Hourly Rate 1 column | for Jerry M Mathew |
| 18. | Type | **80** | in the Hourly Rate 1 column |

This indicates that Jerry M Mathew worked a total of 80 hours during this pay period under his rate of 20.00 per hour (Hourly Rate 1).

| 19. | Press | Tab | |

The Total Hours field is automatically populated with 80:00.

| 20. | Click | Continue | |

The Review & Create Paychecks window opens:

Currently, there are no amounts entered in the Taxes or Deductions columns. Because you have chosen to process your payroll manually, QuickBooks inserts a 0.00 amount for each payroll item associated with a tax. When you process payroll manually, you must enter these tax figures yourself.

Clicking an employees name allows you to view paycheck details and change any information, such as tax figures, before you actually create the paycheck.

21. Click   Jerry M Mathew   in the Employee column

Note: You can also click in any other column in the row for Jerry M Mathew and then click the Open Paycheck Detail button.

The Preview Paycheck window opens:

If you were using a payroll service, QuickBooks would automatically fill in the appropriate employee information in this window and display all deductions from Jerry's paycheck. Because you are processing payroll manually, you will need to enter the tax figures for this employee.

Caution. *Payroll tax information for the federal, state, and local agencies can change at numerous times throughout the tax year. To avoid penalties, you should consult with your tax agencies often to learn about any changes.*

To enter tax information in the Employee Summary (adjusted) area,

22.	Type	**315.20**	in the Amount column for Federal Withholding
23.	Press	Tab	

QuickBooks places a minus (-) sign before the figure entered to indicate it is a deduction that should be subtracted from the employee's check.

24.	Type	**99.20**	in the Amount column for Social Security Employee
25.	Press	Tab	
26.	Type	**23.20**	in the Amount column for Medicare Employee
27.	Press	Tab	
28.	Type	**88.27**	in the Amount column for NY - Withholding
29.	Press	Tab	

A paycheck is not complete unless the company portion of the taxes are entered.

In the Company Summary (adjusted) area,

30.	Select	0.00	in the Amount column for Social Security Company
31.	Type	**99.20**	in the Amount column for Social Security Company
32.	Press	Tab	
33.	Type	**23.20**	in the Amount column for Medicare Company
34.	Press	Tab	

35.	Type	**12.80**	in the Amount column for Federal Unemployment
36.	Select	0.00	in the Amount column for NY - Unemployment Company (scroll down)
37.	Type	**64.00**	
38.	Press	Tab	

The new net amount of the paycheck displays at the bottom of the window:

Preview Paycheck

Jerry M Mathew   PAY PERIOD 10/13/2018 - 10/19/2018

Earnings   ☐ Use Direct Deposit

ITEM NAME	RATE	HOURS	CUSTOMER:JOB				
Hourly Rate 1	20.00	80:00			SICK AVAILABLE		0:00
Hourly Rate 2					VACATION AVAIL		6:45
					SICK ACCRUED		
					VAC. ACCRUED		6:45
TOTALS		1,600.00	80:00 hrs		☐ Do not accrue sick/vac		

Other Payroll Items

ITEM NAME	RATE	QUANTITY
Health Insurance	65.00	

Employee Summary (adjusted)   How are these items calculated?

ITEM NAME	AMOUNT	YTD
Hourly Rate 1	1,600.00	1,600.00
Hourly Rate 2	0.00	0.00
Medicare Employee Addl T...	0.00	0.00
Federal Withholding	-315.20	-315.20
Social Security Employee	-99.20	-99.20
Medicare Employee	-23.20	-23.20
NY - Withholding	-88.27	-88.27
NY - Disability Employee	0.00	0.00

Company Summary (adjusted)   How are these items calculated?

ITEM NAME	AMOUNT	YTD
Medicare Company	23.20	23.20
Federal Unemployment	12.80	12.80
NY - Disability Company	0.00	0.00
NY - Unemployment Com...	64.00	64.00

Check Amount   1,074.13

What's this?

Save & Previous   Save & Next   **Save & Close**   Cancel   Help   ☐ Enter net/Calculate gross

Notice the company-paid taxes and contributions you entered do not affect the amount of the paycheck.

Note: You may need to scroll down to view all company-paid taxes and contributions.

39.	Click	

The Review and Create Paychecks window displays the updated paycheck information for Jerry M Mathew:

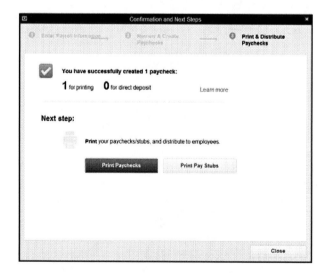

You can choose to print your paychecks directly from QuickBooks or assign check numbers to handwritten checks. For this exercise, you will accept the default selection of Print paychecks on check stock in the Check Options area.

40. Click [Create Paychecks]

A Confirmation and Next Steps window opens:

This window informs you that you have successfully created one paycheck and lists the next steps involved with printing and distributing the paycheck.

You will not print the paycheck at this time.

41. Click [Close] to return to the Employee Center

QuickBooks has automatically written a payroll check for the correct net amount, showing the deductions in the voucher area. The check has been recorded in your QuickBooks Checking account register.

To view the payroll check for Jerry M Mathew,

| 42. | Select | Lists : Chart of Accounts | from the QuickBooks menu bar |

The Chart of Accounts opens:

NAME	TYPE	BALANCE TOTAL	ATTACH
Checking	Bank	5,714.69	
Savings - Money Market	Bank	15,000.00	
Accounts Receivable	Accounts Receivable	11,833.22	
Inventory Asset	Other Current Asset	4,188.00	
Undeposited Funds	Other Current Asset	0.00	
Accounts Payable	Accounts Payable	6,289.00	

| 43. | Double-click | Checking | in the Name column |
| 44. | Click | the paycheck transaction for Jerry M Mathew | |

The paycheck transaction for Jerry M Mathew becomes selected:

Checking

Go to... | Print... | Edit Transaction | QuickReport | Setup Bank Feeds

DATE	NUMBER	PAYEE		PAYMENT	✔	DEPOSIT	BALANCE
	TYPE	ACCOUNT	MEMO				
10/10/2018	2	Fairgrave Gas & Electric		156.33			7,743.67
	CHK	-split-					
10/10/2018	3	Fellows Windows & Doors		639.85			7,103.82
	BILLPMT	Accounts Payable	78787				
10/10/2018	To Print	Smith's Construction Rental		315.00			6,788.82
	CHK	Job Expenses:Equip					
10/26/2018	To Print	Jerry M Mathew		1,074.13			5,714.69
	PAY CHK	-split-					
10/26/2018							

Splits

1-Line

Sort by Date, Type, Number/Ref

ENDING BALANCE   **5,714.69**

Record   Restore

| 45. | Click | Edit Transaction | in the Checking account register toolbar |

Quick Tip. *You can also view paychecks by opening the Employee center, clicking the Transactions tab, and selecting Paychecks from the list of transactions. You then select the appropriate date range from the Date drop-down menu and double-click a paycheck to open the paycheck in the Paycheck - Checking window. From the Paycheck - Checking window, you would then click the Paycheck Detail button.*

The Paycheck - Checking window opens with the check displayed:

The Paycheck Summary area shows a summary of the check's earnings, additions, taxes, and deductions. If you want to see the exact figures that make up these totals, you can click the Paycheck Detail button.

46. Click ⬚ Paycheck Detail...

The Review Paycheck window opens:

The deductions are correct (the same as those in the Preview Paycheck window); therefore, the paycheck created for Jerry M Mathew is acceptable.

47. Click  to return to the Paycheck - Checking window

48. Click to close the Paycheck - Checking window

49. Close the Checking account register and the Chart of Accounts to return to the Employee Center

Printing Paycheck Stubs

You can print paychecks just as you would any QuickBooks check. If you use voucher checks, QuickBooks prints the payroll item detail in the voucher area. If you do not use voucher checks, you can print a pay stub to give to your employees.

Quick Tip. *You can also email pay stubs to employees.*

Note: *You must have a printer driver and printer installed on your computer or network in order to print paycheck stubs.*

To print a pay stub,

1. Click   🖨 **Print** ▾   on the Employee Center toolbar

A drop-down menu displays:

> Print Paychecks
> Print / Send Paystubs
>
> Employee List
> Employee Information
> Employee Transaction List

2. Select   Print / Send Paystubs   from the drop-down menu

The Select Pay Stubs window opens.

3. Type   **10/26/2018**   in the Checks Dated field

4. Press   Tab

The pay stub for Jerry M Mathew displays and is automatically selected:

5. Click   Print

The Print Pay Stubs window opens:

Note: The printer name in your window will be different.

6. Click   Print   to print the pay stub for Jerry M Mathew

The pay stub is sent to the printer and the Employee Center displays.

Note: If you are not set up to print, click Cancel in the Print Pay Stubs window and then click Close in the Select Pay Stubs window.

Tracking Your Tax Liabilities

As an employer, you need to track both payroll expenses and payroll liabilities.

There are two types of company payroll expenses you need to track:

• Employees' gross pay

- Employer payroll taxes, such as contributions to Social Security (FICA), Medicare, federal and state unemployment insurance (SUI), and state disability insurance

QuickBooks uses an expense account called Payroll Expenses to track these actual costs to your company. (The funds you deduct from employee paychecks are not considered an actual cost because they are monies that you hold for the government; they do not come directly from your company's assets.) Whenever you run a payroll, QuickBooks keeps track of your company's expenses for each employee. You can then see totals for these expenses on the Payroll Summary report and on the profit and loss statement.

QuickBooks uses the Payroll Liabilities account (an Other Current Liability account) to track what you owe to the government. When you process payroll, QuickBooks calculates how much you owe for each tax, deduction, or company contribution payroll item and records that information as a transaction in this liability account. With each payroll check you write, the balance of the liability account increases. This produces a record of how much tax you owe at any time, so you can plan to have the cash available for payment. When you pay your payroll taxes or other payroll liabilities, the balance of the liability account decreases.

In this exercise, you will review the payroll expense and liability accounts to see how QuickBooks recorded expenses and liabilities related to Jerry M Mathew's paycheck.

To display the Payroll Expenses QuickReport,

| 1. | Select | Lists : Chart of Accounts | from the QuickBooks menu bar |

The Chart of Accounts opens:

| 2. | Select | Payroll Expenses | in the Name column (scroll down) |

| 3. | Click | Reports ▼ | |

A drop-down menu of reports displays.

| 4. | Select | QuickReport: Payroll Expenses | |

The Account QuickReport window opens:

Note: If data does not display in your report, select the All option from the Dates drop-down menu.

Now you can see all the expense items paid by the company for Jerry M Mathew's paycheck.

5. Close the Account QuickReport window

6. Double-click Payroll Liabilities in the Chart of Accounts (scroll up near the top of the window)

The Payroll Liabilities register opens:

7. Scroll up to view all items in the register

The register shows a separate increase transaction for each item from Jerry's paycheck, such as federal tax, state tax, and FICA. The total balance also shows an increase for every liability.

8. Close the Payroll Liabilities register and the Chart of Accounts

Paying Payroll Taxes

QuickBooks keeps track of all your tax liabilities as they accrue, so you know how much you owe at any time.

Figuring Out What You Owe

If you are about to pay taxes or other liabilities, the Payroll Liability Balances report shows you how much to pay. Suppose you are ready to make a tax payment and want to see how much you owe.

To create a Payroll Liability Balances report,

1. Select   Reports :   from the QuickBooks menu bar
   Employees & Payroll :
   Payroll Liability Balances

Quick Tip. *You can also use the Report Center to access any of the payroll and employee reports.*

The Payroll Liability Balances report opens:

Note: If data does not display in your report, select This Calendar Year-to-date from the Dates drop-down menu.

This report displays the total amount of taxes and other liabilities you must pay for the specified period.

2. Close the Payroll Liability Balances report

Writing a Check for Payroll Taxes

When it's time to deposit payroll taxes with your deposit institution, use the Liability Check window to fill out a QuickBooks check.

1. Click   [Home]   on the Icon Bar

The Home page displays.

2. Click in the Employees section of the Home page

Quick Tip. If you are using QuickBooks enhanced payroll, a Payroll Liability reminder is available to alert you seven days prior to any payroll liability item deadlines, so you don't miss important due dates, such as federal and state taxes and workers' compensation.

The Select Date Range For Liabilities window opens:

Select Date Range For Liabilities	✕

Select the date range for the payroll liabilities you want to pay.

Tip: Base your dates on the dates of the paychecks you issued, not on your pay period dates.

SHOW PAYROLL LIABILITIES

Dates [Custom ▼]   From [01/01/2018 📅]   Through [10/31/2018 📅]

[OK]   [Cancel]   [Help]

3. Press [Tab] twice

The date in the Through field becomes selected.

4. Type **11/1/2018** in the Through field

5. Click [OK]

The Pay Liabilities window opens:

Pay Liabilities	_ □ ✕

☑ To be printed

Bank Account
[Checking ▼]

Check Date
[11/01/2018 📅]

Sort By [Payable To ▼]

○ Review liability check to enter expenses/penalties
○ Create liability check without reviewing

[Create]
[Cancel]
[Payroll Liabilities Report]
[Help]

SHOW PAYROLL LIABILITIES

Dates [Custom ▼]   From [01/01/2018 📅]   Through [11/01/2018 📅]

✓	PAYROLL ITEM	PAYABLE TO	BALANCE	AMT. TO PAY
	Federal Unemployment		12.80	0.00
	Federal Withholding	Eastcoast Bank	315.20	0.00
	Medicare Company	Eastcoast Bank	23.20	0.00
	Medicare Employee	Eastcoast Bank	23.20	0.00
	Medicare Employee Addl T...	Eastcoast Bank	0.00	0.00
	NY - Disability Company	Eastcoast Bank	0.00	0.00
	NY - Disability Employee	Eastcoast Bank	0.00	0.00
	NY - Unemployment Com...	Eastcoast Bank	64.00	0.00
			790.07	0.00

☐ Hide zero balances   Ending Bank Balance   5,714.69

The Pay Liabilities window displays a separate line for each payroll item and includes information about who the item is payable to and the amount to pay. Notice the Review liability check to enter expenses/penalties option is selected. This allows you to review the liability check before actually creating it.

6. Click   in the column   to the left of Federal Withholding

QuickBooks places a check mark in the column to indicate the item will be paid.

7. Click   in the column   to the left of Medicare Company

QuickBooks places a check mark in both the Medicare Company and Medicare Employee columns indicating both items will be paid.

8. Click   in the column   to the left of Social Security Company (scroll down)

QuickBooks places a check mark in both the Social Security Company and Social Security Employee columns indicating both items will be paid.

To create the check for federal withholding,

9. Click   **Create**

Note: If you did not change your computer's date as recommended in the Before You Get Started lesson, the Special Calculation Warning dialog box displays. Click the Continue button to view the Liability Check - Checking window.

The Liability Check - Checking window opens:

QuickBooks has created the check to pay for Jerry M Mathew's federal withholding. You should use a separate check for each type of deposit coupon (for example, 941 or 940). When you make a payment and record a check this way, QuickBooks decreases the balance in your Payroll Liabilities account.

10. Click to close the Liability Check - Checking window

Preparing Payroll Tax Forms

To prepare payroll tax forms from within QuickBooks, you must subscribe to an Intuit Payroll service. However, if you choose not to subscribe to an Intuit Payroll service, you can still use information from QuickBooks to manually prepare your tax forms by importing data from your company file into Excel.

QuickBooks allows you to manually prepare the following tax forms in Excel:

*   Quarterly 941

*   Annual 940

*   Annual W-2/W-3

*   Annual 944

*   Annual 943

*   State SUI Wage Listing

In this exercise, you will manually prepare Form W-2 and Form 941.

Caution. *To manually prepare tax forms, you must have Microsoft Excel 2010 or later installed on your computer. You must also have macros enabled in your Excel application. Refer to the Excel help for information about enabling and setting macro security levels. If you are working on a network and the system administrator set the default macro settings, they will need to change the settings. If macros are disabled in your Excel application, you will not be able to complete this section.*

Form W-2

Form W-2 (Wage and Tax Statement) is the end-of-year form that is sent to each employee and submitted to federal, state, and local tax agencies. It displays an employee's wages and taxes withheld for the year. The IRS requires most employers to file Form W-2 at the beginning of each year.

Note: *If you changed the date on your computer as recommended at the beginning of this lesson and have a Microsoft Office subscription that expires by that date, you will need to change the date on your computer to the current date for this exercise to work properly.*

To prepare Form W-2 by importing data from your company file into Excel,

1. Select   Employees : Payroll   from the QuickBooks menu bar
                            Tax Forms & W-2s :
                            Tax Form Worksheets
                            in Excel

Note: If macros are not enabled, you will be required to enable them.

Note: If you subscribe to an Intuit Payroll service, you would select Employees: Payroll Tax Forms and W-2s: Process Payroll Forms from the menu bar.

The Excel application opens and a QuickBooks Tax Worksheets window opens:

QuickBooks Tax Worksheets

Which worksheet to you want to create?

- ● Quarterly 941
- ○ Annual 940
- ○ Annual W-2/W-3
- ○ Annual 944
- ○ Annual 943
- ○ State SUI Wage Listing

Dates

Last Month
Last Quarter
Last Year
This Month
This Quarter
This Year
Custom

From   7/1/2017

To   9/30/2017

Options / Settings

☑ Refresh from QuickBooks   Cancel   **Create Report**

Note: The dates in your window may be different.

2.	Select	the Annual W-2/W-3 option	in the Which worksheet do you want to create section?
3.	Select	This Year	in the Dates field
4.	Type	1/1/2018	in the From field (if necessary)
5.	Type	12/31/2018	in the To field (if necessary)
6.	Click	**Create Report**	

A QuickBooks Tax Worksheets - Updated dialog box displays informing you that the tax form has been created and you should review the results carefully:

QuickBooks Tax Worksheets - Updated

Finished. Please review the results carefully.

Use the worksheets in this workbook to provide further details on the forms QuickBooks automatically calculates for you, or use them to help complete forms manually, depending on your service option.

☑ Show after each update   OK

7.	Click	OK

The Annual W-2 Summary displays in Excel:

	A	B	C	D
1	Annual W-2 Summary			
2				
3	W3 Summary			1 Employee
4	Compensation			
5	Payroll Category	Item Type	Tax Tracking Type	Amount
6	Hourly Rate 1	Hourly salary	Compensation	1,600.00
7	Hourly Rate 2	Hourly salary	Compensation	0.00
8	Total Box 1			1,600.00
9	Federal Taxes			
10	Tax	Subject Income	Taxed Wages	Tax
11	Federal Withholding	1,600.00	1,600.00	315.20
12	Social Security	1,600.00	1,600.00	99.20
13	Social Security Tips	0.00	0.00	
14	Medicare Employee	1,600.00	1,600.00	23.20
15	State Taxes			
16	Tax	Subject Income	Taxed Wages	Tax
17	NY - State Withholding	1,600.00	1,600.00	88.27
18	NY - SDI Employee	1,600.00	120.00	0.00
19				
20	Jerry M Mathew			987-65-4321
21	22 North Lewis Street			
22	Fairgrave, NY 11111			
23	Compensation			
24	Payroll Category	Item Type	Tax Tracking Type	Amount
25	Hourly Rate 1	Hourly salary	Compensation	1,600.00
26	Hourly Rate 2	Hourly salary	Compensation	0.00
27	Total Box 1			1,600.00
28	Federal Taxes			
29	Tax	Subject Income	Taxed Wages	Tax
30	Federal Withholding	1,600.00	1,600.00	315.20
31	Social Security	1,600.00	1,600.00	99.20
32	Social Security Tips	0.00	0.00	

You should review the W-2 worksheet for each employee who worked for you at any time during the year and make any necessary changes. You should then print the forms on blank perforated paper or preprinted forms and file (or e-file) them appropriately.

Note: For further information about preparing W-2 forms, refer to the QuickBooks Desktop Help or your accountant.

    8. Select   File : Close   from the Excel menu bar

The Excel file closes.

Form 941

Form 941 is an employer's quarterly payroll tax form to report employee wages that have been paid, any tips employees have received, federal income tax withheld, both the employer's and employee's Social Security and Medicare tax, and advanced earned income tax credit (EIC) payments.

Note: You may be required to file a Schedule B with your Form 941. Refer to the QuickBooks Desktop Help for more information.

Note: If you changed the date on your computer as recommended at the beginning of this lesson and have a Microsoft Office subscription that expires by that date, you will need to change the date on your computer to the current date for this exercise to work properly.

To prepare Form 941 by importing data from your company file into Excel,

| 1. | Select | Employees : Payroll Tax Forms & W-2s : Tax Form Worksheets in Excel | from the QuickBooks menu bar |

The Excel application opens and a QuickBooks Tax Worksheets window opens.

| 2. | Select | the Quarterly 941 option | in the Which worksheet do you want to create section? |

The QuickBooks Tax Worksheets window is updated with Form 941 selections:

Note: The dates in your window may be different.

3.	Select	This Quarter	in the Dates field
4.	Type	10/1/2018	in the From field (if necessary)
5.	Type	12/31/2018	in the To field (if necessary)
6.	Click	**Create Report**	

A QuickBooks Tax Worksheets - Updated dialog box displays informing you that the tax form has been created and you should review the results carefully:

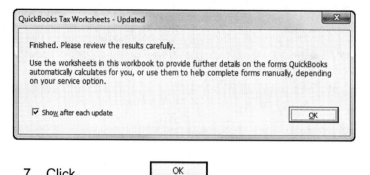

7. Click [OK]

The 941 Summary displays in Excel:

	A	B	C	D	E
1	**941 Summary**				
2	**Wages, Tips, and other Compensation**				
3	*Payroll Category*	*Item Type*	*Tax Tracking Type*		*Amount*
4	Hourly Rate 1	Hourly salary	Compensation		1,600.00
5	Hourly Rate 2	Hourly salary	Compensation		0.00
6					1,600.00
7	*Federal Tax Withholding*	*Subject Income*	*Taxed Wages*		*Tax*
8	Federal Withholding	1,600.00	1,600.00		315.20
9	*Social Security & Medicare*	*Subject Income*	*Taxed Wages*	*Tax Rate*	*Tax*
10	Social Security	1,600.00	1,600.00	0.124	198.40
11	Medicare	1,600.00	1,600.00	0.029	46.40
12					244.80
13	**Total Tax (Calculated)**				560.00
14	*Advance Earned Income Credit*	*Subject Income*	*Taxed Wages*		*Tax Credit*
15					0.00
16	**Total Tax After AEIC (Calculated)**				560.00
17	*COBRA Earned Credit*				*Tax Credit*
18					0.00
19	**Total Due After COBRA Credit**				560.00
20	**Daily Wage Summary**				
21	*Item*	*Date*	*Subject Income*	*Taxed Wages*	*Tax*
22	Federal Withholding	10/26/2018	1,600.00	1,600.00	315.20
23	Social Security Company	10/26/2018	1,600.00	1,600.00	99.20
24	Social Security Employee	10/26/2018	1,600.00	1,600.00	99.20
25	Medicare Company	10/26/2018	1,600.00	1,600.00	23.20
26	Medicare Employee	10/26/2018	1,600.00	1,600.00	23.20
27					560.00
28	**Monthly Total - October**				560.00
29	**Total Tax - Actual**				560.00
30	Taxed Wages by Employee				

You should review the form to ensure it is complete and accurate. You should then print the form and file it appropriately.

Note: For further information about preparing 941 forms, refer to the QuickBooks Desktop Help and your accountant.

8. Close the Excel application to return to the QuickBooks application

Review

In this lesson, you have learned how to:

- ☑ Use payroll tracking
- ☑ Set up for payroll
- ☑ Set up employee payroll information
- ☑ Set up a payroll schedule
- ☑ Write a payroll check
- ☑ Print paycheck stubs
- ☑ Track your tax liabilities
- ☑ Pay payroll taxes
- ☑ Prepare payroll tax forms

Practice:

1. Add a new employee to the employee list using the following criteria:.
   (Do not close the New Employee window when finished)

Legal Name:	Mrs. Amanda A. Mehl
Social Security No:	111-23-4567
Gender:	Female
Date of Birth:	3/1/1976
Marital Status:	Married
U.S. Citizen:	Yes
Disabled:	No
I-9 Form On File:	Yes
U.S. Veteran:	No
Address:	555 Catalina Road Fairgrave, NY 11111
Work Phone:	555-555-5555
Emergency Contact Info	
Contact Name:	Thomas Mehl
Contact Phone:	555-555-1212
Relation:	Spouse
Hourly Rate 1:	$40.00
Filing Status:	Married
State Worked/ Subject to Withholding:	NY
Health Insurance:	$25.00

2. From the New Employee window, add a new payroll schedule using the following information:

What do you want to name this payroll schedule:	Weekly
How often will you pay your employees on this schedule?	Weekly
What is the pay period end date:	10/26/2018
What date should appear on paychecks for this pay period:	11/02/2018
Assign this payroll schedule to all employees with a weekly pay frequency:	Yes

3. Create a paycheck for Amanda, who has worked 70 hours during the pay period ending 10/19/2018. Add the following taxes to the paycheck:

Employee Summary (adjusted)	
Federal Withholding:	-215.85
Social Security Employee:	-62.64
Medicare Employee:	-16.96
NY - Withholding:	-74.27
Company Summary (adjusted)	
Social Security Company	87.60
Medicare Company	23.86
NY - Unemployment Company	56.00

4. Create a Payroll Liability Balances report showing data for the calendar year-to-date.

5. Write a check for the current amount due for NY - Withholding to the State Dept. using the Pay Liabilities and Liability Check windows.

6. Prepare an annual 940 form by importing data from your company file into Excel.

7. Close the Excel application.

8. Close the QuickBooks company file.

A

Using Online Banking

In this appendix, you will learn how to:

❑ Set up an Internet connection

❑ Set up bank feeds for accounts

❑ View, download, and add online transactions

❑ Create online payments

❑ Transfer funds online

❑ Cancel online payments

Concept

QuickBooks allows you to take advantage of online banking, a convenient and timesaving way for small business owners to handle financial transactions and communicate with their banks.

With bank feeds, you can download transactions from your financial institution or credit card provider into QuickBooks. Then, you can see what transactions have cleared your account, find out your current balance, and add transactions that have been processed but aren't in QuickBooks yet.

Scenario

In this appendix, you will learn how to set up an Internet connection and set up bank feeds for your accounts with a financial institution that has online banking capabilities. You will then view statements online and pay a bill by creating and submitting an online payment. You will also complete an online transfer of funds from one account to another. And finally, you will learn how to cancel a payment made online.

Practice Files:

• B18_Using_Online_Banking.qbw

• B18_Sample.qbw

Setting Up an Internet Connection

To use online banking, you need access to the Internet from QuickBooks. This requires you to set up an Internet connection. You will also need a browser to set up your Internet connection. Microsoft® Internet Explorer® is a browser that is automatically loaded on your computer when you install QuickBooks. You must use Internet Explorer in this exercise.

Note: For this lesson, your computer must be set to the current date before opening the QuickBooks file in order to successfully set up your accounts for online services.

To set up an Internet connection in QuickBooks,

1. Open   B18_Using_Online Banking.qbw   using the method described in Before You Get Started

The QuickBooks Login dialog box displays:

```
┌────────────────────────────────────────────────────┐
│            QuickBooks Login                     ✕    │
├────────────────────────────────────────────────────┤
│                                                      │
│  You need to log in as QuickBooks Administrator to   │
│  proceed.  Please enter the admin (owner) password   │
│  for the company:                                    │
│                                                      │
│                   Canalside Corp.                    │
│                                                      │
│   Password: [_____]  I forgot my password │
│                                                      │
│            Passwords are case sensitive.             │
│                                                      │
│        [  OK  ]    [ Cancel ]    [  Help  ]          │
│                                                      │
└────────────────────────────────────────────────────┘
```

This dialog box informs you that you must login as a QuickBooks Administrator in order to open the company file.

2. Type   **Canalside2**   in the Password field

Note: Passwords are case-sensitive.

3. Click   [OK]

QuickBooks opens the file.

4. Click   ✕   to close the Reminders window

QuickBooks opens the Home page:

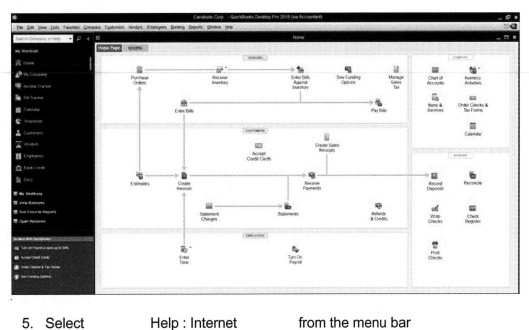

5. Select **Help : Internet Connection Setup** from the menu bar

The Internet Connection Setup window opens:

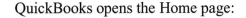

Note: Your window may include additional connection options.

This window asks how you would like to connect to the Internet. QuickBooks simplifies the process of setting up an Internet connection by offering to establish the connection for you automatically whenever you use QuickBooks online.

6. Verify the Use my computer's Internet connection settings to establish a connection when this application accesses the Internet is selected

Note: If you do not want to establish a connection automatically, you can select the "Use the following connection" option and choose another Internet connection.

7. Click | Next > |

The next Internet Connection Setup window displays your connection settings:

Internet Connection Setup

Connection Settings

Your computer is configured to use a direct connection to the Internet.

- Click Done to use these settings whenever an online feature of this product is accessed.

Advanced

- Click Advanced Connection Settings if you want to view or change your preferences.

    Please note that changing these settings may affect how other programs connect to the Internet, including Internet Explorer. | Advanced Connection Settings... |

| < Back | Done | Cancel | Help |

Note: Your window may be slightly different.

8. Click | Done |

You return to the Home page.

Setting Up Bank Feeds for Accounts

In addition to Internet service, you will need a bank account at a financial institution that offers online services for QuickBooks.

Financial institutions provide different levels of bank feed services. While some do not offer any services, others provide enhanced services, such as allowing you to use QuickBooks to transfer money between two online accounts.

Quick Tip. You should check with your financial institution to see what services it offers. You can select Banking : Bank Feeds : Participating Financial Institutions from the menu bar for a list of financial institutions that offer online financial services.

Note: The screens that display when setting up bank feeds for accounts vary between financial institutions. Therefore, the following steps may be different when you set up bank feeds with your financial institution.

To set up bank feeds for an account,

1. Select   Banking : Bank   from the menu bar
Feeds : Set Up Bank
Feed for an Account

QuickBooks displays a message informing you that all open windows must be temporarily closed:

Temporarily Close All Windows

All open QuickBooks windows will be closed temporarily to set up Bank Feeds services. Do you want to continue?

[Yes]   [No]

2. Click   [Yes]   to set up your accounts

QuickBooks closes all open windows and an Update Branding Files dialog box temporarily displays while updating files. When the dialog box closes, Step 1 of the Bank Feed Setup window opens:

Bank Feed Setup

Step 1: Find your bank   ① — ② — ③ — ④
FIND   CONNECT   LINK   DONE

Enter your bank's name

[🔍]

Examples: Bank of America, Citibank, American Express.

Or choose from these popular banks

Bank of America-All Other States
Chase
Fidelity Bank
U.S. Bank - PFM Direct Connect
JPMorgan Chase Bank
Wells Fargo Bank
Capital One Card Services
Citi Cards
Discover Card
American Express

This step in the bank feed set up process allows you to find your bank. You can locate your bank by typing the first few characters of its name in the Enter your bank's name field. QuickBooks displays a list of results matching your entry as you type. You then select your bank from the list of matching results.

You can also select a bank from the list of popular banks. After selecting your bank, you will be presented with options to connect to your bank.

3. Click   Bank of America -   in the Or choose from these popular
All Other States   banks list

The next screen in the Bank Feed Setup window displays:

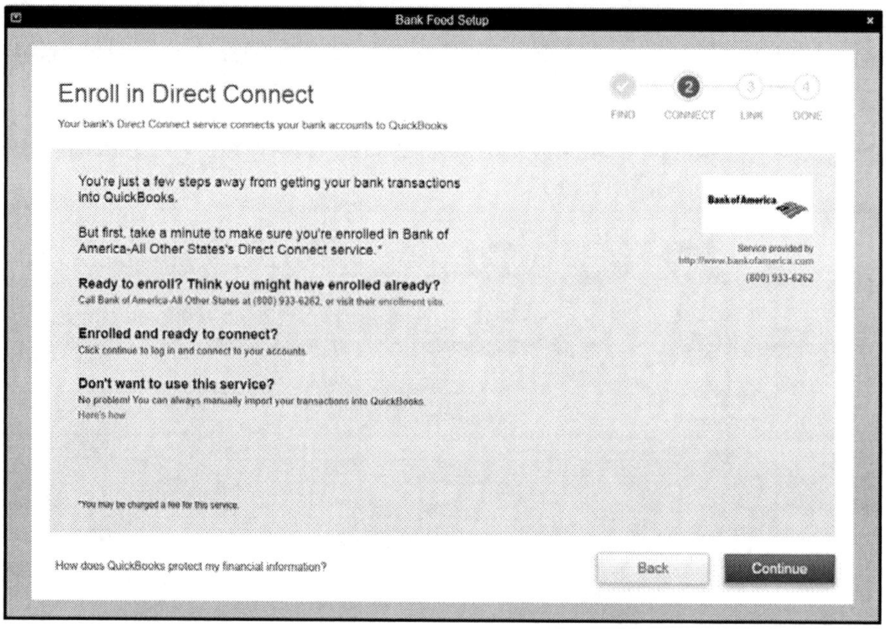

This screen informs you that for the selected bank, you can do one of the following:

- Login and automatically connect to your accounts. This option uses a direct connection to allowing you to download transactions from your bank. Quick-Books provides the contact information for the bank, a phone number and a link to their enrollment site, so that you can easily enroll in their connection services. After you have enrolled and received your logon credentials, you can return to QuickBooks to complete the connection process.

- Manually import your transactions into QuickBooks. For this option, you will need to access your bank's web site and login, locate the statement or transaction you want to import into QuickBooks, download the transactions to your desktop, and then open the downloaded file to manually import your transactions into QuickBooks.

In this exercise, you will click the Continue button to view the next screen for direct connection services.

4. Click **Continue**

Step 2 in the Bank Feed Setup window displays:

This step allows you to enter your bank's credentials in order to connect your bank to QuickBooks. This login information may be different from the credentials you use to sign in to your bank's web site.

Quick Tip. *The Online ID is the credential that you use, along with a passcode, to log in to your financial institution. Your financial institution may also call the Online ID a Customer ID, User ID, User Name, or something similar and the passcode may also be called a password or PIN or something similar.*

Note: *If you do not know your login or have problems logging in, you will need to return to the previous step and contact your bank for assistance.*

Because you do not have an Online ID or Passcode, you will not be able to complete the connection. When you set up bank feeds for your own accounts, you will you need to complete step 3 of the process, which involves selecting the bank accounts you can add to QuickBooks on the Link your Accounts screen of the Bank Feed Setup window.

When setting up your own company file, you can follow the on-screen instructions to activate online services for as many account types as necessary.

Quick Tip. *Click the Help button in the Set Up Account for Online Services window at any time for further information about online banking services and setting up bank feeds.*

5. Close the Bank Feed Setup window

6. Select   File : Close Company   to close the company file

Viewing, Downloading, and Adding Online Transactions

After your accounts are set up for bank feeds, you can view online account balances, download online transactions, and add or match them to transactions in QuickBooks, and create online transactions, such as writing online checks or transferring funds between accounts.

For the following exercises, you will use a QuickBooks sample file created by Intuit.

1. Open   B18_Sample.qbw   using the method described in Before You Get Started

Note: If a Warning dialog box displays with information about the Unit of Measure feature, click OK.

A QuickBooks Information dialog box displays:

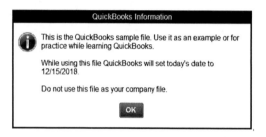

Note: If you are using QuickBooks Premier, your dialog box may be different.

This dialog box informs you that you are using a sample file for practice and while using this file, QuickBooks will set today's date to December 15, 2018.

2. Click   OK

The Home page for the sample file opens:

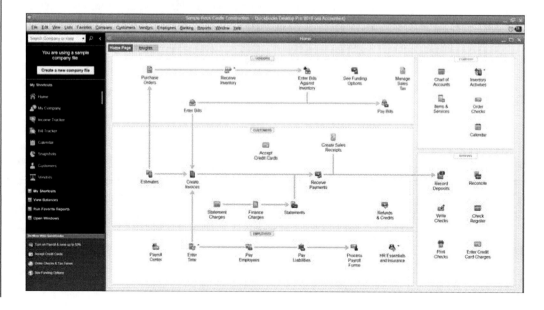

To view online account balances and online transactions,

3. Select   Banking : Bank Feeds : from the menu bar
                 Bank Feeds Center

Note: The Bank Feeds Center option will only be available when you have set up a bank feed for an account.

The Bank Feeds window opens:

Note: You may move or resize the Bank Feeds window as necessary.

The Bank Feeds window can be used to:

• View the most recent online balances for your banking accounts and compare them to your QuickBooks balances

• Download transactions that have cleared your financial institution

• View transactions after they are downloaded and match them to the ones in QuickBooks

• Create transactions to send to your financial institution

The list of bank accounts that have been set up for bank feeds displays in the Bank Accounts pane of the window. Both a QuickBooks Checking and a Savings account have been set up for bank feeds at ANYTIME Financial. The Savings account data for ANYTIME Financial is currently displayed in the window.

To download online transactions,

4. Click   Download Transactions

Because this is a sample QuickBooks file, a Warning dialog box displays:

This dialog box informs you that a sample company file is open, so you cannot use bank feeds. When you have your own company file open, transactions that are downloaded will display in your transaction list.

5. Click [OK] to close the Warning dialog box

After you download transactions, you need to match them to the ones in QuickBooks. Matching allows you to determine which transactions your financial institution has processed and which ones have not yet cleared. You can also tell if your financial institution has processed any transactions that have not yet been added to QuickBooks.

In this exercise, you will view the latest downloaded transactions in the sample file and match them to the transactions in QuickBooks.

To match downloaded transactions,

6. Click
ANYTIME Financial	$5,035.66
Account ending in ***1235	Over a year ago
In QuickBooks	
Checking	$46,969.10
CREDIT CARD	
in the Bank Accounts list

The Bank Feeds window is updated to display Checking account information:

7. Click [Transaction List]

The Transactions List window opens:

When you download transactions, QuickBooks tries to match the transactions to entries in your register automatically. If a match can't be found, QuickBooks tries to create register transactions using renaming rules.

You can use this window to review the downloaded transactions and matches before adding them to the register. Notice that there are 7 total transactions and 1 transaction has been matched to an existing QuickBooks transaction while 6 transactions are unmtached (QuickBooks could not match these to any existing transactions nor create them using renaming rules).

You will now match an unmatched transaction with a transaction in your QuickBooks check register.

8. Select   the check box for the
                   200.00 ATM Withdrawal

9. Click   in the Account field   for the ATM Withdrawal

A drop-down arrow displays.

10. Click   ▼   in the Account field for the ATM
                                                 Withdrawal

QuickBooks displays a drop-down menu of accounts to which you can assign the transaction:

11. Select   the 63000 - Office   from the Account drop-down menu
                  Supplies Expense   (scroll down)
                  account

12. Select   Match to Existing   from the Action drop-down menu
                  Transaction

The Transaction Details - Match to Existing Transaction window opens:

Because this is a sample company file, you will not be able to match the downloaded transaction to an existing transaction. When matching transactions in your company file, you would select the matching transaction from the list of Unmatched transactions in QuickBooks and click the Confirm Match button.

13. Click   [Cancel]   to return to the Transactions List

A Bank Feeds dialog box displays asking if you want to discard changes:

14. Click   [Yes]   to return to the Transactions List

In addition to matching transactions, you can complete a quick add for a an unmatched transaction.

15. Select   the check box for the   in the Transactions List
                  9.00 Bank Service
                  Charge

16. Click   in the Account field   for the Bank Service Charge

A drop-down arrow displays.

17. Select   the 60600 - Bank   from the Account drop-down
      Service Charges   menu for the Bank Service Charge
      Expense account   (scroll down)

18. Select   Quick Add   from the Actions drop-down menu

The Add Transactions dialog box displays:

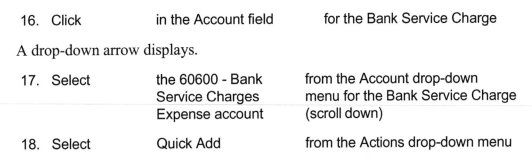

19. Click   [Delete Changes and Continue]

The selected transaction is added and no longer displays in the Transactions List.

20. Click   [⬅ Finish Later]   in the upper-left corner of the
      Transactions List window

A Save and Close dialog box displays:

> **Save and Close**
>
> Do you want QuickBooks to confirm all matched transactions to your register?
> Any unmatched transactions will be left in the workflow to process later.
>
> [Yes]   [No]

This dialog box asks if you want QuickBooks to confirm all matched transactions to your register and leave any unmatched transactions to process later.

21. Click   [Yes]   to confirm the transactions and
      leave the unmatched transactions

You return to the Bank Feeds window.

22. Close the Bank Feeds window

You can now view your checking account register to verify that the transactions have been added.

23. Select   Banking :   from the menu bar
      Use Register

The Use Register dialog box opens:

Use Register	✕
Select Account	10100 · Checking ▾
OK	Cancel

With the Checking account selected,

24. Click   OK

QuickBooks opens the Checking account register:

| | | | 10100 · Checking | | | | − □ ✕ |

◆ Go to... | 🖨 Print... | 📝 Edit Transaction | QuickReport | Download Transactions

DATE	NUMBER	PAYEE		PAYMENT	✔	DEPOSIT	BALANCE
	TYPE	ACCOUNT	MEMO				
12/15/2018	10079	Gregg O. Schneider		1,062.12			46,460.10
	PAY CHK	-split-					
12/15/2018	SEND					500.00	46,960.10
	TRANSFI	10300 · Savings					
2/15/2018 📅	Number	Payee ▾		Payment		Deposit	
		Account ▾	Memo				

Splits

☐ 1-Line

ENDING BALANCE   **46,960.10**

Sort by   Date, Type, Number/Ref ▾   Record   Restore

25. Scroll to the top of the register

At the top of the register, notice the lightening bolt ⚡ displayed next to the 9.00 service charge in the ✓ column. This indicates the transaction has cleared electronically.

26. Close the Checking account register

Creating Online Payments

When you have set up bank feeds with your financial institution, you can write checks and make online payments directly from within QuickBooks. Because you can pay bills without writing paper checks or going to the post office, it's fast and convenient. You can also schedule payments up to one year in advance, to be delivered on or before the date you specify.

To create online payments,

1. Click   Write Checks   in the Banking area of the Home page

The Write Checks - Checking window opens:

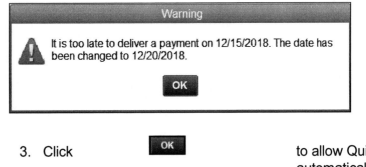

Notice that the Checking account is already selected in the Bank Account field.

2.	Select	the Pay Online check box	in the toolbar of the Write Checks - Checking window

A Warning dialog box displays informing you it is too late to deliver payment by the given date:

3.	Click	OK	to allow QuickBooks to automatically change the date

Quick Tip. *If this is the first time you are making an online payment, you need to allow a minimum of five business days for the delivery of your payment. If you select a date that is not a business day, QuickBooks will automatically enter the closest business date in the Delivery Date field.*

4.	Type	**ABC Telephone Company**	in the Pay to the Order of field
5.	Press	Tab	

A Name Not Found dialog box opens:

You cannot use Quick Add for an online payment. You must complete the setup for ABC Telephone Company in QuickBooks.

6. Click   Set Up

The Select Name Type window opens:

You will accept the default selection of Vendor.

7. Click   OK

The New Vendor window opens:

Notice that ABC Telephone Company already displays in the Vendor Name field.

8. Type **ABC Telephone Company** in the Company Name field

9. Type **Justin M Sullivan** in the First, M.I. and Last fields

10. Type **555-555-5555** in the Main Phone field

11. Type **123 Culver Street Fairgrave, NY 11111** below Justin M Sullivan in the Billed From Address field

The New Vendor window should resemble the figure below:

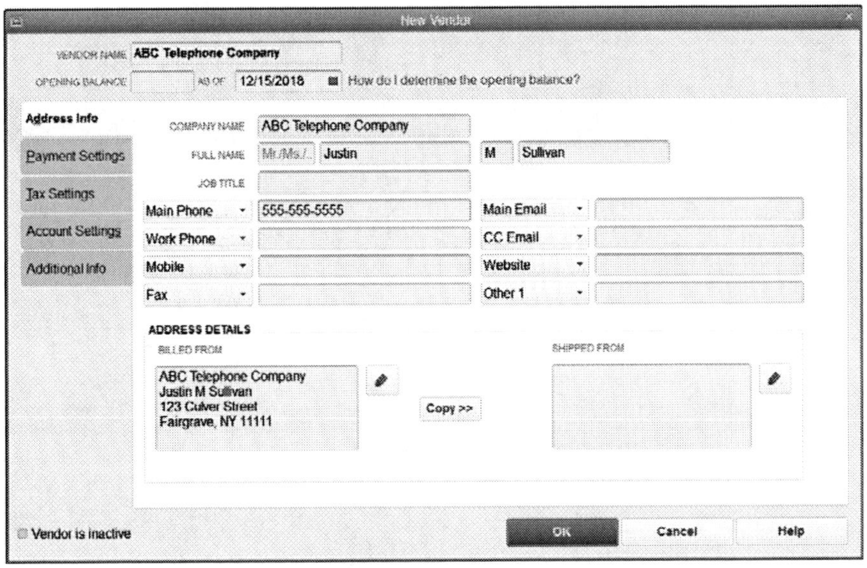

12. Click [Payment Settings]

The Payment Settings tab displays:

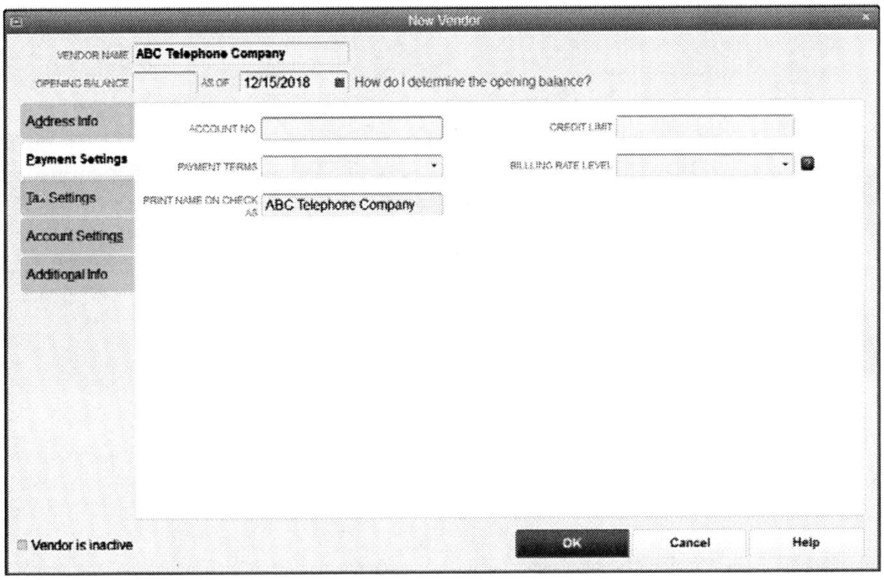

The cursor is automatically positioned in the Account No. field.

13. Type **54321** in the Account No. field

14. Click [OK]

The Write Checks - Checking window opens:

QuickBooks fills in the Send As field with the address of ABC Telephone Company and adds the account number to the check. Because you selected the Pay Online check box, the No. field at the top of the window says SEND.

Note: Your financial institution's logo may display on the check, depending upon the financial institution you use.

15. Type **52.36** in the $ field

16. Click in the first Account field on the Expenses tab at the bottom of the window

17. Click [▾] in the Account field

A drop-down menu displays.

18. Select 65120 - Telephone, below Utilities from the drop-down menu (scroll down)

The Write Checks - Checking window should resemble the figure below:

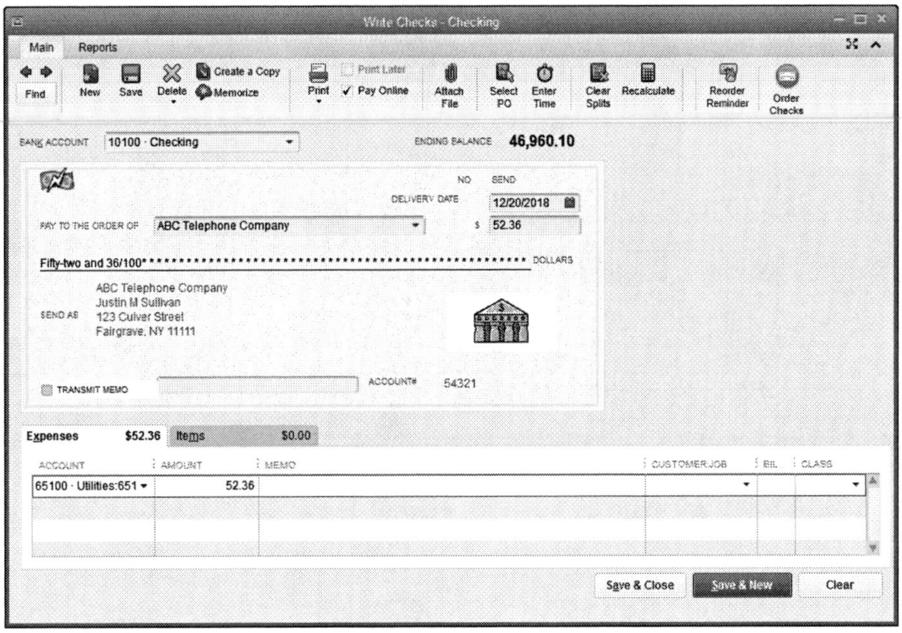

19. Click   [Save & Close]   to return to the Home page

An Online Payment dialog box displays:

20. Select   Do not display this
              message in the future

21. Click   [OK]   to return to the Home page

Because this is a sample company file, you will not be able to go online and submit this payment. If you were submitting an online payment using your own company file, you would open the Bank Feeds window and click the Send Items button to connect to your financial institution and transmit the payment.

Transferring Funds Online

You may want to transfer funds from one account to another using your online banking connection.

To transfer funds online,

1. Select   Banking :   from the menu bar
             Transfer Funds

The Transfer Funds Between Accounts window opens:

2. Select   10100 - Checking   from the Transfer Funds From from drop-down menu

3. Select   10300 - Savings   from the Transfer Funds To drop-down menu

4. Type   **200**   in the Transfer Amount field

5. Select   the Online Funds Transfer check box

The Transfer Funds Between Accounts window is updated for an online transfer:

6. Click   Save & Close

Because this is a sample file, the following Warning dialog box displays:

Quick Fix. *When working in your own company file, if you receive this message or any other message while performing online banking tasks, click the OK button and refer to the QuickBooks Desktop Help for further information about bank feeds.*

7. Click **OK** to close the Warning dialog box

To send the transfer to your financial institution,

8. Select **Banking :** from the menu bar
   Bank Feeds :
   Bank Feeds Center

The Bank Feeds window opens:

The transfer displays in the Send items to your bank area.

9. Click _____ in the Bank Accounts list

The Bank Feeds window is updated to display transactions for the ANYTIME Financial Checking Account:

In the Send items to your bank area, QuickBooks lists the two items ready to send for the checking account - the online check and the transfer.

10. Click   Transfers (1 of 1)   in the Send items to your bank area

The Funds Transfers To Be Sent window opens:

This window displays all online transfers ready to be sent.

11. Click   OK   to return to the Bank Feeds window

To transfer the funds electronically, you must go online and connect to your financial institution.

12. Click   Send Items

A Warning dialog box displays:

> **Warning**
>
> Problem: You cannot use online banking because a sample company file is open. Solution: Go to the File menu and click Close Company to close the sample company file. Then, in the No Company Open window, locate your company file and click the Open button.
>
> OK

Because this is a sample company file, you will not be able to go online and transfer the funds.

13. Click   OK   to close the Warning dialog box

When you have completed reading through the Canceling Online Payments section, close the Bank Feeds window and the sample company file.

Canceling Online Payments

When you create an online payment, you include a delivery date. Because your financial institution does not process the payment until that delivery date, there may be a short period of time where you can cancel a payment instruction even after it has been sent to the financial institution.

Note: You will not be able to cancel a payment unless you have actually sent an instruction to your bank setting up that payment. Therefore, you cannot actually perform the steps in this exercise using the sample file.

To cancel an online payment,

1. Select | Cancel Payments | from the Create New drop-down menu in the Items ready to send area

All online transactions that have been sent are displayed.

2. Click | the Send check box | for the online payment transaction you want to cancel

3. Click | the Close button

The Items ready to send area of the window will now display one cancelled payment. The next time you send transactions, the cancellation will be sent to the financial institution.

Caution. Canceling a payment instruction is not the same as stopping a payment. It does not stop payment when the payment has already been processed. To stop a payment, you will need to contact your financial institution.

4. Close the Bank Feeds window and the company file

Review

In this appendix, you have learned how to:

- ☑ Set up an Internet connection
- ☑ Set up bank feeds for accounts
- ☑ View, download, and add online transactions
- ☑ Create online payments
- ☑ Transfer funds online
- ☑ Cancel online payments

Practice: None

B | Managing Company Files

In this appendix, you will learn how to:

- ❑ Use QuickBooks in multi-user mode
- ❑ Set up users and passwords
- ❑ Set a closing date
- ❑ Share files with an accountant
- ❑ Update QuickBooks
- ❑ Back up and restore a company file
- ❑ Condense a company file

Concept

QuickBooks provides many features that allow you to maintain and manage your company files. For example, if you have multiple people on a network that need to work simultaneously in the same company file, you can open the file in multi-user mode and set up the users who need access to the file. To protect your data, you can set up an administrator with a password, as well as passwords for the individual users. When it's time to close your books, you can set a closing date to identify the specific date when your company's books were closed. Setting a password with this closing date prevents transactions from being modified within the closed period. QuickBooks also includes a feature that allows you to save a copy of your company file and share it with your accountant. And, in addition to being able to easily update QuickBooks with the latest software enhancements, you can back up and restore company files, and even condense a company file.

Scenario

In this appendix, you will learn how to set up QuickBooks in multi-user mode and how to set up users and passwords. You will also learn how to set a company closing date and how to share files with an accountant, including saving an Accountant's Copy of your company file, importing an accountant's changes back into your company file, removing Accountant's Copy restrictions from your company file, and sending a copy of your company file directly to your accountant. Finally, you will learn how to update QuickBooks, back up and restore a company file, and condense a company file.

Practice Files: B18_Managing_Company_Files.qbw

Using QuickBooks in Multi-User Mode

Multi-user mode allows multiple people on a network to work in a QuickBooks company file at the same time. For example, a business owner may use QuickBooks and may also want their assistant, office manager, and payroll manager to have access to the QuickBooks company file. In this mode, every user of QuickBooks on a network must have a separate licensed copy of QuickBooks installed on his or her computer.

Note: You must set your computer to the current date before opening the QuickBooks file in order to successfully complete the exercises in this lesson.

To open a QuickBooks file in multi-user mode,

1. Select   File : Open or Restore   from the QuickBooks menu bar
                     Company

The Open or Restore Company window opens:

Open or Restore Company   ✕

What type of file do you want to open or restore?

◉ Open a **c**ompany file
   • Open a regular company file (.qbw)

○ Restore a bac**k**up copy
   • Restore a backup file (.qbb)
   • Restore files from an online backup

○ Restore a portable file
   • Re-create a company file that was stored as a portable file (.qbm)

   Back   Next   Finish   Help   Cancel

Note: If you are using the QuickBooks Premier version, the Open or Restore Company window may display an additional option to Convert an Accountant's Copy Transfer file.

2. Verify that Open a company file is selected

3. Click   Next

The Open a Company window displays:

Note: If the Books2018 folder does not display, click the Browse button and navigate to the folder.

4.	Select	B18_Managing Company_Files	from the list of files
5.	Select	the Open file in multi-user mode check box	
6.	Click	Open	

The QuickBooks Login dialog box displays:

QuickBooks Login ✕

You need to log in as QuickBooks Administrator to proceed. Please enter the admin (owner) password for the company:

Canalside Corp.

Password: _____ I forgot my password

Passwords are case sensitive.

OK   Cancel   Help

This dialog box informs you that you must login as a QuickBooks Administrator in order to open the company file.

7.	Type	**Canalside2**	in the Password field

Note: Passwords are case-sensitive.

8.	Click	OK

Note: A multi-user hosting dialog box may display if this is the first time you are setting up your computer for multi-user access. This dialog box informs you that QuickBooks must set up this computer to host multi-user access. By clicking the Yes button, you are allowing other users to open company files located on this computer, as long as they have valid user names and passwords. If this dialog box does display, click Yes. When the Set up multiple users dialog box displays, click OK.

QuickBooks opens the file and displays the Create New Users dialog box:

Create New Users

You have opened the company file in multi-user mode. For additional users to access this company file, you must first set them up as users.

Do you want to set up users now?

☐ Do not display this message in the future

Yes   No

This dialog box informs you that you have opened the company file in multi-user mode and asks if you want to set up additional users now. You will be setting up users and passwords in the next exercise, so you will close this dialog box.

9. Select   the Do not display this message in the future check box

10. Click   No

QuickBooks displays the Home page:

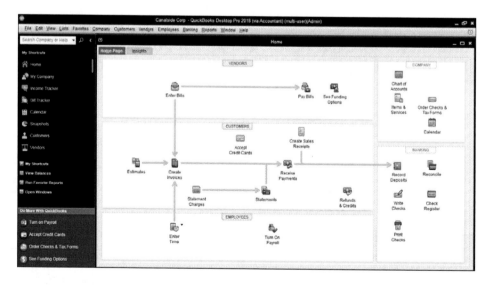

When you open a file in multi-user mode, (multi-user)(Admin) displays in the Title bar after the QuickBooks software version.

Note: For further information about multi-user mode, including installation instructions, refer to the QuickBooks Desktop Help.

Setting Up Users and Passwords

To use QuickBooks multi-user mode, you must set up an administrator for your QuickBooks file. The administrator must then set up the users who will use QuickBooks on the network.

To keep your company data safe, QuickBooks strongly recommends setting up an administrator password, as well as passwords for any other users that will have access to your company file.

To set up users and passwords,

1. Select   Company : Set Up   from the menu bar
                             Users and Passwords:
                             Set Up Users

The QuickBooks Desktop Login dialog box displays:

```
┌─────────────────────────────────────────────────┐
│            QuickBooks Desktop Login          ✖   │
├─────────────────────────────────────────────────┤
│  You need to log in as QuickBooks Desktop        │
│  Administrator to proceed.  Please enter the     │
│  admin (owner) password for the company:         │
│                                                  │
│       Password: [                            ]   │
│              Passwords are case sensitive.       │
│                                                  │
│     [   OK   ]   [  Cancel  ]   [   Help   ]     │
└─────────────────────────────────────────────────┘
```

This dialog box informs you that you must login as a QuickBooks Desktop Administrator in order to open the company file.

2. Type   **Canalside2**   in the Password field

Note: Passwords are case-sensitive.

3. Click   [OK]

The User List window opens:

```
┌─────────────────────────────────────────────────┐
│                  User List                   ✖   │
├─────────────────────────────────────────────────┤
│  ┌──────────────────────────┐   [  Add User... ] │
│  │ Admin (logged on)        │                    │
│  │                          │   [  Edit User... ]│
│  │                          │                    │
│  │                          │   [ Delete User  ] │
│  │                          │                    │
│  │                          │   [  View User   ] │
│  │                          │                    │
│  │                          │   [   Close      ] │
│  └──────────────────────────┘                    │
│  Set the closing date: [Closing Date...] [ Help ]│
└─────────────────────────────────────────────────┘
```

This window allows you to add, edit, and delete users, as well as view the areas of QuickBooks a user can access. Notice that QuickBooks has automatically added an Administrator (Admin) to the User List.

To edit the administrator settings,

4. Click   Edit User...

The Change user password and access window opens:

Change user password and access

Admin Name and Password

Provide a name and an optional password for this user.

User Name: Admin

Password: ●●●●●●●●

Confirm Password: ●●●●●●●●

Select a challenge question and enter answer.

How will this help me recover my password?

Challenge Question: Name of oldest nephew ▼

Challenge Answer: ●●●●●●●●

Back   Next   Finish   Help   Cancel

From this window, you can set up a user name and password. You are the administrator of this file, so you will leave the default of Admin in the User Name field.

5. Type   **\<a password\>**   in the Password field

6. Retype   **\<the password\>**   in the Confirm Password field

7. Select   [a question]   from the Challenge Question drop-down menu

8. Type   **[the answer to the**   in the Challenge Answer field
              challenge question]

If you forget your administrator password or want to reset it, QuickBooks will ask you for the answer to the challenge question to prove your identity.

9. Click

The next screen in the Change user password and access window displays:

```
┌─────────────────────────────────────────────────────────────────┐
│              Change user password and access                  ✗  │
├─────────────────────────────────────────────────────────────────┤
│ ┌──────┐                                                         │
│ │Tracking│                                                       │
│ │Banking │   The QuickBooks Administrator has access to all areas in QuickBooks.  This │
│ │Reports │   user's access cannot be modified.                   │
│ │PASSWORD│                                                        │
│ │ ★★★★  │   Click the Finish button to save your changes or the Cancel button to exit without │
│ │  ⚷    │   saving.                                              │
│ └──────┘                                                         │
│                                                                  │
│                                                                  │
│                                                                  │
│                                                                  │
│                                                                  │
│   ┌────────┐   ┌────────┐   ┌──────────┐          ┌──────────┐  │
│   │  Back  │   │  Next  │   │  Finish  │          │  Cancel  │  │
│   └────────┘   └────────┘   └──────────┘          └──────────┘  │
└─────────────────────────────────────────────────────────────────┘
```

This window informs you that, as the QuickBooks administrator, you have access to all areas of QuickBooks and your access cannot be modified.

10. Click   [Finish]   to save your settings

Note: You should also set up an administrator password for company files used in single-user mode.

The User List window displays:

```
┌─────────────────────────────────────────────────────┐
│                    User List                     ✗   │
├─────────────────────────────────────────────────────┤
│ ┌─────────────────────────────┐   ┌──────────────┐  │
│ │ Admin (logged on)           │   │  Add User... │  │
│ │                             │   └──────────────┘  │
│ │                             │   ┌──────────────┐  │
│ │                             │   │  Edit User...│  │
│ │                             │   └──────────────┘  │
│ │                             │   ┌──────────────┐  │
│ │                             │   │  Delete User │  │
│ │                             │   └──────────────┘  │
│ │                             │   ┌──────────────┐  │
│ │                             │   │  View User   │  │
│ │                             │   └──────────────┘  │
│ │                             │   ┌──────────────┐  │
│ │                             │   │    Close     │  │
│ └─────────────────────────────┘   └──────────────┘  │
│ Set the closing date:  [Closing Date...]  ┌────────┐│
│                                           │  Help  ││
│                                           └────────┘│
└─────────────────────────────────────────────────────┘
```

Now, you need to set up the users who will use this QuickBooks file on the network.

11. Click   [Add User...]   in the User List window

The first Set up user password and access screen opens:

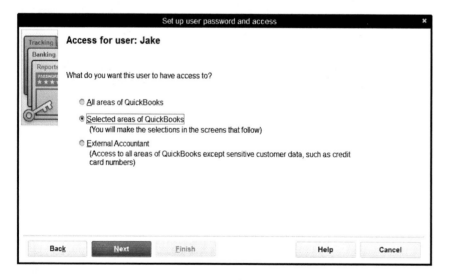

12.	Type	**Jake**	in the User Name field
13.	Type	**[a password]**	in the Password field
14.	Retype	**[the password]**	in the Confirm Password field
15.	Click	Next	

The next Set up user password and access screen displays:

This screen allows you to grant the user access to all areas of QuickBooks or only selected areas of QuickBooks. You also have the option to provide external accountant-level access, which allows the user to access all areas of QuickBooks except sensitive customer data.

| 16. | Select | All areas of QuickBooks |
| 17. | Click | Next |

A Warning dialog box displays asking you if you are sure you want to give Jake access to all areas of QuickBooks, including payroll, check writing, customer credit card numbers, and other sensitive information:

Warning
⚠ Are you sure you want to give Jake access to all areas of QuickBooks, including payroll, check writing, customer credit card numbers, and other sensitive information?
Yes   **No**

18. Click

The next Set up user password and access screen displays, displaying a summary of the areas to which Jake now has access:

Set up user password and access			✕
Access for user: Jake			Page 1 of 1
You have finished setting this user's access rights and password. Below is a summary of this user's access rights. Click the Finish button to complete this task.			

AREA	CREATE	PRINT	REP...
Sales and Accounts Receivable	Y	Y	Y
Purchases and Accounts Payable	Y	Y	Y
Checking and Credit Cards	Y	Y	n/a
Inventory	Y	Y	Y
Payroll and Employees	Y	Y	Y
Sensitive Accounting Activities	Y	Y	Y
Sensitive Financial Reports	Y	Y	n/a

Back   Next   **Finish**   Help   Cancel

If you chose to allow access to only selected areas, QuickBooks provides additional screens from which you may choose the level of access for your QuickBooks network user, including a final screen summarizing your choices. You may assign access levels in the following areas:

- Sales and Accounts Receivable

- Purchases and Accounts Payable

- Checking and Credit Cards

- Time Tracking

- Payroll and Employees

- Sensitive Accounting Activities

- Sensitive Financial Reports

- Changing or Deleting Transactions

- Changing Closed Transactions

19. Click [**Finish**]

The User List window displays:

User List	✕
Admin (logged on)	Add User...
Jake	Edit User...
	Delete User
	View User
	Close
Set the closing date: [Closing Date...]	Help

Jake has been added to the User List. You can follow the same procedure to add as many licensed network users as necessary.

20. Click [**Close**] to close the User List window

Setting a Closing Date

When it's time for you to close your books, you will want to set a closing date. A closing date identifies specifically when your company's books have been closed. A closing date allows you to restrict access to data from the prior accounting period by setting a password. This prevents transactions from being changed without you being aware, because in order to modify or delete a transaction in a closed period, a user must know the closing date password and have the appropriate permissions.

Caution. *You should always discuss your closing date with your accountant prior to setting it. You should also consult with your accountant for more information about making changes that affect closed periods.*

You cannot set a closing date when a file is open in multi-user mode. Therefore, in order to complete this exercise, you will first switch the file to single-user mode.

To switch the file to single-user mode,

1. Select   File : Switch to   from the menu bar
                 Single-user Mode

A QuickBooks dialog box displays indicating you are now in single-user mode:

2. Click

The file opens in single-user mode.

Quick Tip. *When a file is open in single-user mode, you can switch to multi-user mode by selecting File : Switch to Multi-user Mode from the menu bar.*

3. Select Company : Set from the menu bar
          Closing Date

The Preferences window opens displaying the Company Preferences tab of the Accounting category:

Preferences

| Accounting | My Preferences | **Company Preferences** | OK |

ACCOUNTS
☐ Use account numbers ☑ Require accounts
☐ Show lowest subaccount only

Cancel
Help
Default

CLASS
☐ Use class tracking for transactions
☐ Prompt to assign classes

Also See:
General
Payroll and Employees

☑ Automatically assign general journal entry number
☑ Warn when posting a transaction to Retained Earnings
DATE WARNINGS
☑ Warn if transactions are 90 day(s) in the past
☑ Warn if transactions are 30 day(s) in the future

CLOSING DATE
Date through which books are closed: (not set)

Set Date/Password

Left sidebar list: Bills, Calendar, Checking, Desktop View, Finance Charge, General, Integrated Applications, Items & Inventory, Jobs & Estimates, Multiple Currencies, Payments, Payroll & Employees, Reminders, Reports & Graphs, Sales & Customers, Sales Tax, Search, Send Forms, Service Connection, Spelling

4. Click   **Set Date/Password**   in the Closing Date section

The Set Closing Date and Password window opens:

Set Closing Date and Password

To keep your financial data secure, QuickBooks recommends assigning all other users their own username and password, in Company > Set Up Users.

DATE
QuickBooks will display a warning, or require a password, when saving a transaction dated on or before the closing date. More details...

☐ Exclude estimates, sales orders and purchase orders from closing date restrictions

Closing Date [   ] 📅

PASSWORD
QuickBooks strongly recommends setting a password to protect transactions dated on or before the closing date.

Closing Date Password [   ]
Confirm Password [   ]

OK   Cancel

You now need to enter the closing date through which you want your books to be closed. Typical closing dates are the end of the prior month, quarter, or year.

5. Type **[the last day of the** in the Closing Date field
previous month in
mm/dd/yyyy format]

You can also limit access to the closed accounting period by setting a closing date password. If you decide to set a password, QuickBooks requires the password for any changes that would alter balances for the accounting period you have closed. This includes adding, editing, or deleting transactions dated on or before the closing date.

6. Press Tab to move to the Closing Date Password field

7. Type **[a password]** in the Closing Date Password field

8. Press Tab to move to the Confirm Password field

9. Retype **[the password]** in the Confirm Password field

Note: The closing date password can be different from the Administrator password.

10. Click OK

The closing date now displays in the Closing Date section of the Preferences window:

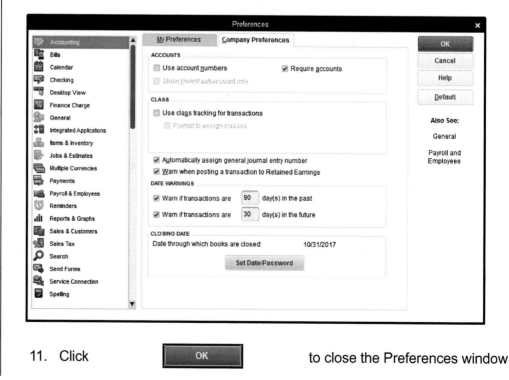

11. Click OK to close the Preferences window

Sharing Files with an Accountant

QuickBooks includes a feature that allows you to easily save a copy of your company file and share it with your accountant. This version of your company file is known as an Accountant's Copy. An Accountant's Copy is designed for your accountant to do end-of-the-year work on your books. It is different from creating a backup file for your accountant, because you can continue working in your company file while your accountant is working in the Accountant's Copy. When your accountant's work is complete, they send you an Accountant's Copy change file, and you automatically import their changes into your company file.

Saving an Accountant's Copy

An Accountant's Copy is a saved version of your company file that you can share with your accountant. QuickBooks allows you to easily create an Accountant's Copy in a few simple steps. After you have created an Accountant's Copy, you can deliver it to your accountant using any method you prefer, such as via e-mail or on a USB drive. Your accountant can make changes to the Accountant's Copy, while at the same time, you can continue to work in your company file.

Note: You must be in single-user mode to save an accountant's copy.

To save an Accountant's Copy,

1. Select   File : Send Company   from the menu bar
   File : Accountants
   Copy : Save File

Note: Depending on the version of QuickBooks you are using, you may need to select File : Send Company File: Accountant's Copy : Client Activities : Save File.

The Save Accountant's Copy window opens:

This window explains the differences between an Accountant's Copy and a portable or backup file.

Caution. *If your accountant needs to set up your books, perform daily bookkeeping tasks, or work on payroll, it may be better to create a portable or backup file, rather than an Accountant's Copy because creating an accountant's copy will require you to stop working in your company file and manually enter changes from your accountant at a later date.*

To confirm you want to save an Accountant's Copy,

2. Click   

The next Save Accountant's Copy window displays:

Save Accountant's Copy

Set the dividing date

Set the date that divides the transactions that you can change from the ones your accountant can change. Please discuss a suitable date with your accountant.

Your company file

You can view, but not change transactions	You work on transactions dated **after** dividing date

Accountant's copy of your company file

Your accountant works **on or before** dividing date	Accountant can view, but not change transactions

Before   *After*

Dividing Date

Back	Next		Help	Cancel

When you save an Accountant's Copy, you must choose a dividing date. The dividing date determines the fiscal period your accountant can work on. After an Accountant's Copy is created, your accountant works with transactions dated on or before the dividing date, while you continue to work with transactions dated after the dividing date.

It is recommended that you consult with your accountant when choosing a dividing date. Generally, an appropriate dividing date to choose is one that is a couple of weeks following the last day of the fiscal period, such as the end of the year or the end of a quarter. This will allow your accountant to move transactions between periods.

Caution. *Although you will be able to view transactions dated on or before the dividing date, you will not be able to make changes to those transactions. Your accountant will be able to view transactions dated after the dividing date, but they will not be able to make changes to those transactions.*

3. Click   ▼   in the Dividing Date field

A drop-down menu of dividing dates displays:

End of Last Month
2 Weeks Ago
4 weeks Ago
Custom

QuickBooks includes three pre-defined dividing dates you can choose from: End of Last Month, 2 Weeks Ago, and 4 Weeks Ago, There is also a Custom option, which allows you to enter a specific date.

4. Select   End of Last Month   from the drop-down menu

5. Click   `Next`

A Close All Windows dialog box displays informing you that QuickBooks must close all windows to create an Accountant's Copy:

Close All Windows

⚠ QuickBooks must close all windows to create an Accountant's Copy.

`OK`   `Cancel`

6. Click   `OK`

The Save Accountant's Copy window opens:

Save Accountant's Copy ✖

Save in:	Books2018	▾

Name	Type	Size
	No items match your search.	

Recent Places

Desktop

Libraries

Computer

Network

File name:	looks2018 Acct Transfer Nov 18,2017 10 30 PM).QBX ▾	Save
Save as type:	QuickBooks Accountant's Copy Transfer Files (*.QBX) ▾	Cancel
		Help

The Save Accountant's Copy window is similar to the Save As window in that it allows you to specify a name and location for your Accountant's Copy on your computer. By default, QuickBooks names the new file using the company file name, along with the date and time and the required .QBX extension.

Note: If the Books2018 folder does not display, click the drop-down arrow in the Save in field and navigate to the folder.

You will accept the suggested file name and directory settings.

7. Click | Save |

A Create Accountant's Copy dialog box displays while the file is saved. When the process is complete, an Accountant's Copy Created dialog box displays:

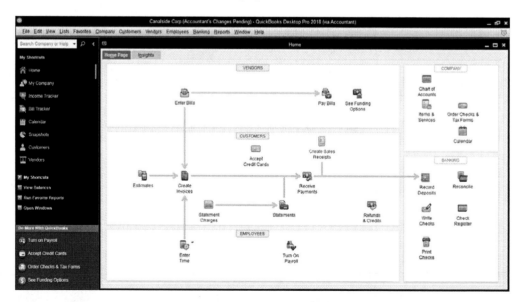

This dialog box informs you that you have successfully created an Accountant's Copy file, which has been saved to the specified folder (in this example, the Books2018 folder). Your next step would be to deliver this file to your accountant.

8. Click | OK |

You return to the QuickBooks home page:

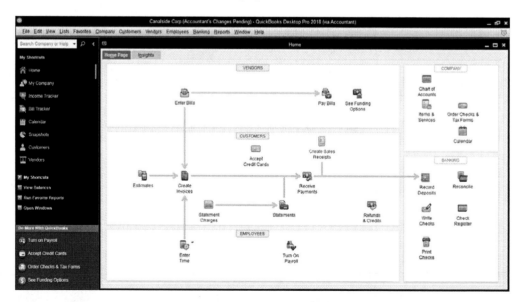

Notice that "Accountant's Changes Pending" displays in the title bar. This indicates you are working in a file with an Accountant's Copy.

You can now provide your accountant with the Accountant's Copy (.QBX file) using any method you prefer, such as via e-mail, disk, or FTP server.

Although you can continue to work in your company file after providing your accountant with an Accountant's Copy, there are limitations to what you can do after creating the copy.

While your accountant is working with the Accountant's Copy, you can continue to work in the current period (after the dividing date). To prevent your work from conflicting with your accountant's work:

- You can work only on transactions dated after the dividing date.

- You can add a new account, but you cannot add a new subaccount to an existing account. Also, you cannot edit, merge, or inactivate an existing account. However, you can edit or inactivate new accounts you create while your accountant has the Accountant's Copy.

- You can edit, inactivate, and sort list items (other than in the Chart of Accounts). You cannot delete or merge list items.

- You can reconcile your accounts. All reconciliations that include transactions in the current period (after the dividing date) will be saved. However, to prevent conflicts with your accountant's changes, reconciliations that include transactions dated on or before the dividing date will be undone when you import your accountant's changes. Also, if your accountant has reconciled or undone a reconciliation for any period, any reconciliation you have completed will be undone when you import your accountant's changes.

Importing an Accountant's Changes

After you provide your accountant with an Accountant's Copy, they can make any necessary changes to the file. When their work is complete, the accountant will save their changes to an Accountant's Copy change file (.QBY file) and send the change file back to you. You can then use this file to review and import your accountant's changes into your company file.

An accountant can send you an Accountant's Copy change file:

- Via the Web. When this occurs, you will receive an e-mail from your accountant informing you they have sent changes for you to import. You then have 30 days to download the changes from the Intuit Web server.

- Using another method, such as e-mailing the file.

Quick Tip. *It is recommended that you print a copy of your accountant's changes or save them to a PDF file, so that you have a record of the changes.*

In this exercise, you will assume the accountant has provided you with an Accountant's Copy change file on an external device, rather then the web.

1. Select   File : Send Company   from the menu bar
   File : Accountants Copy :
   Import Accountant's
   Changes from File

Note: Depending on the version of QuickBooks you are using, you may need to select File : Send Company File: Accountant's Copy : Client Activities : Import Accountant's Changes from File.

Note: You must have an Accountant's Copy file open to select the Import Accountant's Changes menu option.

The Import Accountant's Changes window opens:

	Import Accountant's Changes		✖
Look in:	📁 Books2018 ▼ 📀 📁 📄 📰▼		
	Name ▲	Type	Size
Recent Places	No items match your search.		
Desktop			
Libraries			
Computer			
Network	◀ ▶		
	File name:	*.QBY ▼	Open
	Files of type:	QuickBooks Accountant Change Files(*.QBY) ▼	Cancel
			Help

Note: If you set up your company file with an Administrator, only the Administrator will be able to import an accountant's changes.

From this window, you would locate the Accountant's Copy change file (.QBY file) and click the Open button. For this lesson, you will not import an accountant's changes.

2. Click   Cancel   to close the Import Accountant's Changes window

When you import an accountant's changes into your own company file, you will be able to review all changes prior to importing them. If any of your accountant's changes conflict with work you've done since saving the Accountant's Copy, a message will display below the change with an explanation of what to do. After reviewing the changes, you can choose whether or not to import the changes.

Note: If you choose not to import an accountant's changes, you will have to remove the Accountant's Copy restrictions and enter any changes manually. You should check with your accountant before you decide not to import the changes.

Quick Tip. *When importing an accountant's changes into your own company file, refer to the QuickBooks Help for step-by-step instructions.*

Removing Accountant's Copy Restrictions

If you find using an Accountant's Copy is not suitable for you, you have the ability to remove Accountant's Copy restrictions and continue to work as if you did not create an Accountant's Copy. However, if your accountant continues to work with the Accountant's Copy, you will not be able to import their changes. Rather, you will have to manually enter any changes made by your accountant.

Caution. You should always consult with your accountant before you remove restrictions from an Accountant's Copy. You and your accountant will no longer be able to work independently, so be sure you coordinate with them on which of you has the main copy of the company file prior to removing restrictions.

To remove Accountant's Copy restrictions,

1. Select   File : Send Company   from the menu bar
                      File : Accountant's
                      Copy : Remove Restrictions

Note: Depending on the version of QuickBooks you are using, you may need to select File : Send Company File: Accountant's Copy : Client Activities : Remove Restrictions.

A Remove Restrictions dialog box displays:

Remove Restrictions   ✕

⚠ Doing this will remove the restrictions on your file that prevent you from editing transactions dated on or before 10/31/2017

However, if your accountant sends you a file of changes, you will **NOT** be able to import the changes into this QuickBooks file. You will need to get a listing of the changes and enter them manually.
Please discuss this with your accountant before proceeding.

☐ Yes, I want to remove the Accountant's Copy restrictions.

[OK]   [Cancel]   [Help]

---

2. Select   Yes, I want to remove
               the Accountant's Copy restrictions

3. Click   [OK]

The Accountant's Copy restrictions are removed. Notice that "Accountant's Changes Pending" no longer displays in the title bar.

Using the Accountant's Copy File Transfer Service

If you have Internet access and an e-mail address for your accountant, you can send an Accountant's Copy directly to your accountant using Intuit's Copy File Transfer service. With this feature, you don't have to save the Accountant's Copy to your computer and then deliver it to your accountant. Instead, your Accountant's Copy is automatically sent to an Intuit server. Your accountant will receive an e-mail notification with a link to automatically download your file.

Note: You must have Microsoft® Internet Explorer® installed on your computer and an Internet connection to complete this exercise. It is also recommended that you have a working e-mail address. In addition, if you did not remove the Accountant's Copy restrictions as instructed in the previous exercise, you will not be able to use the Accountant's Copy File Transfer service.

1. Select   File : Send Company   from the menu bar
                             File : Accountants
                             Copy : Send to Accountant

Note: Depending on the version of QuickBooks you are using, you may need to select File : Send Company File: Accountant's Copy : Client Activities : Send to Accountant.

The Send Accountant's Copy window opens:

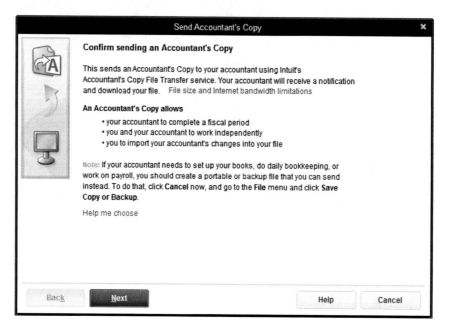

The Send Accountant's Copy window displays information about using the Accountant's Copy File Transfer service.

Caution. In order to use the Accountant's Copy File Transfer service, your company file must be under 200 MB. Also, a dial-up connection may be too slow to send your file over the Internet. If you are using a dial-up connection or your company file is over 200 MB, you will need to save your Accountant's Copy to your computer and deliver it to your accountant using another method, such as via a USB drive. Click the File size and Internet bandwidth limitations link in this window for further information on how to troubleshoot problems when sending an accountants copy.

To confirm you want to send an Accountant's Copy,

2. Click   [Next]

The next Send Accountant's Copy window displays:

As mentioned previously, when you create an Accountant's Copy to send, you must set a dividing date. You work with transactions dated after the dividing date, and your accountant works with transactions dated on or before the dividing date.

3. Select   End of Last Month   from the Dividing Date drop-down menu

4. Click   **Next**

The next Send Accountant's Copy window displays:

On this window, you enter your accountant's e-mail address, as well as your name and e-mail address. For this exercise, you will use your personal e-mail address.

Note: If you do not have a working e-mail address, you may enter a fictitious one.

5. Type   **[your e-mail address]**   in the Accountant's e-mail address field

To confirm the e-mail address is correct,

6. Retype   **[your e-mail address]**   in the Reenter the accountant's e-mail address field

QuickBooks will send your Accountant's Copy to this e-mail address.

7. Type   **[your name]**   in the Your name field

This allows your accountant to identify who has sent the Accountant's Copy.

8. Type   **[a secondary e-mail address]**   in the Your e-mail address field to replace the canalsidecorp@email.com text

This enables you to receive a confirmation e-mail when the Accountant's Copy is successfully uploaded to the Intuit server.

Note: If you do not have a second e-mail address to use, you can leave canalsidecorp@email.com in the Your e-mail address field.

9. Click   [Next]

The next Send Accountant's Copy window displays:

This window allows you to enter a file transfer password for security purposes. Your accountant will use this password to access the Accountant's Copy.

Note: Passwords are case-sensitive and must be at least seven characters in length. At least one character must be an uppercase letter and at least one character must be a number. You will receive a warning message if your password is not a strong password and you will then have to enter another password.

10.	Type	**[a password]**	in the Create file transfer password to encrypt file for security field
11.	Retype	**[the password]**	in the Reenter password field
12.	Click	Send	

A Close All Windows dialog box displays:

> **Close All Windows**
>
> ⚠ QuickBooks must close all windows to create an Accountant's Copy.
>
> [OK] [Cancel]

13.	Click	OK	to close all windows

A Create Accountant's Copy dialog box and a Sending QBX Transfer File dialog box display while the file is being uploaded to the Intuit Accountant's Copy File Transfer server. When the file has been successfully uploaded, a Send Accountant's Copy dialog box displays:

> **Send Accountant's Copy**
>
> ⓘ Your Accountant's Copy file has been successfully uploaded to the Intuit Accountant's Copy File Transfer server. Your accountant will be notified and will be able to download the file.
>
> Next step: Be sure to provide the file transfer password to your accountant, so he or she can retrieve the file.
>
> [OK]

14.	Click	OK	to return to the Home page

After your Accountant's Copy is sent, you will receive a confirmation e-mail and your accountant will receive an e-mail with a link to download your Accountant's Copy. They will need to use the password you created to open the file.

Updating QuickBooks

Intuit regularly provides updates to QuickBooks, such as maintenance releases, that you can download from the Internet.

To update QuickBooks,

1.	Select	Help : Update QuickBooks Desktop	from the menu bar

The Overview tab of the Update QuickBooks Desktop window displays:

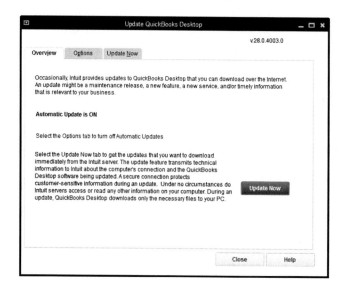

Notice the version number that displays in the upper-right corner of the window. When you update QuickBooks, this number will also be updated accordingly. Notice also that the Automatic Update feature is turned on. This feature ensures that you have the latest QuickBooks improvements and is automatically turned on by default. When this feature is turned on, the QuickBooks software will be automatically updated via an Internet connection. Automatic updates to the software may cause very slight variances between what is displayed in this guide and what you see on screen when using QuickBooks. It is still strongly recommended that you leave this feature turned on.

2. Click   **Update Now**

Quick Tip. *If you would like to learn more about what versions and editions of QuickBooks are available, you can access the QuickBooks.com web site and click the Products tab at the bottom of the page.*

The Update Now tab of the Update QuickBooks window displays:

Note: The Last Checked column in your window will display different dates.

Quick Tip. If you would like to view detailed information about your QuickBooks product, such as the license number and product number, press the F2 key to display a Product Information window. The version and release number are also displayed in the top line of this window.

From this tab, you would select the updates you want to download and then click the Get Updates button. For this exercise, you will not update QuickBooks.

3. Click [Close] in the Update QuickBooks window

The Update QuickBooks window closes and you return to the Home page.

Backing Up and Restoring a Company File

You should always create a backup of your company file to protect it in case of loss or damage to your file. If you create a backup file and lose data for any reason, you can restore the data from your backup copy.

Creating a Local Backup File

QuickBooks allows you to create an online backup of your company file or a local backup. In this exercise, you will create a local backup.

To create a local backup file,

1. Select   File : Back Up   from the menu bar
     Company : Create
     Local Backup

Quick Tip. For larger QuickBooks company files, you can also create a portable version of the file. A portable file is a compact version of a company file, allowing you to more easily email or move company data. See the QuickBooks Desktop Help for more information.

The first screen in the Create Backup wizard displays:

The Create Backup wizard allows you to make a backup copy of everything you need to recreate your company file. This first screen in the wizard allows you to determine how you want to save your backup file; either online or locally to a network folder or a removable storage device, such as a CD or USB flash drive.

You will accept the default selection and save a local backup of your company file.

2. Click   [Options]

The Backup Options window opens:

Backup Options ✖

Use this window to set default options for your manual and automatic backups.

LOCAL BACKUP ONLY

Tell us where to save your backup copies **(required)**

[   ] [Bro_wse...]

☑ Add the date and time of the backup to the file name (recommended)

    ☑ Limit the number of backup copies in this folder to [3]

ONLINE AND LOCAL BACKUP

☑ _R_emind me to back up when I close my company file every [4] times.

Select an option to verify that your company data is OK (that is, not corrupted) when you save.

⦿ Com_p_lete verification (recommended)

○ _Q_uicker verification

○ _N_o verification   Help me choose

[_O_K]   [Cancel]   [Help]

This window allows you to set default options for manual and automatic backups. From here, you can specify where to save local backup copies, set reminders to backup your company file, and set verification levels to verify that your company data is not corrupted when you save it.

Note: If you use an online backup service, such as Intuit Data Protect or QuickBooks Online Backup, you can use this window to set reminders and verification settings. All other options specified will affect local backups only.

For the purpose of this exercise, you will save your backup copy to the Books2018 folder.

Note: If the Books2018 folder does not display, click the Browse button and navigate to the folder.

3. Click

A QuickBooks dialog box displays:

> **QuickBooks**
>
> ⚠ You've told us to save backup copies to the same hard drive (drive: C:) that holds your company file. We do not recommend this.
>
> Instead, we recommend that you save to a different drive or to a removable storage device to avoid losing the backup due to an unexpected hard-drive failure.
>
> [Change Location] [Use this Location]

This dialog box informs you that QuickBooks does not recommend saving backup files to the same hard drive that holds your company file. Typically, you would not save a backup file to the same hard drive as your company file, but for the purpose of this exercise, you will.

4. Click **[Use this Location]** to return to the Create Backup wizard

5. Click **[Next]**

The next screen in the Create Backup wizard displays:

> **Create Backup** ✕
>
> **When do you want to save your backup copy?**
>
> ⦿ Save it now
>
> ○ Save it now and schedule future backups
>
> ○ Only schedule future backups
>
> Note: If you are saving your backup copy to a removable storage device such as a CD or USB flash drive, insert the CD or connect the device now.
>
> [Back] [Next] [Finish]   [Help] [Cancel]

This window allows you to specify when to save your back up copy. You can choose to save it now, save it now and schedule future backups, or only schedule future backups.

6. Verify the Save it now option is selected

Quick Tip. If you choose to schedule future backups, QuickBooks provides you with options for scheduling backups automatically after closing QuickBooks a specified amount of times or to occur on specific dates and times.

7. Click **[Next]**

A Save Backup Copy window displays:

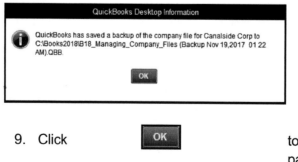

Note: If your company file is stored on a remote computer, a dialog box displays informing you that QuickBooks may not be able to back up all associated files. If this dialog box displays, click the OK button.

By default, QuickBooks names the new file using the company name and the date and time of the backup and places it in the directory you specified. The backup copy will have a .QBB file extension.

8. Click [Save]

A Working dialog box displays while the company file is saved to a backup file. The file will include all of your company data up to the date the backup is made.

When the backup is complete, a QuickBooks Desktop Information dialog box displays:

> **QuickBooks Desktop Information**
>
> ⓘ QuickBooks has saved a backup of the company file for Canalside Corp to
> C:\Books2018\B18_Managing_Company_Files (Backup Nov 19,2017 01 22
> AM).QBB.
>
> [OK]

9. Click [OK]   to return to the QuickBooks Home
                     page

Restoring a Local Backup File

After you have created a local back up file, you can restore the file and bring your data back into QuickBooks. Because a backup copy is in a compressed file format, you will need to use the Open or Restore Company wizard to restore the file.

Note: If you backed up your company file using Intuit Data Protect, you must restore it through that service. If you created a local backup file and it is not on your hard disk or in a network folder, you should first insert the CD, USB drive, or other storage device in the appropriate drive.

To restore a local backup from a network folder or removable storage device, such as a CD or USB drive,

1. Select   File : Open or   from the menu bar
   Restore Company

The first screen in the Open or Restore Company wizard displays:

Open or Restore Company	✕
What type of file do you want to open or restore?	
⦿ **Open a company file**	
• Open a regular company file (.qbw)	
○ **Restore a backup copy**	
• Restore a backup file (.qbb)	
• Restore files from an online backup	
○ **Restore a portable file**	
• Re-create a company file that was stored as a portable file (.qbm)	

Back   Next   Finish   Help   Cancel

Note: *If you are using the QuickBooks Premier version, the Open or Restore Company window may display an additional option to Convert an Accountant's Copy Transfer file.*

This screen allows you to open or restore a QuickBooks file.

2. Select   the Restore a backup
   copy option

3. Click   Next

The next screen in the Open or Restore Company wizard displays:

Open or Restore Company	✕
Is the backup copy stored locally or online?	
⦿ Local backup	
Backup copy is saved on this computer, on a removable storage device, or on a network drive.	
○ Online backup	
Backup copy is stored online.	

Back   Next   Finish   Help   Cancel

4. Verify the Local backup option is selected

5. Click   Next

The Open Backup Copy window displays:

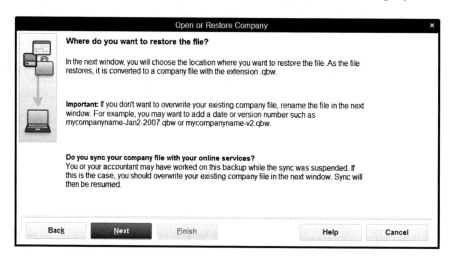

By default, QuickBooks displays the folder where you last saved a file and selects the most recent backup copy in that folder.

Note: If the Books2018 folder does not display, click the drop-down arrow in the Look in field and navigate to the folder. The list of backup files that display in your window may be different. If there are multiple files displayed, you may have to scroll down to locate the back up file.

6. Click   Open

The next screen in the Open or Restore Company wizard displays:

This screen informs you that the next window allows you to choose where to restore your company file.

7. Click [Next]

The Save Company File as window displays:

By default, the folder where you last saved your company file displays.

Note: If the Books2018 folder does not display, click the drop-down arrow in the Look in field and navigate to the folder.

8. Click [Save]   to accept the default selections

A Confirm Save As dialog box displays:

9. Click [Yes]

Because QuickBooks located a company file with the same name in the folder, a Delete Entire File dialog box displays:

This dialog box enables QuickBooks to delete the existing file and replace it with the file you're restoring.

Note: If you were not sure if you wanted to erase the existing file, you would click the Cancel button and rename the file you are restoring.

10. Type **YES** in the text field

11. Click

A Working dialog box displays while the company file is converted to a regular company file, with a .QBW extension (or a .QBA extension if the backup was made from an Accountant's Copy). The company file and all of its related files are stored in this location.

When the restore is complete, a QuickBooks Desktop Login dialog box displays:

This dialog box informs you that you must login to the company file.

12. Type **<the administrator password you created>** in the Password field

Note: Passwords are case-sensitive. If your password does not work, type Canalside2 in the Password field.

13. Click ` OK `

A QuickBooks Information dialog box displays informing you that your data has been restored successfully:

14. Click ` OK `

The QuickBooks Home page displays.

Condensing a Company File

Condensing your company file allows you to get rid of unnecessary detail, in order to decrease file size and improve performance. It can also be used to clean up company data by removing unused items, names, and accounts.

Most QuickBooks users do not need to condense their company files. However, you may want to consider condensing your company file if you don't need the details of transactions anymore or if you have many unused list entries.

Caution. Careful consideration should be given before condensing a company file. It is suggested that you contact Intuit support before using this feature.

In this exercise, you will learn how to condense a company file to remove old transactions, while keeping unused list entries.

Caution. Due to critical payroll information within payroll files, this feature is not available to payroll users. This feature is also not available to QuickBooks online banking users, due to security and time-related data from the financial institution.

Note: You must be in single-user mode to condense a company file.

1. Select   File : Utilities :   from the menu bar
                        Condense Data

The first screen in the Condense Data wizard opens:

Note: The date displayed on your screen may be different. Also, depending on the version of QuickBooks you are using, this window may display additional options.

2. Verify that the Transactions before a specific date option is selected

3. Type   **01/01/2005**   in the Remove transactions before field

4. Click [Next]

Note: If you are using the QuickBooks Premier version, a How Should Transactions be Summarized screen displays next. Verify the Create one summary journal entry option is selected and click the Next button.

Note: If you condense a file that includes inventory transactions, an additional window will display asking how inventory should be condensed.

The next screen in the Condense Data wizard displays:

Condense Data   ✖

Do You Want To Remove The Following Transactions?

QuickBooks recommends that you remove the following transactions:

☑ Uncleared (unreconciled) bank and credit card transactions

☑ Transactions marked 'To be printed'

☑ Invoices and Estimates marked 'To be sent'

☑ ALL Estimates, Sales Orders, Purchase Orders, and Pending Invoices

☑ ALL Time and Mileage activities

☑ Transactions containing unbilled expenses and items

[Select None]

[Back]   [Next]   [Begin Condense]   [Help]   [Cancel]

---

5. Click [Next]   to remove the selected transactions

The next screen in the Condense Data wizard displays:

Condense Data   ✖

Do You Want To Remove Unused List Entries?

After condensing, some list entries will not be used in transactions. QuickBooks recommends removing the unused entries for the following lists:

☑ Accounts   ☑ Items

☑ Customers and Jobs   ☑ 'Done' To Do notes

☑ Vendors   ☑ Classes

☑ Other Names

[Select None]

[Back]   [Next]   [Begin Condense]   [Help]   [Cancel]

---

6. Click [Select None]   to clear all check boxes

This allows you to keep unused list entries in the file.

7. Click [Next]

The next screen in the Condense Data wizard displays:

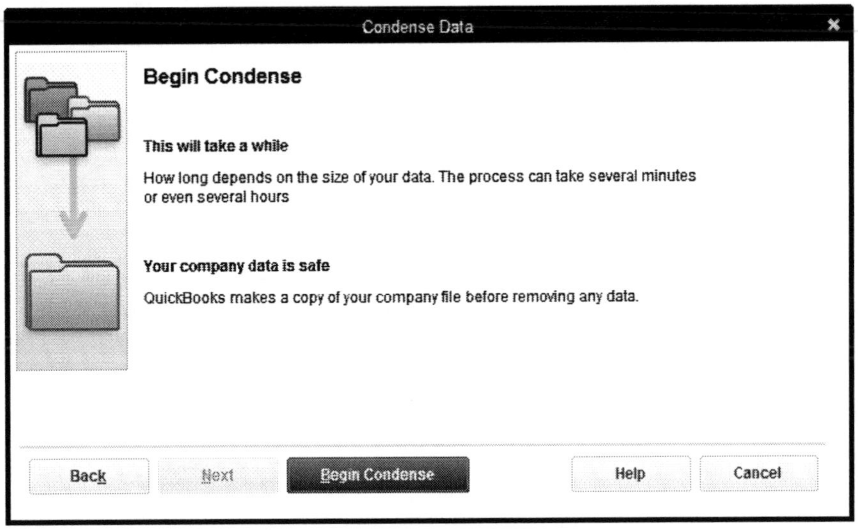

Condense Data ✕

Begin Condense

This will take a while

How long depends on the size of your data. The process can take several minutes or even several hours

Your company data is safe

QuickBooks makes a copy of your company file before removing any data.

[Back] [Next] [Begin Condense] [Help] [Cancel]

When you click the Begin Condense button, QuickBooks creates a copy of your company file before condensing in case you need the transaction detail later. However, you'll work in the condensed file moving forward.

For this exercise, you will not actually condense the company file.

8. Click [Cancel] to close the Condense Data wizard

You return to the Home page.

Review

In this appendix, you have learned how to:

- ☑ Use QuickBooks in multi-user mode
- ☑ Set up users and passwords
- ☑ Set a closing date
- ☑ Share files with an accountant
- ☑ Update QuickBooks
- ☑ Back up and restore a company file
- ☑ Condense a company file

Practice:

1. Switch to multi-user mode.
2. Set up a new user with a password.
3. Change the administrator password.
4. Change your closing date and password.
5. Save an accountant's copy of the company file and then remove accountant's copy restrictions.
6. Back up and restore the company file.
7. Close the company file.

Estimating, Time Tracking, and Job Costing

In this lesson, you will learn how to:

- ❑ Create job estimates
- ❑ Create an invoice from an estimate
- ❑ Display reports for estimates
- ❑ Update the job status
- ❑ Track time
- ❑ Display reports for time tracking
- ❑ Track vehicle mileage
- ❑ Display vehicle mileage reports
- ❑ Display other job reports

Concept

QuickBooks integrates estimating, time tracking, and advanced job costing with accounting and payroll. QuickBooks is ideal for businesses that are time or project based, such as accounting firms, construction companies, or consultants. Time can be entered either directly into QuickBooks on the weekly or single activity timesheet form or by using the QuickBooks Timer program. The Timer program is a stand-alone program that allows employees or contractors who do not have access to QuickBooks to track their time and then export it to QuickBooks as desired. Time entered directly into QuickBooks or imported from the Timer program can easily be transferred to invoices or paychecks. Estimates and billable vehicle mileage, can be transferred to an invoice with just a few mouse clicks. QuickBooks tracks profitability by job, service, activity, or item, so you know instantly which projects or activities are most profitable for your business.

Scenario

In this appendix, you will create a job estimate for an existing customer. From the estimate, you will create an invoice to bill for one-third of the job before starting work. After work begins, you will update the job status. You will then track time spent on a repair job and transfer the hours from that timesheet to an invoice. You will also track vehicle mileage spent on a job and then bill the customer for the vehicle mileage. Finally, you will display project reports that show job estimates versus actual costs, as well as reports that track job profitability.

Practice Files: B18_Estimating_Time_Tracking_And_Job_Costing.qbw

Creating Job Estimates

An estimate is a description of work you propose to do for, or products you propose to sell to, a current or prospective customer. If a customer accepts an estimate, you can turn the estimate into an invoice, modifying it as necessary. When you have actual costs and revenues, you can compare them with your estimated costs and revenues to see if you were over or under the estimate.

Estimates are "non-posting" transactions; they will not affect any financial reports or income and expense balances. QuickBooks allows you to create invoices from estimates either by transferring the entire estimate to an invoice or by allowing you to choose a percentage or selected items for which to invoice from the estimate. The ability to bill for only a percentage of the estimate or selected items on an estimate is called progress invoicing.

When you create a new QuickBooks company, you are asked if you use estimates and/or time tracking. If you respond yes, these features will be available. If you respond no, you will need to turn these features on in order to use them. Canalside Corp. already has estimates and time tracking turned on, but you will review how to do this, so you become familiar with these QuickBooks preferences.

Note: For this lesson, be sure to set your computer's date to 11/1/2018 before opening the QuickBooks file, as recommended in the Before You Get Started lesson. This will ensure that the dates you see on your screen match the dates in this lesson. In addition, your company file must be open in single-user mode.

Setting Preferences

1. Open   B18_Estimating   using the method described in
   Time_Tracking_And   Before You Get Started
   Job_Costing.qbw

The QuickBooks Login dialog box displays:

QuickBooks Login	✖
You need to log in as QuickBooks Administrator to proceed. Please enter the admin (owner) password for the company:	
Canalside Corp.	
Password: [_____] I forgot my password	
Passwords are case sensitive.	
OK Cancel Help	

This dialog box informs you that you must login as a QuickBooks Administrator in order to open the company file.

2. Type   **Canalside2**   in the Password field

Note: Passwords are case-sensitive.

3. Click   OK

QuickBooks opens the file.

4. Click   ✖   to close the Reminders window

QuickBooks displays the Home page:

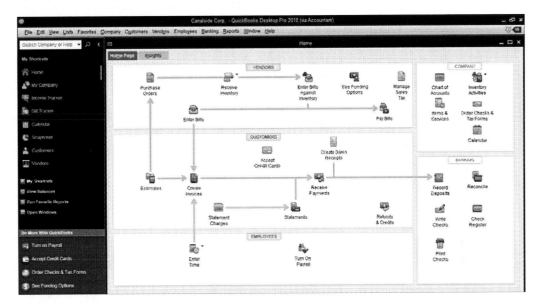

To turn on the estimates and time tracking features,

5. Select   Edit : Preferences   from the menu bar

The Preferences window opens with the General category displayed:

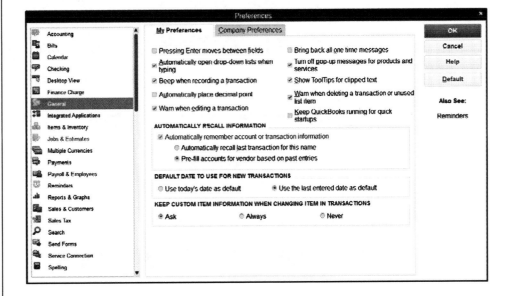

Note: Your Preferences window may display a different selected category.

6. Select   the Jobs & Estimates category

The My Preferences tab for Jobs & Estimates displays.

7. Click   the Company Preferences tab

The Company Preferences tab for Jobs & Estimates displays:

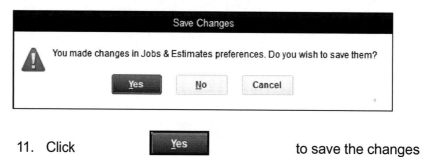

8. Verify that Yes is selected for Do You Create Estimates?

9. Select   the Yes option   in the Do You Do Progress
                                               Invoicing? section

10. Select   Time & Expenses   on the left side of the window (scroll
                                               down, if necessary)

Because you have made changes to your Jobs & Estimates preferences, the Save
Changes dialog box displays:

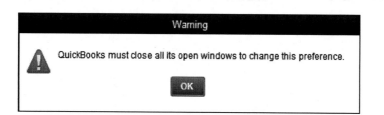

11. Click   [Yes]   to save the changes

A Warning dialog box displays informing you that QuickBooks must close all
open windows to change this preference:

12. Click   **OK**

The Company Preferences tab for Time & Expenses displays:

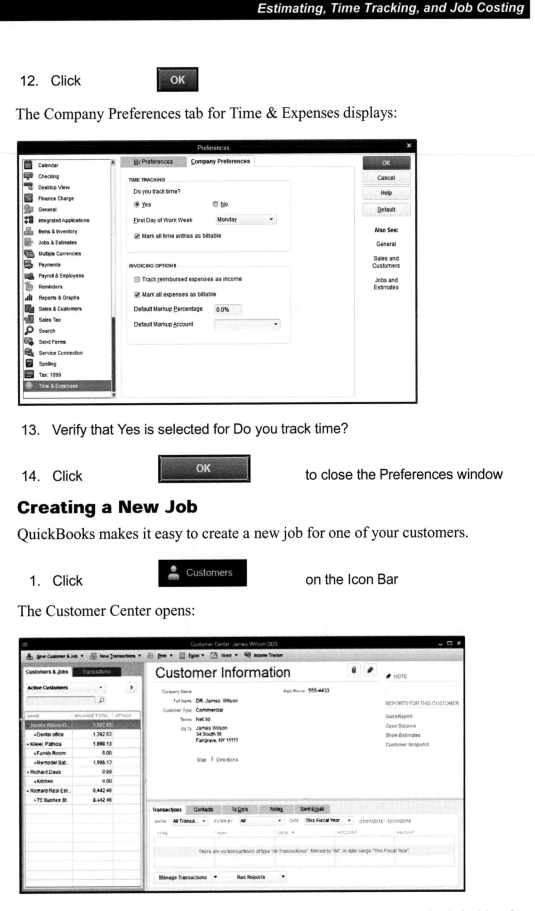

13. Verify that Yes is selected for Do you track time?

14. Click   **OK**   to close the Preferences window

Creating a New Job

QuickBooks makes it easy to create a new job for one of your customers.

1. Click   **Customers**   on the Icon Bar

The Customer Center opens:

All customers and jobs are listed on the Customers & Jobs tab on the left side of the window.

2. Select   James Wilson DDS   (if necessary)

3. Click   👍 **New Customer & Job ▼**   on the Customer Center toolbar

A drop-down menu displays:

> New Customer
> Add Job
> Add Multiple Customer:Jobs

4. Select   Add Job   from the drop-down menu

The New Job window opens:

5. Type   **Bathroom**   in the Job Name field

6. Click   Job Info

The Job Info tab displays:

This tab allows you to add or edit information about a job as it progresses. For example, you can record a change in job status or enter a new projection for the end date of the job.

Note: If you performed a previous job for this customer, dates would already display in the date fields.

7.	Type	**Remodel Bathroom**	in the Job Description field
8.	Select	Remodel	from the Job Type drop-down menu
9.	Select	Pending	from the Job Status drop-down menu
10.	Type	**11/05/2018**	in the Start Date field
11.	Type	**11/16/2018**	in the Projected End field
12.	Click	OK	to save the new job information and return to the Customer Center

Your Customer Center should resemble the figure below:

The new Bathroom job is listed below James Wilson DDS in the Customers & Jobs list and Pending is displayed as the Job Status in the Job Information area. Keep in mind that you can have only one estimate per job, but each customer can have an unlimited number of jobs.

Creating an Estimate

Creating an estimate is very similar to creating an invoice.

To create a job estimate,

1.	Select	Bathroom	under James Wilson DDS to highlight it (if necessary)

2. Click   **New Transactions ▼**   on the Customer Center toolbar

A drop-down menu of transactions displays:

Estimates
Invoices   Ctrl+I
Sales Receipts
Statement Charges
Receive Payments
Credit Memos/Refunds

Note: If you are using QuickBooks Premier, a Sales Orders option will display below the Estimates option.

3. Select   Estimates   from the drop-down menu

The Create Estimates window opens with James Wilson DDS:Bathroom entered in the Customer:Job field:

Note: If your window does not display the custom estimate, select Custom Estimate from the Template drop-down menu.

4. Click   in the first row of the Item column

QuickBooks automatically enters the customer information in the Name / Address area of the estimate.

5. Type   **i (for installation)**

6. Press   Tab

QuickBooks automatically fills in the Item column with the word **Installation** and the default information for installation is automatically added to the estimate.

7. Press   `Tab`   to move to the Qty column

8. Type   **10**   in the Qty column to indicate the estimated number of installation hours

9. Click   below Installation   in the Item column

The total cost for installation is automatically calculated by QuickBooks.

10. Type   **Fr (for Framing)**   in the Item column

11. Press   `Tab`

QuickBooks automatically fills in the Item column with the word **Framing**.

12. Press   `Tab`   to move to the Qty column

13. Type   **48**   in the Qty column

14. Click   below Framing   in the Item column

The total cost for framing is automatically calculated by QuickBooks.

15. Type   **Ro (for Rough)**   in the Item column

16. Press   `Tab`

QuickBooks automatically fills in the Item column with **Lumber:Rough**.

17. Select   0.00   in the Cost field to highlight it

18. Type   **2500**   to replace 0.00

19. Type   **15%**   in the Markup field

20. Press   `Tab`

Note: If a dialog box displays informing you about setting price levels, close it.

Your Create Estimates window should resemble the figure below:

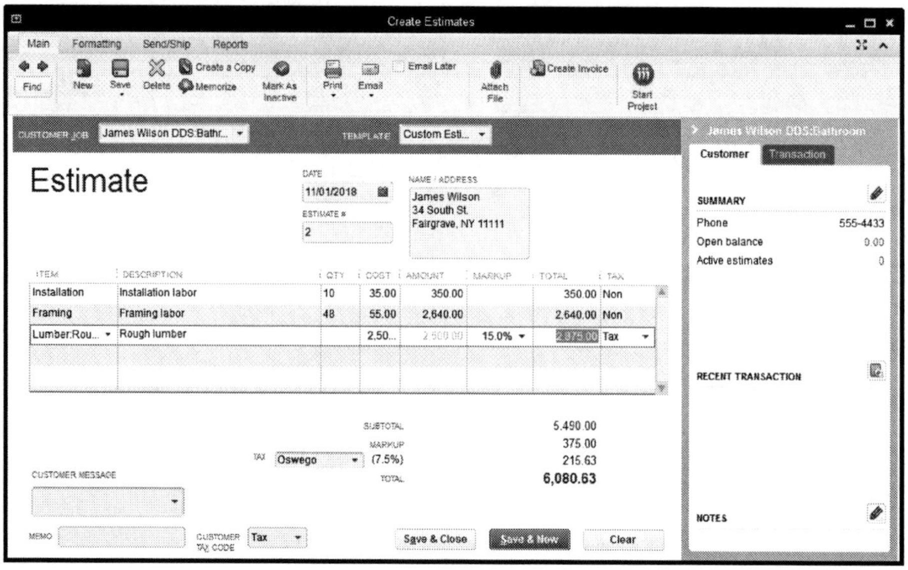

QuickBooks filled in most of the information for the estimate based on the selections in the Item column.

21. Click [Save & Close]

The Customer Center displays:

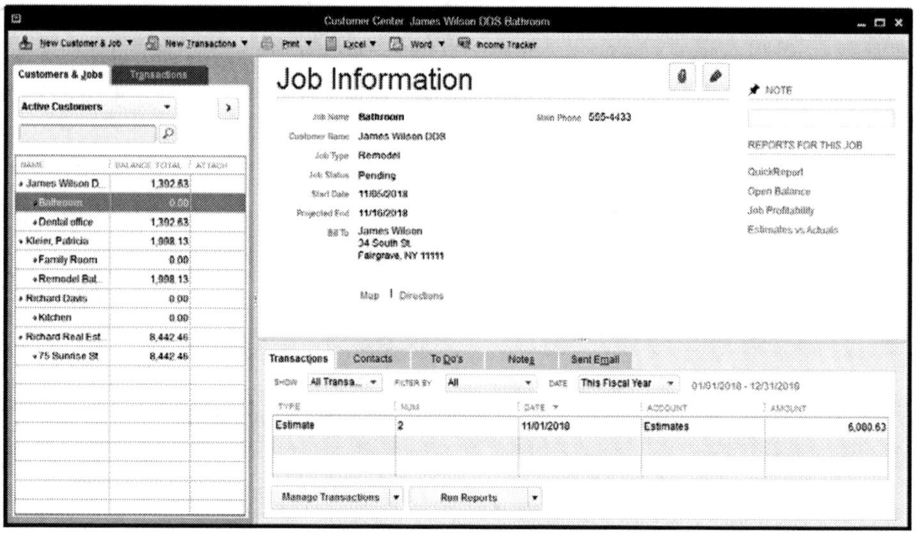

The Amount column in the Transactions table for the pending bathroom job for James Wilson DDS now has a balance of $6,080.63.

Creating an Invoice from an Estimate

When you create an estimate in QuickBooks, you can easily turn it into an invoice after the customer accepts the job. QuickBooks allows you to create invoices from estimates either by transferring the entire estimate to an invoice or by allowing you to choose a percentage or selected items for which to invoice from the estimate. Turning an estimate into multiple invoices enables you to bill for parts of a large job as the work progresses.

1. Select **Bathroom** under James Wilson DDS to highlight it (if necessary)

2. Click [New Transactions ▾] on the Customer Center toolbar

A drop-down menu of transactions displays.

3. Select **Invoices** from the drop-down menu

The Create Invoices window opens with James Wilson DDS:Bathroom displayed in the Customer:Job field:

Note: Your Create Invoices window may display a different Template selection.

4. Press [Tab] to leave the Customer:Job field

Because you have an existing estimate for this job, the Available Estimates window opens:

5. Click **the estimate for James Wilson DDS Bathroom** to select it

6. Click

The Create Progress Invoice Based On Estimate window opens:

> **Create Progress Invoice Based On Estimate** ✕
>
> Specify what to include on the invoice.
>
> ⦿ Create invoice for the entire estimate (100%).
>
> ○ Create invoice for a percentage of the entire estimate.
>
> % of estimate
>
> ○ Create invoice for selected items or for different percentages of each item.
>
> [OK]   [Cancel]   [Help]

Canalside Corp. typically bills for one third of the job before starting the work, then one third when the project is halfway complete, and the final one third when the job has been completed.

To bill for the first third of the job,

7. Click   Create invoice for a percentage of the entire estimate

The % of estimate field becomes active.

8. Type   **33.333**   in the % of estimate field

Quick Tip. If you need to invoice for only part of an estimate, select Create invoice for selected items or for different percentages of each item. QuickBooks will display a table containing all items in the estimate and allow you to select which items you want to include and the amounts for each item.

9. Click   [OK]

QuickBooks creates an invoice for one-third of the bathroom remodeling job:

QuickBooks automatically changed the invoice template to Progress Invoice and added fields for Est Amt (Estimate Amount), Prior Amt, and Total %. QuickBooks will also track that one third of the James Wilson bathroom remodeling job has been invoiced and that two thirds has not yet been invoiced.

10. Click **Save & Close** to return to the Customer Center

Displaying Reports for Estimates

QuickBooks provides five reports on estimates: Job Estimates vs. Actuals Summary, Job Estimates vs. Actuals Detail, Job Progress Invoices vs. Estimates, Item Estimates vs. Actuals, and Estimates by Jobs. These reports can be accessed from the Jobs, Time & Mileage section of the Report Center or from the Jobs, Time & Mileage submenu under Reports.

Displaying the Job Estimates vs. Actuals Summary Report

To display the Job Estimates vs. Actuals Summary report,

1. Select Reports : Jobs, Time & Mileage : Job Estimates vs. Actuals Summary from the menu bar

The Job Estimates vs. Actuals Summary report opens:

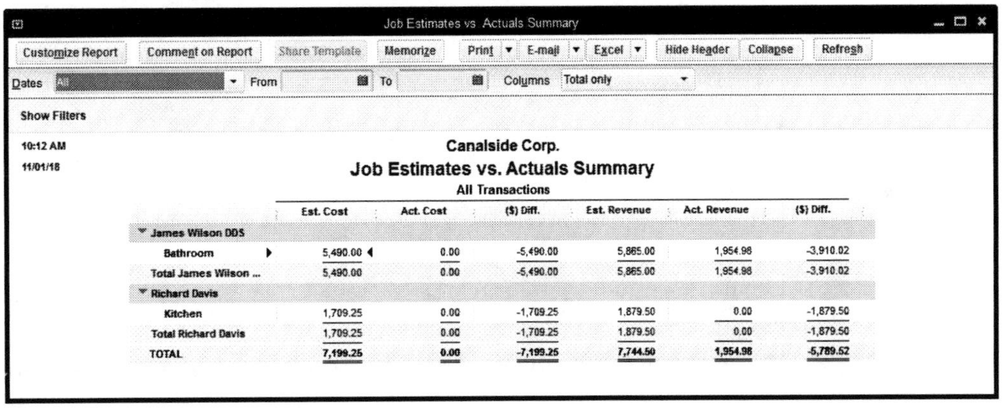

	Est. Cost	Act. Cost	($) Diff.	Est. Revenue	Act. Revenue	($) Diff.
James Wilson DDS						
Bathroom	5,490.00	0.00	-5,490.00	5,865.00	1,954.98	-3,910.02
Total James Wilson ...	5,490.00	0.00	-5,490.00	5,865.00	1,954.98	-3,910.02
Richard Davis						
Kitchen	1,709.25	0.00	-1,709.25	1,879.50	0.00	-1,879.50
Total Richard Davis	1,709.25	0.00	-1,709.25	1,879.50	0.00	-1,879.50
TOTAL	7,199.25	0.00	-7,199.25	7,744.50	1,954.98	-5,789.52

Note: *If All is not displayed in the Dates field, select it from the drop-down menu.*

This report summarizes how accurately your company estimated job-related costs and revenues. The report compares estimated cost to actual cost and estimated revenue to actual revenue for all customers.

2. Close the Job Estimates vs. Actuals Summary report window

Displaying the Job Estimates vs. Actuals Detail Report

To display the Job Estimates vs. Actuals Detail report,

1. Select   Reports : Jobs, Time &   from the menu bar
   Mileage : Job Estimates
   vs. Actuals Detail

The Filter Report by Job window opens:

Filter Report by Job   ✕
Customer:Job   [James Wilson DDS   ▼]
[OK]   [Cancel]   [Help]

This window allows you to create a report for a particular customer/job. James Wilson DDS is already selected.

2. Click   [OK]

The Job Estimates vs. Actuals Detail for James Wilson DDS report opens:

Job Estimates vs. Actuals Detail for James Wilson DDS   — ☐ ✕

Customize Report   Comment on Report   Share Template   Memorize   Print ▼   E-mail ▼   Excel ▼   Hide Header   Collapse   Refresh

Dates All   ▼   From   🗓 To   🗓   Columns Total only   ▼

Show Filters

10:16 AM
11/01/18

Canalside Corp.
Job Estimates vs. Actuals Detail for James Wilson DDS
All Transactions

	Est. Cost	Act. Cost	($) Diff.	Est. Revenue	Act. Revenue	($) Diff.
▼ Parts						
▼ Lumber (Lumber)						
Rough (Rough lumber) ▶	2,500.00 ◀	0.00	-2,500.00	2,875.00	958.32	-1,916.68
Total Lumber (Lumber)	2,500.00	0.00	-2,500.00	2,875.00	958.32	-1,916.68
Total Parts	2,500.00	0.00	-2,500.00	2,875.00	958.32	-1,916.68
▼ Service						
Framing (Framing labor)	2,640.00	0.00	-2,640.00	2,640.00	879.99	-1,760.01
Installation (Installation la...	350.00	0.00	-350.00	350.00	116.67	-233.33
Total Service	2,990.00	0.00	-2,990.00	2,990.00	996.66	-1,993.34
TOTAL	5,490.00	0.00	-5,490.00	5,865.00	1,954.98	-3,910.02

Note: If All is not displayed in the Dates field, select it from the drop-down menu.

This report shows how accurately costs and revenues were estimated for a specific customer/job. The report compares estimated and actual costs—and estimated and actual revenues—for each item billed. This enables you to quickly see which portions of a job were estimated accurately and which portions were not.

3. Close the Job Estimates vs. Actuals Detail for James Wilson DDS report window to return to the Customer Center

You can generate the other estimate reports by selecting them from the Jobs, Time & Mileage submenu under Reports or the Jobs, Time & Mileage section in the Report Center.

Updating the Job Status

Every time you change the status of a job, you must update it in the Customers & Jobs list. In this example, the estimate for the bathroom remodel job is no longer pending. James Wilson DDS awarded you the job, and you have begun work on it.

To update the status of a job,

1. Select **Bathroom** under James Wilson DDS in the Customers & Jobs list (if necessary)

2. Click [pencil icon] in the Job Information area

The Edit Job window opens:

3. Click the Job Info tab

The Job Info tab displays:

4. Select   In progress   from the Job Status drop-down menu

5. Click | OK |

The Edit Job window closes and the Customer Center displays:

The Job Status field in the Job Information area now shows the status of the bathroom remodeling job as being in progress. Notice also that the transactions table now displays both the estimate and the invoice that were created for this job.

Tracking Time

QuickBooks provides time tracking for all jobs. Time tracking allows you to keep track of the time a person spends on each job, including sick and vacation time and time spent for general overhead. The person can be an employee, an owner or partner, or a subcontractor.

You can use this information to:

• Invoice the customer for the time spent doing a job

• Automatically fill in hours worked on an employee's paycheck

• Track the cost of employees' gross pay by job

• Report on the number of hours worked by person, by job, or by item

There are various ways to enter time into a QuickBooks company file:

Method	Description
Stopwatch	Allows you to time an activity while it is being performed.
Manual Entry	Allows you to manually enter time either on a weekly timesheet or activity by activity.
Timer	Allows you to track time spent on various projects and then import the time directly into QuickBooks. The Timer program is useful when you have employees or subcontractors who need to track their time, but do not need or want to run QuickBooks. When time is imported into QuickBooks from the Timer application, you view the imported time data on the same timesheets you would use if you entered the data directly into QuickBooks.
Time Tracker	Allows your employees and vendors to track their own time online - they can even submit billable time to Time Tracker from their Microsoft® Outlook® calendar. The timesheets can then be downloaded and added to your QuickBooks timesheets. Time Tracker is a subscription-based service that works with QuickBooks.

This exercise will cover manually entering time data into QuickBooks. For information about the other time tracking methods, refer to the QuickBooks Help.

Using the Weekly Timesheet

To manually track time in QuickBooks,

1. Click   🏠 Home   on the Icon Bar

The Home page displays.

2. Click   [Enter Time]   in the Employees area of the Home page

A drop-down menu displays:

> Use Weekly Timesheet
> Time / Enter Single Activity

When you track time with QuickBooks, you have a choice of two forms on which to enter time: Weekly Timesheet or Time/Enter Single Activity. If you want to enter time for multiple jobs or multiple days; Weekly Timesheet is the best choice.

3. Select   Use Weekly   from the drop-down menu
                          Timesheet

The Weekly Timesheet window opens:

Note: *You can maximize the window to enlarge the timesheet if necessary.*

4. Select   Joseph Rogers   from the Name drop-down menu
                                    (scroll down to the bottom of the list)

The Transfer Activities to Payroll dialog box displays:

Because Canalside Corp. plans to generate paychecks based on time data entered
in QuickBooks,

5. Click   **Yes**

The dialog box closes and the Weekly Timesheet opens with Joseph Rogers
displayed in the Name field.

6. Click   in the first row   of the Customer:Job column

7. Click   ▼   in the Customer:Job column

A drop-down menu of customers and jobs displays:

8. Select   Richard Real Estate, 75 Sunrise St.

QuickBooks will associate the time that you enter in this window with the 75 Sunrise St. job for Richard Real Estate.

9. Press | Tab | to move to the Service Item column

10. Type   **i (for installation)**

11. Press | Tab |

QuickBooks automatically fills in the Service Item column with the word **Installation**.

12. Select   Hourly 1   from the Payroll Item drop-down menu

13. Click   in the M column   (M stands for Monday)

Quick Tip. *To change the first day of your work week, select the Time & Expenses category in the Preferences window and click the Company Preferences tab. You can then change the first day of the work week by selecting the appropriate day from the drop-down menu.*

14. Type   **8**   to enter the number of hours worked on Monday

15. Press | Tab | to move to the Tu column

16. Repeat steps 14-15 to enter 8 in the columns for Tuesday through Friday on the timesheet

17. Press | Tab | to move to Sa (if necessary)

Note: The Billable check box to the right of the Total column allows you to tell QuickBooks if the hours will be transferred onto an invoice as billable time. If you do not plan on creating an invoice using time worked, then you can deselect the Billable check box. This means that QuickBooks will not display that time in the Choose Billable Time and Costs window for the invoice.

18. Click | Save & Close | to record the timesheet

The Weekly Timesheet window closes and the Home page displays. QuickBooks records the time for the Richard Real Estate 75 Sunrise St. job. This time can now be transferred to an invoice for this job or used to create a paycheck for the employee.

Invoicing for Time

To invoice Richard Real Estate for the time Canalside Corporation's employee Joseph Rogers spent on the remodel job,

1. Click [Create Invoices] in the Customers area of the Home page

The Create Invoices window opens:

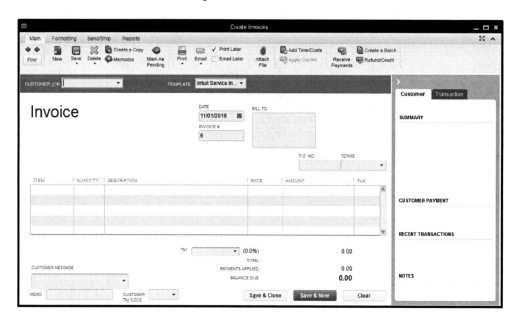

2. Select **Richard Real Estate : 75 Sunrise St.** from the Customer:Job drop-down menu

A Billable Time/Costs window opens:

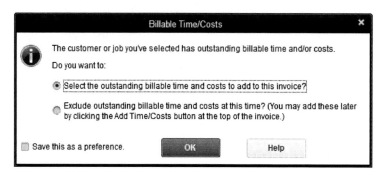

This window informs you that the customer has outstanding billable time or costs. You can choose to select the outstanding billable time and costs to add to the invoice or exclude the outstanding billable time and costs at this time.

3. Click [OK] to add the outstanding billable time and costs to the invoice

The Choose Billable Time and Costs window opens with the Time tab selected:

This window allows you to select the billable time you would like transferred to the invoice.

Quick Tip. By default, QuickBooks lists each individual line from the timesheet on the invoice. If you prefer to have QuickBooks combine time for activities with the same service item, click the Options button and select the Combine activities with the same service items option. For example, if you select this option, QuickBooks would display one line on the invoice for Installation with a total of 40 hours.

4. Click **Select All**

QuickBooks places a check mark in the column to the left of all entries to indicate they are selected.

5. Click **OK**

The billable time is transferred to the invoice:

Note: If your window displays the Intuit Product Invoice, select Intuit Service Invoice from the Template drop-down menu.

6. Click | Save & Close | to record the invoice and return to the Home page

Displaying Reports for Time Tracking

QuickBooks has four time reports that you can use to monitor the hours associated with the elements of a job: Time by Job Summary, Time by Job Detail, Time by Name, and Time by Item.

To display the Time by Job Summary report,

1. Select   Reports :   from the menu bar
    Jobs, Time & Mileage :
    Time by Job Summary

The Time by Job Summary report opens.

2. Select   All   from the Dates drop-down menu (scroll up)

The report is updated to display all dates:

This report displays the amount of time your company spent on various jobs. For each customer or job, the report lists the type of work performed. Currently, there is only one customer and job in this report that has time billed against it - the installation job for Richard Real Estate: 75 Sunrise St.

3. Close the Time by Job Summary report

Note: When the Memorize Report dialog box displays asking if you would like to memorize this report, click the Do not display this message in the future check box and click the No button.

You can generate the other time reports by selecting them from the Jobs, Time & Mileage submenu under Reports or the Jobs, Time & Mileage section in the Report Center.

Tracking Vehicle Mileage

QuickBooks can track mileage for your business vehicles. You can use the mileage information for tax deductions for your vehicles, and to bill customers for mileage expenses. You cannot use vehicle mileage tracking to reimburse your employees or vendors for mileage.

Quick Tip. *It is recommended that you consult with your accountant to determine if you can deduct the costs of operating and maintaining your vehicle.*

Entering Vehicle Mileage Rates

QuickBooks calculates appropriate mileage expenses based on the dates and rates you enter in the Mileage Rates window. Therefore, you should keep your mileage rates up-to-date, so you can always take advantage of the latest IRS deduction rates for your business vehicles.

To enter vehicle mileage rates,

1. Select   Company : Enter   from menu bar
                     Vehicle Mileage

The Enter Vehicle Mileage window opens:

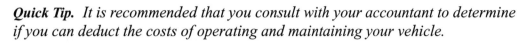

This window allows you to record the mileage cost for your business vehicles.

2. Click   [Mileage Rates]   on the toolbar

The Mileage Rates window opens:

This window allows you to record the mileage cost for your business vehicles.

This window allows you to enter the IRS rates for vehicle mileage costs. QuickBooks calculates the appropriate mileage cost based on the dates and rates entered in this window. The most current date displays at the top of the list.

3. Highlight   01/01/2011   in the Effective Date column (if necessary)

4. Type   **01/01/2018**   to replace 01/01/2011

5. Press   to move to the Rate column

6. Type   **.56**   in the Rate column to replace .52

Note: The IRS specifies the standard mileage rate per mile for the use of a car (including vans, pickups, and panel trucks) for business miles driven. You should check with the IRS for the latest rates and enter each date and rate change as it becomes effective. Visit the IRS web site at www.irs.gov for further information.

7. Click   Close

You return to the Enter Vehicle Mileage window.

Adding a Vehicle to the Vehicle List

To track mileage for a vehicle, you must first add the vehicle to the Vehicle list.

To add a vehicle to the vehicle list,

1. Click   Vehicle List   in the Enter Vehicle Mileage window

Quick Tip. You can also display the vehicle list by selecting Lists : Customer & Vendor Profile Lists : Vehicle List from the menu bar.

The Vehicle List opens:

NAME	DESCRIPTION
2014 Chevy Bl...	Four-wheel drive
2016 Chevy Ta...	Equipped with plow, All-wheel drive

Vehicle ▾ | Reports ▾ | Include inactive

The Vehicle List stores the names and descriptions of your business vehicles. To track mileage for a vehicle, the vehicle must be entered in this list.

From this window you can add, edit, or delete vehicles. You can also make a vehicle inactive, print the list, and even view reports on vehicles.

2. Click   [Vehicle ▼]   in the bottom-left corner of the Vehicle List

A drop-down menu displays:

```
New                 Ctrl+N
Edit Vehicle        Ctrl+E
Delete Vehicle      Ctrl+D

Make Vehicle Inactive
Show Inactive Vehicles
Customize Columns...

Use                 Ctrl+U

Print List...       Ctrl+P
Re-sort List
```

3. Select   New   from the drop-down menu

The New Vehicle window opens:

```
New Vehicle                                    —  □  ✖

Enter the name or identification number of the vehicle for which you    [   OK   ]
want to track mileage.

Vehicle    [                          ]                                  [ Cancel ]

Description                                                              [  Next  ]
[                          ]
[                          ]

☐ Vehicle is inactive
```

4. Type   **2018 Ford F-350**   in the Vehicle field

5. Type   **Four-wheel drive pick-up truck**   in the Description field

6. Click   [OK]

The vehicle is added to the Vehicle List:

```
Vehicle List                              —  □  ✖

NAME             ┊ DESCRIPTION

2014 Chevy Bl... │ Four-wheel drive
2016 Chevy Ta... │ Equipped with plow, All-wheel drive
2018 Ford F-350 │ Four-wheel drive pick-up truck




[ Vehicle ▼ ]  [ Reports ▼ ]  ☐ Include inactive
```

7. Close the Vehicle List to return to the Enter Vehicle Mileage window

Entering Mileage for a Vehicle

Now that you have entered the IRS mileage rate and added a vehicle to the vehicle list, you can enter mileage for the vehicle.

To enter mileage for a vehicle,

1. Select   2018 Ford F-350   from the Vehicle drop-down menu in the Enter Vehicle Mileage window

2. Leave the dates in the Trip Start Date and Trip End Date fields

You now need to enter the beginning and ending vehicle mileage as shown on the odometer for this vehicle, for this trip.

3. Type   **28,363**   to replace 0 in the Odometer Start field

4. Press   `Tab`

5. Type   **28,478**   to replace 0 in the Odometer End field

6. Press   `Tab`   to move to the Total Miles field

QuickBooks automatically calculates the total miles based on the odometer readings.

Because this trip involved you traveling to pick up materials for a specific job, you will be charging the customer for the vehicle mileage expense.

7. Select   the Billable check box

8. Select   Richard Davis:Kitchen   from the Customer:Job drop-down menu

9. Select   Mileage   from the Item drop-down menu

Caution. *The mileage rates you enter in the Item List should not be confused with the mileage rates specified by the IRS that you entered previously in the Mileage Rates window. If you want to charge your customers for mileage, you need to create a Service or Other Charge item type in the Item List.*

The Enter Vehicle Mileage window should resemble the figure below:

10. Click   Save & New

The fields in the Enter Vehicle Mileage window are cleared.

11. Repeat steps 1-8 using the following information:

Vehicle	2016 Chevy Tahoe
Trip Start Date	10/19/2018
Trip End Date	10/19/2018
Odometer Start	62,654
Odometer End	62,776
Total Miles	122
Billable check box	Selected
Customer:Job	Richard Davis:Kitchen
Item	Mileage

The Enter Vehicle Mileage window should resemble the figure below:

12. Click   Save & Close

Billing a Customer for Vehicle Mileage

After you have entered mileage for a vehicle and assigned it to a specific customer:job, you can bill the customer for the mileage.

To bill a customer for vehicle mileage,

1. Click in the Customers area of the home page

The Create Invoices window opens:

Note: *If your window displays the Intuit Product Invoice, select Intuit Service Invoice from the Template drop-down menu.*

2. Select   Richard Davis: from the Customer:Job drop-down
   Kitchen   menu

An estimate for this job already exists, so the Available Estimates window opens:

3. Click   the estimate for   to select it
   Richard Davis: Kitchen

4. Click  to transfer the estimate to the invoice

A Create Progress Invoice Based on Estimate window opens:

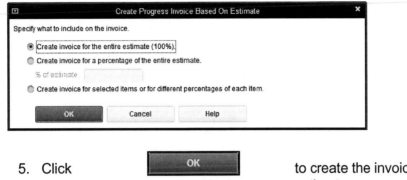

5. Click  to create the invoice for the entire estimate

Because you recently entered billable vehicle mileage for this customer, a Billable Time/Costs window opens:

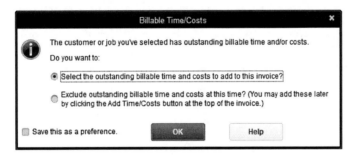

This window informs you that the customer has outstanding billable time or costs.

6. Click  to add the outstanding billable costs to the invoice

The Choose Billable Time and Costs window opens with the Time tab selected:

7. Click   the Mileage tab

The Mileage tab of the Choose Billable Time and Costs window displays:

This tab allows you to select the billable mileage you would like transferred to the invoice. The two mileage entries you just created are displayed in the list. The amount you are billing for the mileage is also displayed.

8. Click   [Select All]

QuickBooks places a check mark in the column to the left of all entries to indicate they are selected.

9. Click   [Options...]

The Options for Transferring Billable Mileage window opens:

This window allows you to determine how you want the mileage expenses to display on the invoice. You can choose to enter a separate line item on the invoice for each activity and transfer activity notes, item descriptions, or both, or you can choose to combine several mileage items into one activity.

To collapse all mileage entries for the same job into a single entry on the invoice,

10. Select   Combine activities with the same service items

11. Click   [OK]   to return to the Mileage tab of the Choose Billable Time and Costs window

Now, the two entries for mileage, each with a different number of miles, will be combined into one single entry for 237 miles on the invoice.

12. Click   [OK]

The billable mileage is transferred to the invoice:

13. Scroll to the last entry in the table of Items

Note: To delete extra lines in an invoice, position the cursor in the line, right-click, and select Delete Line from the drop-down menu that displays.

The total amount of miles (237) and the total cost billable to the customer ($118.50) is listed on the invoice.

14. Click   [Save & Close]   to record the invoice and return to the Home page

Note: If an Information Missing Or Invalid dialog box displays, enter your email address in the Email address(es) field and click the OK button. Then, click the Save & Close button in the Create Invoices window again.

Displaying Vehicle Mileage Reports

QuickBooks has four vehicle mileage reports that you can use: Mileage by Vehicle Summary, Mileage by Vehicle Detail, Mileage by Job Summary, and Mileage by Job Detail reports.

Displaying the Mileage by Vehicle Detail Report

To display the Mileage by Vehicle Detail report,

1. Select   Reports : Jobs, Time   from the menu bar
                           & Mileage: Mileage
                           by Vehicle Detail

The Mileage by Vehicle Detail report opens:

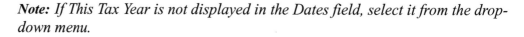

Note: If This Tax Year is not displayed in the Dates field, select it from the drop-down menu.

This report shows the miles for each trip per vehicle and includes the trip date, total miles, mileage rate, and mileage expense. If you deduct your mileage expenses on your income taxes, you can use this report for reference.

2. Close the Mileage by Vehicle Detail report to return to the Home page

Displaying the Mileage by Job Summary Report

To display the Mileage by Job Summary report,

1. Select   Reports : Jobs, Time   from the menu bar
                           & Mileage: Mileage
                           by Job Summary

The Mileage by Job Summary report opens:

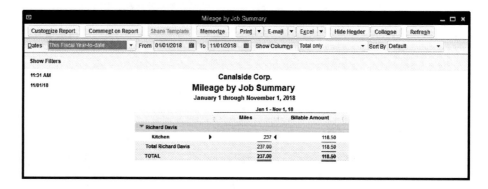

Note: If This Fiscal Year-to-date is not displayed in the Dates field, select it from the drop-down menu.

This report shows the total miles you've accumulated per customer : job and the billable amount for both billed and unbilled trips.

Note: This report does not include trips for which you did not assign an item or that you did not mark as billable.

You can generate the other mileage reports by selecting them from the Jobs, Time & Mileage submenu under Reports or the Jobs, Time & Mileage section in the Report Center.

   2. Close the Mileage by Job Summary report to return to the Home page

Displaying Other Job Reports

In addition to the estimate and time reports, QuickBooks provides several reports to track job profitability.

Displaying the Job Profitability Summary Report

To display the Job Profitability Summary report,

| 1. | Select | Reports : Jobs, Time & Mileage: Job Profitability Summary | from the menu bar |

The Job Profitability Summary report opens:

Quick Tip. If All is not displayed in the Dates field, select it from the drop-down menu.

This report summarizes how much money your company has made to date from each customer.

- The Act. Cost column displays the costs your company incurred for each customer or job.

- The Act. Revenue column displays the revenue your company received from each customer and job.

• The ($) Diff column displays the difference between costs and revenues. A positive amount in this column indicates your company made money; a negative amount indicates that your company lost money.

This report is a great tool to use to determine which jobs have been profitable and which have not, so that you are more informed when creating future job estimates.

2. Review the report and then close the Job Profitability Summary report window

Displaying the Job Profitability Detail Report

You can generate a job profitability detail report for any customer. This report presents detailed information about cost and revenue for each service and/or part for a customer or job.

To display the Job Profitability Detail report,

1. Select   Reports : Jobs, Time from the menu bar
       & Mileage : Job
       Profitability Detail

The Filter Report by Job window opens:

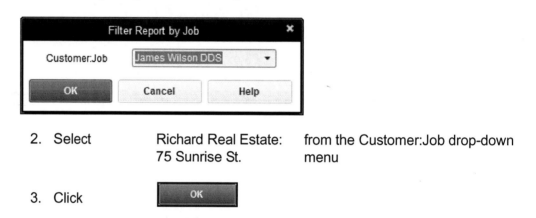

2. Select   Richard Real Estate: from the Customer:Job drop-down
       75 Sunrise St. menu

3. Click   OK

The Job Profitability Detail for Richard Real Estate:75 Sunrise St. report opens:

Quick Tip. *If All is not displayed in the Dates field, select it from the drop-down menu.*

This report displays how much money your company has made to date for a specific customer or job. The report lists costs and revenues for each item you billed to the customer, so you can see which portions of the job were profitable and which were not.

- The Act. Cost column displays your company's cost for each item billed.

- The Act. Revenue column displays the revenue your company earned for each item billed.

- The ($) Diff column displays the difference between costs and revenues. A positive amount in this column means that your company made money; a negative amount means that your company lost money.

No actual cost displays on this report because you invoiced for the time that Canalside Corp.'s employee Joseph Rogers worked, but have not yet paid Joseph for that work. When you generate a paycheck for Joseph, the cost of the work will be reflected in the report.

4. Review the report and close the report window

Quick Tip. *You can also display the Item Profitability report from the Jobs, Time & Mileage submenu so you know which services that you provide or what goods you sell are most profitable.*

Review

In this lesson, you have learned how to:

☑ Create job estimates

☑ Create an invoice from an estimate

☑ Display reports for estimates

☑ Update the job status

☑ Track time

☑ Display reports for time tracking

☑ Track vehicle mileage

☑ Display vehicle mileage reports

☑ Display other job reports

Practice:

1. Create a new job for Patricia Kleier with the following criteria:

Job Name:	Sunroom
Job Description:	Sunroom Addition
Job Type:	New Construction
Job Status:	Pending
Start Date:	11/12/2018
Projected End Date:	11/21/2018

2. Create an estimate for the Sunroom job for Patricia Kleier. The estimate is for 6 hours of installation labor, 18.5 hours of framing work, and 4 hours of drywall work.

3. Create a progress invoice for the Sunroom job for Patricia Kleier using 50% of the existing estimate.

4. Update the Patricia Kleier Sunroom job to show an in progress status.

5. Create a weekly timesheet for Joseph Rogers for 8 hours worked each on Monday, November 12th and Tuesday, November 13th, 2018 on the Patricia Kleier Sunroom job. The Service Item is Framing and the Payroll Item is Hourly 1.

6. Create an invoice based on the time Joseph Rogers spent on the Patricia Kleier Sunroom job. *(Hint: Click Cancel when the Available Estimates window displays)*.

7. Display a Time by Name project report to see how many hours Joseph Rogers has worked on each job *(Hint: Select the All option from the Dates drop-down menu on the report)*.

8. Add a 2018 Ford F-150 to the Vehicle List with a description of White, four-wheel drive pick-up truck.

9. Enter mileage for the 2018 Ford F-150 using the following data:

Vehicle	2018 Ford F-150
Trip Start Date	11/01/2018
Trip End Date	11/01/2018
Odometer Start	48,234
Odometer End	48,322
Total Miles	88
Billable check box	Selected
Customer:Job	Richard Davis:Kitchen
Item	Mileage

10. Create an invoice billing Richard Davis for the 88 miles.

11. Display the Mileage by Job Detail report.

12. Close the company file.

Notes:

D

Writing Letters

In this lesson, you will learn how to:

❑ Use the Letters and Envelopes wizard

❑ Customize letter templates

Concept

The QuickBooks Letters and Envelopes wizard helps you compose letters to customers, employees, and vendors using QuickBooks letter templates and Microsoft® Word. The wizard allows you to select the type of letter you want to send and to whom you want it sent. QuickBooks then creates the letter in Microsoft Word. You may also choose from a large variety of prewritten, preformatted business letters, including collection letters, thank you notes, and more. These letters can be customized to meet your specific business needs.

Scenario

In this appendix, you will prepare a collection letter to one of your customers using the Letters and Envelopes wizard feature of QuickBooks. You will then learn about customizing letter templates.

Note: You must have Microsoft Word 2010 or higher to complete this lesson.

Practice Files: B18_Writing_Letters.qbw

Using the Letters and Envelopes Wizard

You can use the Letters and Envelopes wizard to create the following types of letters:

Collection Letters: Letters to customers and jobs with overdue payments.

Customer Letters: Letters to customers, such as apology letters, bounced check letters, and thanks for your business letters for both product and service industries.

Vendor Letters: Letters to vendors, such as credit request letters or letters to dispute charges.

Employee Letters: Letters to employees, such as employee birthday letters, memos, or vacation accrued letters.

Letters to Other Names: Pre-written and pre-formatted letters to other names you have identified in QuickBooks.

Customize Letter Templates: Letters you design to better suit the needs of your business.

In this exercise, you will create a friendly collection letter to Patricia Kleier, who has fallen more than 30 days behind on her payments.

Note: For this lesson, set your computer to the current date before opening the QuickBooks file in order to successfully use the Letters and Envelopes wizard.

To start the Letters and Envelopes wizard,

1. Open   B18_Writing Letters.qbw   using the method described in Before You Get Started

The QuickBooks Login dialog box displays:

This dialog box informs you that you must login as a QuickBooks Administrator in order to open the company file.

2. Type   **Canalside2**   in the Password field

Note: Passwords are case-sensitive.

3. Click   [OK]

QuickBooks opens the file.

4. Click to close the Reminders window

QuickBooks displays the Home page:

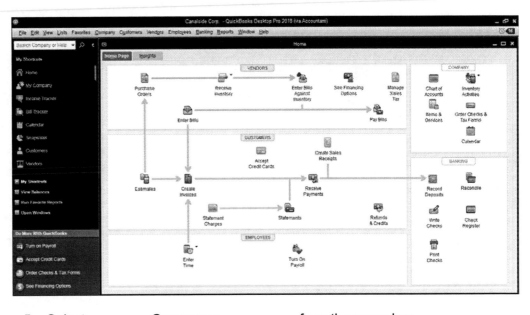

5. Select   Company :   from the menu bar
                 Prepare Letters
                 with Envelopes :
                 Collection Letters

If QuickBooks cannot locate the preinstalled letter templates in your company file folder, the Find Letter Templates window opens:

Note: If the Letters and Envelopes wizard opens instead of this window, proceed to step 7.

6. Click   [Copy]   to copy the preinstalled letter templates from the QuickBooks program folder to the Books2018 folder

The Letters and Envelopes wizard opens, allowing you to choose the recipients of the letter:

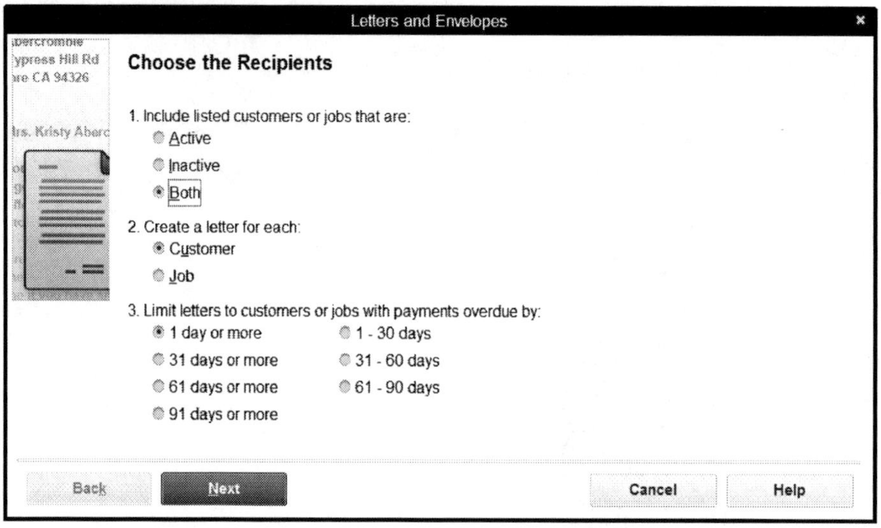

For this exercise, you will leave the default selection of Both below option 1 and Customer below option 2.

7. Click   31 days or more   below option 3

The options now selected indicate that QuickBooks should create letters for both active and inactive jobs, for each customer who has payments that are more than 30 days overdue.

8. Click   Next

The next screen in the wizard displays, allowing you to review the customers who met the criteria:

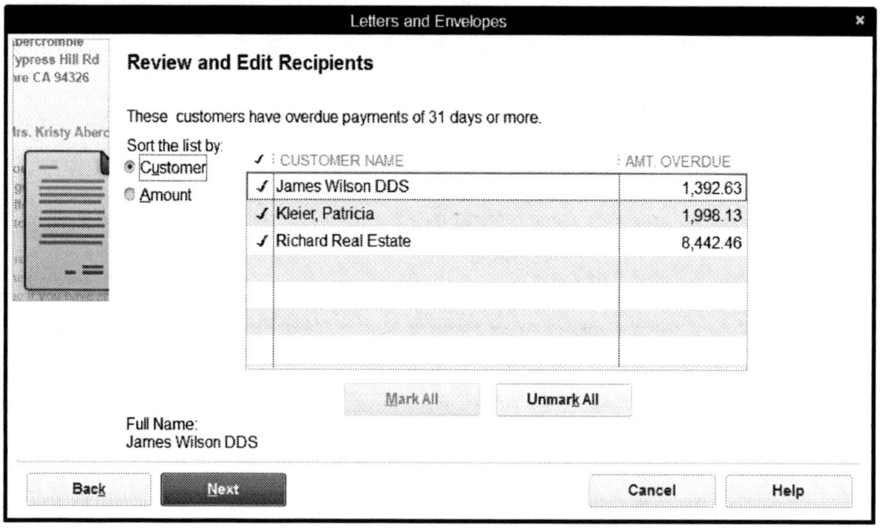

9. Click   the check mark   to the left of James Wilson DDS to
                                        deselect this customer

10. Click   the check mark   to the left of Richard Real Estate to deselect this customer

Your Letter and Envelopes wizard should resemble the figure below:

11. Click   Next

The next screen in the wizard displays, allowing you to choose the letter template to use:

12. Select   Friendly collection   from the list of templates

Quick Tip. *You can select the Create or Edit a letter template option to customize a letter to better suit your needs.*

13. Click   Next

The next screen in the wizard displays allowing you to enter a name and title to use for the signature:

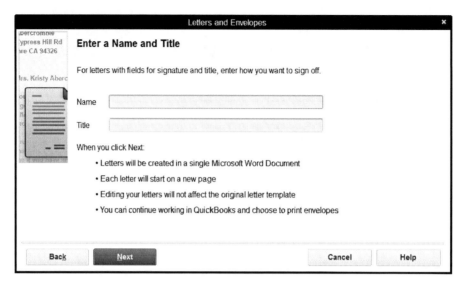

Notice that the insertion point is already in the Name field.

14. Type   **Brian M. Smith**   in the Name field

15. Type   **Accountant**   in the Title field

When you click the Next button, your letter will be created in Microsoft Word. If multiple letters met the criteria specified, the letters would be created in a single Microsoft Word document and each letter would start on a new page.

Caution. *You must have Microsoft Word 2010 or higher for QuickBooks to create the letter. If you do not have a compatible version of Microsoft Word, a Warning dialog box will display and you will not be able to create the letter. In addition, you must enable macros in Word in order for this feature to work properly. Refer to the Microsoft Word help for information about enabling and setting macro security levels. If you are working on a network and the system administrator has set the default macro settings, they will need to change the settings.*

16. Click   Next

A Creating Letters dialog box displays while the letter is created.

Caution. *The Creating Letters dialog box may display for a prolonged period of time or a Server Busy error may display if you are working on a network with multiple users accessing the file, or if you are running other programs that interfere with QuickBooks processes. If the Creating Letters dialog box does not close or if the Server Busy error displays, and you cannot create the Microsoft Word letter, you may be required to restart the QuickBooks application.*

After the letter creation process is complete, QuickBooks launches Microsoft Word and displays the letter:

Canalside Corp.
401 Utica St.
Fairgrave, NY 11111

November 1, 2018

Patricia Kleier
43 Bethany St.
Fairgrave, NY 11111

Dear Patricia,

Just a friendly reminder that you have 1 overdue invoice(s), with an overdue balance of $1,998.13. If you have any questions about the amount you owe, please give us a call and we'll be happy to discuss it. If you've already sent your payment, please disregard this reminder.

We appreciate your continuing business, and we look forward to hearing from you shortly.

Sincerely,

Brian M. Smoth
Accountant
Canalside Corp.

Note: You may have to click on the Microsoft Word application on the taskbar to view the Microsoft Word letter.

Notice that the information you provided in the Letters and Envelopes wizard (name of recipient and signature) displays in the letter. It also includes information associated with that customer, including the address and the amount overdue. You can edit any part of the letter as necessary.

When you have finished viewing the letter,

17. Select   File : Exit   from the Microsoft Word menu bar

Note: If a Microsoft Word dialog box displays asking you to save the letter, click the No or Don't Save button.

Microsoft Word closes, you return to QuickBooks, and the next screen in the Letters and Envelopes wizard displays:

Print Letters and Envelopes

Your options for printing letters and envelopes are:

- Print letters you've created by selecting Print in the Microsoft Word File menu

- Print envelopes in Microsoft Word by selecting Next on this screen

- Choose not to print envelopes by selecting Cancel on this screen

Back   Next   Cancel   Help

This screen displays options for printing letters and envelopes. If you choose to print letters and envelopes, you can click the Next button to continue using the wizard. For this exercise, you will not print letters and envelopes.

18. Click   Cancel

The Letters and Envelopes wizard closes.

Customizing Letter Templates

In this exercise, you will view the options that QuickBooks offers for customizing letter templates in order to design your own letter.

1. Select   Company :   from the menu bar
                  Prepare Letters
                  with Envelopes :
                  Customize Letter
                  Templates

The first screen in the Letters and Envelopes wizard displays, allowing you to select the type of letter template you want to work with:

QuickBooks offers you four different options for customizing letter templates:

Create a New Letter Template From Scratch: This option allows you to choose the letter type and name the template. When you create the new template, Microsoft Word opens with a QuickBooks toolbar in it so that you may insert QuickBooks data fields into the letter template. When you save the new letter template, QuickBooks places it in the letter folder for the letter type you selected.

Convert an Existing Microsoft Word Document to a Letter Template: This option allows you to open an existing Microsoft Word document with the QuickBooks toolbar in it so that you can insert QuickBooks data fields into the existing letter. You can then save the letter with a new name and QuickBooks will place it in the letter folder for the letter type you selected.

View or Edit Existing Letter Templates: This option allows you to view and edit existing QuickBooks letter templates.

Organize Existing Letter Templates (Delete, Rename, Duplicate, or Move): This option allows you to delete, rename, duplicate, or move QuickBooks letter templates. All QuickBooks letter templates are assigned to the list for which they were created. You can duplicate a letter template used for one list and then move the duplicate letter to another list.

You would now select the action you would like to take and then use the Letters and Envelopes wizard to create, convert, edit, or organize the letter templates. You will not customize a letter template at this time.

2. Click   [Cancel]   to close the Letters and Envelopes wizard

Review

In this lesson, you have learned how to:

 ☑ Use the Letters and Envelopes wizard

 ☑ Customize letter templates

Practice:

1. Using the Customer Letters option of the Letters and Envelopes wizard, create a thank you letter to James Wilson DDS. Use the following criteria for the thank you letter:

   Review and Edit Recipients:

   Deselect: Kleier, Patricia
                                  Richard Davis
                                  Richard Real Estate

   Choose a Letter Template:

   Select   Thanks for business (service)

   Enter a Name and Title:

   Name: **[your name]**
   Title: **[your title]**

2. View the letter in Microsoft Word.

3. Close Microsoft Word.

4. Close the Letters and Envelopes wizard.

5. Close the company file.

Before Training Skill Evaluation

This training guide is designed to meet the following course objectives. Prior to using the guide, rate your skill level for each objective using the numbered scale on the right. If you have not had prior experience with the objective, indicate as not applicable (n/a). This evaluation helps to determine whether the objectives of the training have been met.

| COURSE OBJECTIVES | SKILL LEVEL | | | | | |
| Keep Going With QuickBooks® 2018 | low | | | | | high |
	n/a	1	2	3	4	5
Memorize transactions	❑	❑	❑	❑	❑	❑
Customize forms	❑	❑	❑	❑	❑	❑
Use other QuickBooks accounts	❑	❑	❑	❑	❑	❑
Create reports	❑	❑	❑	❑	❑	❑
Create graphs	❑	❑	❑	❑	❑	❑
Track and pay sales tax	❑	❑	❑	❑	❑	❑
Prepare payroll with QuickBooks	❑	❑	❑	❑	❑	❑
Use online banking	❑	❑	❑	❑	❑	❑
Manage company files	❑	❑	❑	❑	❑	❑
Estimate, time track, and job cost	❑	❑	❑	❑	❑	❑
Write letters	❑	❑	❑	❑	❑	❑

Company Name:

User/Student Name: E-mail: Date:

Instructor's Name:

Comments:

After Training Skill Evaluation

This training guide is designed to meet the following course objectives. After completing the guide, rate your skill level for each objective using the numbered scale on the right. If you did not work on the objective, indicate as not applicable (n/a). This evaluation helps to determine whether the objectives of the training have been met.

COURSE OBJECTIVES	SKILL LEVEL					
Keep Going With QuickBooks® 2018	low					high
	n/a	1	2	3	4	5
Memorize transactions	❑	❑	❑	❑	❑	❑
Customize forms	❑	❑	❑	❑	❑	❑
Use other QuickBooks accounts	❑	❑	❑	❑	❑	❑
Create reports	❑	❑	❑	❑	❑	❑
Create graphs	❑	❑	❑	❑	❑	❑
Track and pay sales tax	❑	❑	❑	❑	❑	❑
Prepare payroll with QuickBooks	❑	❑	❑	❑	❑	❑
Use online banking	❑	❑	❑	❑	❑	❑
Manage company files	❑	❑	❑	❑	❑	❑
Estimate, time track, and job cost	❑	❑	❑	❑	❑	❑
Write letters	❑	❑	❑	❑	❑	❑

Company Name:

User/Student Name: E-mail: Date:

Instructor's Name:

Comments: